Social Banks and the Futur Sustainable Finance

Social banking describes a way of value-driven banking that has a positive social and ecological impact at its heart, as well as its own economic sustainability. Although it has a long and successful history, it has arguably never been more topical than it is now in the aftermath of the latest financial crisis. Most social banks came out of this crisis not only unscathed but much stronger and bigger than they were before. And contrary to their conventional peers, none of the social banks had to be bailed out with public funds. This increasingly attracts the interest not only of clients searching for safe and sensible ways to deposit their funds but also of conventional banks that begin to understand the potential of a more socially oriented approach towards banking.

Social Banks and the Future of Sustainable Finance is the first book to deliver a comprehensive and detailed overview about the past, present and possible future of social and sustainable banking for researchers, students and a professional audience. The authors are experts from research and practice and have been involved in social banking for many years. Thus they combine state-of-the-art expertise with valuable insider knowledge.

The book covers the following topics: the history of social banking, the need for social banking in the current economy, the particular issues of managing a social bank as business enterprise, social banking products and services, the special role of donations and foundations for financing change, the opportunities and challenges for social banks lying ahead, and concrete directions for the future of social banking. In addition to these respective analyses are many real-world examples and interviews with representatives of social banks. As such, this comprehensive collection delivers valuable insights for academics, students and professionals who are interested in the growing field of social banking.

Olaf Weber is Associate Professor at the University of Waterloo, Canada.
Sven Remer is Manager of Training and Research at the Institute for Social Banking, Germany.

Routledge international studies in money and banking

1 **Private Banking in Europe**
Lynn Bicker

2 **Bank Deregulation and Monetary Order**
George Selgin

3 **Money in Islam**
A study in Islamic political economy
Masudul Alam Choudhury

4 **The Future of European Financial Centres**
Kirsten Bindemann

5 **Payment Systems in Global Perspective**
Maxwell J. Fry, Isaak Kilato, Sandra Roger, Krzysztof Senderowicz, David Sheppard, Francisco Solis and John Trundle

6 **What is Money?**
John Smithin

7 **Finance**
A characteristics approach
Edited by David Blake

8 **Organisational Change and Retail Finance**
An ethnographic perspective
Richard Harper, Dave Randall and Mark Rouncefield

9 **The History of the Bundesbank**
Lessons for the European central bank
Jakob de Haan

10 **The Euro**
A challenge and opportunity for financial markets
Published on behalf of *Société Universitaire Européenne de Recherches Financières (SUERF)*
Edited by Michael Artis, Axel Weber and Elizabeth Hennessy

11 **Central Banking in Eastern Europe**
Edited by Nigel Healey and Barry Harrison

12 **Money, Credit and Prices Stability**
Paul Dalziel

13 **Monetary Policy, Capital Flows and Exchange Rates**
Essays in memory of Maxwell Fry
Edited by William Allen and David Dickinson

14 Adapting to Financial Globalisation
Published on behalf of *Société Universitaire Européenne de Recherches Financières (SUERF)*
Edited by Morten Balling, Eduard H. Hochreiter and Elizabeth Hennessy

15 Monetary Macroeconomics
A new approach
Alvaro Cencini

16 Monetary Stability in Europe
Stefan Collignon

17 Technology and Finance
Challenges for financial markets, business strategies and policy makers
Published on behalf of *Société Universitaire Européenne de Recherches Financières (SUERF)*
Edited by Morten Balling, Frank Lierman and Andrew Mullineux

18 Monetary Unions
Theory, history, public choice
Edited by Forrest H. Capie and Geoffrey E. Wood

19 HRM and Occupational Health and Safety
Carol Boyd

20 Central Banking Systems Compared
The ECB, the pre-Euro Bundesbank and the Federal Reserve System
Emmanuel Apel

21 A History of Monetary Unions
John Chown

22 Dollarization
Lessons from Europe and the Americas
Edited by Louis-Philippe Rochon and Mario Seccareccia

23 Islamic Economics and Finance
A glossary, 2nd edition
Muhammad Akram Khan

24 Financial Market Risk
Measurement and analysis
Cornelis A. Los

25 Financial Geography
A banker's view
Risto Laulajainen

26 Money Doctors
The experience of international financial advising 1850–2000
Edited by Marc Flandreau

27 Exchange Rate Dynamics
A new open economy macroeconomics perspective
Edited by Jean-Oliver Hairault and Thepthida Sopraseuth

28 Fixing Financial Crises in the 21st Century
Edited by Andrew G. Haldane

29 Monetary Policy and Unemployment
The U.S., Euro-area and Japan
Edited by Willi Semmler

30 Exchange Rates, Capital Flows and Policy
Edited by Peter Sinclair, Rebecca Driver and Christoph Thoenissen

31 **Great Architects of International Finance**
The Bretton Woods era
Anthony M. Endres

32 **The Means to Prosperity**
Fiscal policy reconsidered
Edited by Per Gunnar Berglund and Matias Vernengo

33 **Competition and Profitability in European Financial Services**
Strategic, systemic and policy issues
Edited by Morten Balling, Frank Lierman and Andy Mullineux

34 **Tax Systems and Tax Reforms in South and East Asia**
Edited by Luigi Bernardi, Angela Fraschini and Parthasarathi Shome

35 **Institutional Change in the Payments System and Monetary Policy**
Edited by Stefan W. Schmitz and Geoffrey E. Wood

36 **The Lender of Last Resort**
Edited by F.H. Capie and G.E. Wood

37 **The Structure of Financial Regulation**
Edited by David G. Mayes and Geoffrey E. Wood

38 **Monetary Policy in Central Europe**
Miroslav Beblavý

39 **Money and Payments in Theory and Practice**
Sergio Rossi

40 **Open Market Operations and Financial Markets**
Edited by David G. Mayes and Jan Toporowski

41 **Banking in Central and Eastern Europe 1980–2006**
A comprehensive analysis of banking sector transformation in the former Soviet Union, Czechoslovakia, East Germany, Yugoslavia, Belarus, Bulgaria, Croatia, the Czech Republic, Hungary, Kazakhstan, Poland, Romania, the Russian Federation, Serbia and Montenegro, Slovakia, Ukraine and Uzbekistan
Stephan Barisitz

42 **Debt, Risk and Liquidity in Futures Markets**
Edited by Barry A. Goss

43 **The Future of Payment Systems**
Edited by Stephen Millard, Andrew G. Haldane and Victoria Saporta

44 **Credit and Collateral**
Vania Sena

45 **Tax Systems and Tax Reforms in Latin America**
Edited by Luigi Bernardi, Alberto Barreix, Anna Marenzi and Paola Profeta

46 **The Dynamics of Organizational Collapse**
The case of Barings Bank
Helga Drummond

47 **International Financial Co-operation**
Political economics of compliance with the 1988 Basel Accord
Bryce Quillin

48 **Bank Performance**
A theoretical and empirical framework for the analysis of profitability, competition and efficiency
Jacob Bikker and Jaap W.B. Bos

49 **Monetary Growth Theory**
Money, interest, prices, capital, knowledge and economic structure over time and space
Wei-Bin Zhang

50 **Money, Uncertainty and Time**
Giuseppe Fontana

51 **Central Banking, Asset Prices and Financial Fragility**
Éric Tymoigne

52 **Financial Markets and the Macroeconomy**
Willi Semmler, Peter Flaschel, Carl Chiarella and Reiner Franke

53 **Inflation Theory in Economics**
Welfare, velocity, growth and business cycles
Max Gillman

54 **Monetary Policy Over Fifty Years**
Heinz Herrman (Deutsche Bundesbank)

55 **Designing Central Banks**
David Mayes and Geoffrey Wood

56 **Inflation Expectations**
Peter J.N. Sinclair

57 **The New International Monetary System**
Essays in honour of Alexander Swoboda
Edited by Charles Wyplosz

58 **Taxation and Gender Equity**
A comparative analysis of direct and indirect taxes in developing and developed countries
Edited by Caren Grown and Imraan Valodia

59 **Developing Alternative Frameworks for Explaining Tax Compliance**
Edited by James Alm, Jorge Martinez-Vazquez and Benno Torgler

60 **International Tax Coordination**
An interdisciplinary perspective on virtues and pitfalls
Edited by Martin Zagler

61 **The Capital Needs of Central Banks**
Edited by Sue Milton and Peter Sinclair

62 **Monetary and Banking History**
Edited by Geoffrey E. Wood, Terence Mills and Nicholas Crafts

63 **New Approaches to Monetary Economics and Theory**
Interdisciplinary perspectives
Edited by Heiner Ganßmann

64 **Social Banks and the Future of Sustainable Finance**
Edited by Olaf Weber and Sven Remer

Social Banks and the Future of Sustainable Finance

Edited by Olaf Weber and Sven Remer

LONDON AND NEW YORK

First published 2011
by Routledge
2 Park Square, Milton Park, Abingdon, Oxfordshire OX14 4RN

Simultaneously published in the USA and Canada
by Routledge
711 Third Avenue, New York, NY 10017

First issued in paperback 2014

Routledge is an imprint of the Taylor & Francis Group, an informa business

© 2011 Selection and editorial matter, Olaf Weber and Sven Remer; individual chapters, the contributors

The right of Olaf Weber and Sven Remer to be identified as authors of the editorial material and of the authors for their individual chapters has been asserted in accordance with the Copyright, Designs and Patent Act 1988.

All rights reserved. No part of this book may be reprinted or reproduced or utilized in any form or by any electronic, mechanical, or other means, now known or hereafter invented, including photocopying and recording, or in any information storage or retrieval system, without permission in writing from the publishers.

Trademark notice: Product or corporate names may be trademarks or registered trademarks, and are used only for identification and explanation without intent to infringe.

British Library Cataloguing in Publication Data
A catalogue record for this book is available from the British Library

Library of Congress Cataloging in Publication Data
Social banks and the future of sustainable finance/edited by Olaf Weber and Sven Remer.
p. cm.
Includes bibliographical references and index.
1. Banks and banking–Social aspects. 2. Development banks. 3. Social responsibility of business. 4. Community development–Finance. 5. Finance–Social aspects. I. Weber, Olaf, 1965– II. Remer, Sven.
HG1601.S58 2010
332.1–dc22

2010040394

ISBN 978-0-415-58329-9 (hbk)
ISBN 978-1-138-79949-3 (pbk)
ISBN 978-0-203-82787-1 (ebk)

Typeset in Times
by Wearset Ltd, Boldon, Tyne and Wear

Contents

Figures

Tables

Boxes

Contributors

Leonardo Becchetti, Professor of Economics, University of Rome 'Tor Vergata', Italy and President of the Ethical Committee of Banca Popolare Etica.

Riccardo Milano, responsible for Cultural Relations in Banca Popolare Etica. He is also Contract Professor of 'Ethics and Business Finance', 'Ethics and Economy' in numerous Master courses and Italian universities and Professor of 'Ethics of Enterprise and Social Doctrine of the Catholic Church' in Vatican University.

Christina von Passavant, Consultant in Organizational Development and Leadership. Former board member of the Alternative Bank Schweiz; president of the board of two enterprises.

Sven Remer, Training and Research, Institute for Social Banking, Bochum, Germany

Antje Toennis, Head of Communications, GLS Treuhand, Bochum, Germany.

Olaf Weber, Associate Professor, Export Development Canada Chair in Environmental Finance, School of Environment, Enterprise and Development, University of Waterloo, Canada and Managing Partner of GOE – Gesellschaft für Organisation und Entscheidung, Thalwil, Switzerland.

Preface

In this book, we have striven to contribute to closing a gap in the banking and finance literature that has become increasingly noteworthy over the past years. Having worked in field of social banking for several years, to our best knowledge, there is hardly any literature available to provide an overview of this sector, not to mention a closer look at the organizations within this sector. Until recently, this did not come as a surprise. There simply was no perceived need for such literature. Social banking as we know it today has been around for some 40 years. But for most of this time, it only attracted the interest of a small group of dedicated co-workers, owners and customers of social banks. These early stakeholders, who shared relatively similar worldviews and objectives, were more interested in practising and developing further social banking and less in reading about it. Furthermore, as the term suggests, *social banking* always was very much about direct human relations – *relationship banking* at its best. Social banks were small organizations with sufficient time for meetings and discussions, both internal and external. New customers were referred to them mainly by word of mouth from within the community, and new co-workers could learn their trade on the job, based on a regular exchange with their more experienced colleagues. So, overall, the early stakeholders felt sufficiently informed about what was going on in and around their social bank and consequently felt little need for treatises on social banking in general.

However, with the rapid growth of (the public interest in) social banking, which came also as a result of the recent dramatic events in the financial markets, the situation changed completely. The apparent 'good' performance of most social banks put them 'on the radar screens' of the media and the general public. Soon this resulted in substantial growth in the number of stakeholders, including customers and new co-workers, who realized that social banking not only makes social and ecological sense, but also economic sense. As compared to the earlier (old) stakeholders, most of these new stakeholders are less informed about social banking in general and individual social banks in particular. New customers now come from outside of the community of people with shared worldviews and objectives, and new staff now often have been trained and socialized in very different organizations. Clearly, the growing group of new stakeholders of social banks have a growing interest in information on what social banking is all about.

Furthermore, new banks that define themselves as social banks appear and some criteria are needed to classify banks as social banks.

Thus, we feel, the time is ripe for some in-depth work that takes a closer look at the 'phenomenon' of social banking. This should serve the informational needs of both practitioners and these generally interested in the sector. We would hope that this book, as the first of its kind, not only contributes to the information of all those interested in social banking but also inspires more discussions and more literature to develop this exciting and promising sector further.

Acknowledgements

We express our gratitude to Export Development Canada (EDC) for the financial support of the Export Development Canada Chair in Environmental Finance at the University of Waterloo. Without EDC's support the foundation of this chair and consequently the necessary research for writing this book would not have been possible. Furthermore, we thank GOE – Gesellschaft für Organisation und Entscheidung m.b.H., Zurich, Switzerland for financially supporting some of the translations needed to create this book.

Equally important, we thank the Institute for Social Banking (ISB) in Bochum, Germany and its founder, Mr Julian Kühn. Not only did the ISB provide vital financial resources for this project (without making any prescriptions on the specific contents and perspectives of this project), it also provided an invaluable platform to meet and network with people, some of whom became contributors to this book, either indirectly by inspiring us in many conversations, or directly by writing individual chapters of this book.

The thoughts and opinions of representatives of social banks are an integrative part of the book. Thus we want express our gratitude to Malcolm Hayday, Head of Charity Bank, United Kingdom; Lars Hektoen, CEO, Cultura Bank, Norway; David Niven, Head of Public Affairs at Triodos Bank; Eric Nussbaumer, President of the Board of Directors of Alternative Bank Schweiz AG; Lars Pehrson, CEO, Merkur Bank, Denmark, and Edy Walker, member of the executive board of Alternative Bank Switzerland for their valuable and exciting inputs on the present and future of social banking.

The book, however, would not have been possible without the contributing authors. They invested a significant part of their valuable time to bring to fruition a book that concentrates only on social banking and thus gives insights into this new and fascinating part of banking and its history and future. Many thanks to Riccardo Milano, Leonardo Becchetti, Christina von Passavant, and Antje Toennis for their respective contributions.

A big thank you to our publisher, Routledge, and its staff who not only were patient and understanding when the events turned such that we couldn't keep our agreed deadline, but also provided very valuable assistance in the final editing of this book.

Finally, all mistakes are ours.

Olaf Weber and Sven Remer

1 Social banking

Introduction

Olaf Weber and Sven Remer

What is social banking?

To state it clearly upfront: there is not only one definition of social banking. Many people use different words to mean the same, and many mean different things when they use the same phrase.

To many, social banking sounds like an oxymoron, combining what does not belong together. To others banking is inherently social and to them the phrase social banking is almost tautological. Some refer to social banks as those that serve socially oriented or charitable clients. Others use the term social banking to refer to banking based on the new social media, such as the Internet and related software. In some regions social banking is equated with government banking, in others it is equated with microfinance. Finally, some argue the social part in social banking could and should be replaced by sustainable or ethical, whilst others insist that these terms are not to be used interchangeably.

Thus, Frans de Clerck (2009), co-founder of Triodos Belgium and former head of the supervisory board of the Institute for Social Banking, concludes that there is no clear definition of social banking because

> social, ethical, alternative, sustainable development and solidarity banking and finance are denominations that are currently used to express particular ways of working with money based on non-financial deliberations. A precise and unified definition of these types of finance as such is not available and perhaps not possible because of the different traditions from which the ethical finance actors have emerged.
>
> (de Clerck 2009)

We agree with de Clerck and we acknowledge the existence of these different perspectives on and definitions of social banking.

For the purpose of this book, however, we will adhere to a definition of social banking that is well summarized by James Niven, from the Global Alliance for Banking on Values (GABV). He defines the purpose of the social bank as follows:

> to make an impact directly – by increasing our lending and investing to people and organisations that benefit people, the environment and culture. Making an impact by influencing others indirectly, both by showing that a different approach to banking is both possible and necessary and by actively engaging in important wider discussions about the future of the financial industry.
>
> (James Niven in a personal interview)

Thus, in line with Niven, we would define social banking as banking that aims to have a positive impact on people, the environment and culture by means of banking, i.e. savings accounts, loans, investments and other banking products and services, including 'gift money'.

This also reflects the self-perception of the group of banks we consider 'core social banks', and which will therefore form the basis of much of our subsequent discussions in this book. These are the banks that are members of the Global Alliance for Banking on Values (GABV; www.gabv.org), an independent network of banks using finance to deliver sustainable development for unserved people, communities and the environment, or the Institute for Social Banking (ISB; www.social-banking.org), an institute founded by a group of European social banks and financial service providers to offer training and education in the field of social banking.

But to specify our definition of social banks further, in this context, we also follow Scheire and de Maertelaere (2009) who note that there are two main clusters of social banks – *poverty alleviation banks* (in the South) and *ethical banks* (in the North). As Scheire and de Maertelaere (2009) point out, there are some fundamental differences between these two clusters not only with respect to their missions but also with respect to the funding and organizational structures as such.

But let us take a more detailed look at the current situation of social banks, their missions and products. This analysis will support the understanding of social banking from a practical point of view. We will describe and characterize the missions, products and services, and some financial figures of member banks of the ISB and/or of the GABV. The ISB is funded by a group of European social banks and offers training and education in the field of social banking. The GABV is an independent network of banks using finance to deliver sustainable development for unserved people, communities and the environment (see www.gabv.org). Thus we analysed the following banks (these banks are also characterized as the main social banks globally by de Clerck (2009)):

- Alternative Bank Schweiz (ABS), Switzerland
- Banca Popolare Etica, Italy
- Banex, Nicaragua
- BRAC, Bangladesh
- Charity Bank, UK
- Cultura Sparebank, Norway

- Ekobanken, Sweden
- GLS Gemeinschaftsbank and GLS Treuhand, Germany
- HERMES, Austria
- Merkur, Denmark
- Mibanco, Peru
- New Resource Bank, USA
- ShoreBank, USA
- Société financiere de la NEF, France
- Triodos Bank, the Netherlands
- XAC Bank, Mongolia.

In the following, a brief overview of these banks, with a particular focus on their missions, products and services, strives to provide a better idea of what we consider key features of social banks, and thus a good foundation for putting the subsequent chapters into context.

Alternative Bank Schweiz AG (ABS), Switzerland (www.abs.ch)

The mission of ABS is for ethical principles to take precedence over maximizing profits. The banking activities are based on transparency and all approved loans are published. Tax evasion is expressly excluded at the start of any business relationship. Loans are granted to support ecological and social projects. Solidarity is encouraged between depositors and borrowers: it enables loans to be granted at reduced rates of interest. Internal operations are largely democratic. Clients and the public are informed about the role and the effect of money in society. Ensuring equality of opportunity for both sexes is part of the bank's strategy.

Products and services: ABS is a savings and loan bank that offers mainly a range of savings accounts, deposits and basic banking. ABS issues loans, principally in the areas of social or ecological housing, organic agriculture, renewable energies, small and medium-size companies, etc. Additionally the bank offers investment advice and sale of a selection of sustainable investment funds.

The balance sheet was approximately €650 million (end of 2009) with €479 million in loans outstanding (74 per cent of the total balance sheet). The net profit in 2009 was €0.63 million.

Banca Popolare Etica, Italy (www.bancaetica.com)

Mission: Banca Popolare Etica is a place where savers, driven by the common desire for the more transparent and responsible management of financial resources, may meet socio-economic initiatives, inspired by the values of sustainable social and human development (www.gabv.org).

Products and services: the bank manages savings and invests them in initiatives pursuing both social and economic objectives, operating in full respect of human dignity and the environment. Thus it is mainly a savings and loan bank.

The balance sheet of Banca Popolare Etica at the end of 2008 was approximately €612 million with €280 million of loans outstanding (46 per cent of the balance sheet). In 2008 the net profit was €1.2 million.

Banex, Nicaragua (www.banex.com.ni)

Mission: Banco del Exito (Banex) is a Nicaraguan bank dedicated to providing prompt and long-term financial services to its clients in a sustainable way. The vision of Banex is to become a world-class bank with social sensitivity, serving regional micro, small and medium enterprises. Its corporate values are related to the policies and practices of sustainability: integrity, commitment, quality, service and social sensitivity. Banex, through its leadership in the small and medium enterprises (SME) sector, develops products and services that meet the financial needs of its clients. It also strives for the development of long-term relationships and a better quality of life for its customers.

Products and services: Banex is a savings and loan bank that offers the financing of mostly rural micro, small and medium enterprises nationwide.

At the end of 2008 the balance sheet was approximately €147 million with €114 million in loans outstanding (77.6 per cent of the balance sheet). The net profit was €2.3 million (end of 2008).

BRAC, Bangladesh (www.brac.net)

Mission: BRAC bank is a profitable and socially responsible financial institution focused on markets and businesses with growth potential, thereby assisting BRAC and its stakeholders build a 'just, enlightened, healthy, democratic and poverty free Bangladesh'.

Products and services: BRAC offers collateral-free financing to the poor, especially women, in both rural and urban areas, in a simple, efficient and affordable manner, as well as savings accounts. Furthermore it offers assistance to its borrowers. Savings opportunities with BRAC provide members with funds for consumption, children's education and other investments. It also provides security for old age and serves as a contingency fund during natural disasters.

The balance sheet at the end of 2008 was approximately €860 million with €625 million in loans outstanding (73 per cent of the balance sheet). The net profit in 2008 was €11.6 million.

Charity Bank, UK (www.charitybank.org)

Mission: Charity Bank is a regulated bank that is also a registered general charity. It tackles marginalization, social injustice and exclusion, and facilitates social change through investment. It wants to change the perceptions of how personal and corporate wealth can provide finance for the benefit of society.

Products and services: Charity Bank provides affordable loan finance and advice to enable charities, community associations, voluntary organizations, community businesses and social enterprises across the UK to grow. Of the depositors' money, 100 per cent is invested in supporting charities and communities.

The balance sheet of 2009 was approximately €68 million with €42 million in loans outstanding (62 per cent of the balance sheet). At the end of 2009 the net loss was €1.67 million.

Cultura Sparebank, Norway (www.cultura.no)

Mission: Cultura promotes projects with a social and ethical quality. Profitability is secondary but the economic viability of the projects is a prerequisite for financing them.

Products and services: Cultura offers current accounts with overdraft facilities, loans for new working capital as well as investment loans.

The balance sheet at the end of 2008 was approximately €46 million with €32 million in loans outstanding (70 per cent of the balance sheet). The net profit in 2008 was €0.24 million.

Ekobanken, Sweden (www.ekobanken.se)

Mission: Ekobanken is an ethical bank open to all who want to encourage opportunities for people to take free initiatives that enrich society in the form of a wider variety of healthcare forms, educational methods and artistic expression. Ekobanken considers money to be a social medium through which cooperation among people and groups is made easier. The individual is the starting point for Ekobanken's operations. The public good and the benefit of its members are the main driving forces and the reason why Ekobanken finances initiatives within the social economy. The bank is also interested in sustainable business that takes the environment and the individual into account.

Products and services: Ekobanken is a savings and loan bank that grants loans to initiatives that have social, environmental and cultural value. It offers thematic accounts such as eco, healthcare or cultural accounts.

At the end of 2008 the balance sheet was approximately €34 million with €22 million in loans outstanding (65 per cent of the balance sheet). The net profit in 2008 was €0.07 million.

GLS Gemeinschaftsbank, Germany (www.gls.de)

Mission: the activities of GLS are geared towards sustainable development and it aims for a responsible exposure to money in favour of human beings and nature.

Products and services: GLS is a savings and loan bank. It focuses on financing cultural, social and ecological projects that try to tackle challenges in society by developing creative solutions. It offers financial investments, the entire range of payment services, as well as investment funds and securities brokerage. Loans are offered to companies and projects such as independent schools and kindergartens, organic farms, organic food stores, or institutions using therapeutic pedagogy. Through cooperation with GLS Treuhand and GLS Beteiligungsaktiengesellschaft, foundation and endowment products can also be provided.

The balance sheet was approximately €1 billion at the end of 2008 with €624 million in loans outstanding (60 per cent of the balance sheet). The net profit in 2008 was €0.2 million.

HERMES, Austria (www.hermes-oesterreich.at)

Mission: HERMES-Austria deals with the deliberate design of financial business such as savings, loans, gifts, pledges and fiduciary administration.

Products and services: HERMES-Austria offers accounts and interest-free thematic accounts. Loans are especially provided for anthroposophist education and institutions, healthcare, organic farming, green enterprises, renewable energies, etc.

The balance sheet at the end of 2008 was approximately €8.1 million with €3.5 million in loans outstanding (43 per cent of the balance sheet). The net profit in 2008 was €0.06 million.

Merkur Bank, Denmark (www.merkur.dk)

Mission: Merkur Bank is founded on the idea of conscious handling of money, and on criteria that include environmental, social and ethical aspects in addition to financial considerations. The bank pursues a situation where the individual, based on his own insight, meets the needs of others in a dignified way.

Products and services: Merkur offers combined loan finance projects in the environmental, social and cultural sectors. As a secondary activity, Merkur approves loans and arranges mortgages for private customers. The bank provides other financial services, including savings accounts and current accounts (available with credit or debit cards), payment services, online banking, and pensioners' and children's savings accounts, as well as a full range of financial services for business customers.

The balance sheet at the end of 2008 was approximately €184 million with €141 million in loans outstanding (77 per cent of the balance sheet). The net profit in 2008 was €0.8 million.

Mibanco, Peru (www.mibanco.com.pe)

Mission: Mibanco provides opportunities and support to microbusiness owners and entrepreneurs in their growth, through specialized financial services.

Products and services: Mibanco provides working capital, investment loans and accommodation loans to small businesses. It also offers current accounts, savings accounts and deposit accounts to private individuals.

In 2009 the balance sheet was approximately €902 million with €738 million in loans outstanding (82 per cent of the balance sheet). The net profit in 2009 was €9.7 million.

New Resource Bank, USA (www.newresourcebank.com)

Mission: New Resource Bank is dedicated to providing a new standard in customer service while promoting sustainable and efficient resources. It does so by providing attentive full-service solutions to entrepreneurial businesses and personal banking clients, and developing new programmes to more efficiently finance green projects and green businesses and to introduce green incentives to everyday community banking clients that it serves. The bank is active in market development for green businesses and green projects through the engagement of its people in sustainability related policies and movements.

Products and services: New Resource Bank offers a full range of financial services such as checking, money market and savings accounts, online banking, bill paying and the financing of residential solar installations and energy efficiency upgrades for individuals. For businesses it offers corporate cash management, commercial credit lines, real estate loans and construction loans as well as project finance. The bank also serves as advisor to its business clients. For non-profit organizations it offers banking services and other strategic services. Furthermore it offers a community rewards programme from which mission-aligned non-profit organizations can generate income from New Resource Bank donations that are funded by its clients' exchange fees collected from debit-card activities. In addition to operating as a full-service community bank, New Resource Bank provides innovative loans for green projects, including alternative energy, clean tech, organic food production, and sustainable home and office construction.

The balance sheet at the end of 2009 was approximately €139.4 million with €92 million in loans outstanding (66 per cent of the balance sheet). The net loss at the end of 2009 was €10.6 million.

ShoreBank, USA (www.shorebankcorp.com)

Mission: ShoreBank invests in people and their communities to create economic equity and a healthy environment. Its triple-bottom-line mission aims to build wealth in economically and racially diverse communities, to promote sustainability and to operate profitably.

Products and services: ShoreBank is a savings and loan bank that provides financial and information services to customers through residential real estate loans, loans to small businesses, faith-based and non-profit organizations, conservation loans addressing, among others, energy, land and water use, as well as bank deposits and retail services.

At the end of 2008 the balance sheet was approximately €2.2 billion with €1.34 billion of loans outstanding (61 per cent of the balance sheet). The net loss at the end of 2008 was €1.8 million.

Société financiere de la NEF, France (www.lanef.com)

Mission: La Nef builds a direct link between savers and borrowers who carry out sustainable projects meeting social and ecological criteria.

Products and services: La Nef is a savings and loan cooperative that collects savings from its cooperators through current accounts and deposit accounts; it grants loans to professionals and non-governmental organizations in the social, environmental and cultural sectors.

The balance sheet was approximately €192 million at the end of 2009, with €68 million in loans outstanding (35 per cent of the balance sheet). There is no information about the net profit available.

Triodos Bank, the Netherlands (www.triodos.com)

Mission: Triodos Bank's mission is to help create a society that promotes quality of life and that has human dignity at its core; to enable individuals, institutions and businesses to use money more consciously in ways that benefit people and the environment, and promote sustainable development; to offer customers sustainable financial products and high-quality services.

Products and services: Triodos offers dedicated savings products and specific investment funds. Clients have access to payment services, debit and credit cards, Internet banking, investment and private banking services as well as mortgages. Furthermore it creates and offers a high number of investment funds.

The balance sheet was approximately €2.7 billion at the end of 2008 with €1.47 billion in loans outstanding (54 per cent of the balance sheet). Additionally Triodos has €1.55 million in funds under management. The net profit at the end of 2008 was €11.5 million.

XAC Bank, Mongolia (www.xacbank.mn)

Mission: XAC's mission is to contribute to sustainable development in Mongolia that can come only from educated and skilled people and competitive and dynamic businesses concerned equally about Planet, People and Profit. The Bank will provide equitable access to transparent, reliable and responsive banking products and services to its clients, including its traditional micro-entrepreneurs as well as small and medium businesses.

Products and services: XAC is a microfinance, savings and loan bank. The Bank provides financial services for micro-enterprises and SMEs, as well as for the low-income segment of the population in urban and remote rural areas.

At the end of 2008 the balance sheet was approximately €134 million with €97 million in loans outstanding (72 per cent of the balance sheet). The net profit at the end of 2008 was €2.65 million.

Having presented the missions, products and services, and the balance sheets of the social banks, we would like to analyse the current state of social banking on this basis.

There are mainly two groups of banks, social banks from Europe or the United States based on the savings and loan business (N=12) and four microfinance institutions. All banks integrate social, ethical or sustainability aspects into their mission. Though most of the missions integrate banking issues, only the microfinance institution BRAC stresses the profitability of its business. To describe their mission the term sustainability is used by six banks, microfinance is used by four, the term ethical and social is used twice respectively, one bank used conscious handling of money and one bank uses 'deliberate design of financial business' to describe its mission. Thus sustainability seems to be a concept that is often used to define the social impact of these banks. Social impact, therefore, is defined in an intergenerational responsibility for the society, the environment and the economy (Brundtland 1987).

With respect to the size of social banks we have to confess that none of these banks is comparable to the important players in the financial business with respect to its size measured in the amount of the balance sheet, in numbers of clients or in the amount of loans outstanding. With a balance sheet of €2.7 billion at the end of 2008 Triodos is the biggest social bank in the sample (see Figure 1.1). It is the only social bank from Europe and the United States that provides international business with branches in different European countries, including the Netherlands, UK, Spain, Belgium and Germany. The other international bank is BRAC, which is active in Bangladesh and in African countries. Only seven social banks provide a balance sheet higher than €600 million (Banca Etica provides €612 million). This is comparable to ranking 365 out of the 431 savings banks that are members of the German Savings Banks Association. However, in contrast to a regional savings bank social banks of that size are operating at least on a national level and often even maintain a number of regional branches.

Furthermore, most of the banks characterize themselves as savings and loan banks or microfinance institutions. The amount of loans outstanding and the balance sheet in millions of Euros is presented in Figure 1.1. The total balance sum of all the banks is $10.2 billion.

In order to provide a social impact, a high amount of the savings and other assets at social banks should be invested in their main business, especially in loans to social enterprises or other social entities. Thus we analysed the relation of the loans outstanding to the balance sheet. Figure 1.2 shows that at La Nef only 35 per cent of the balance sheet is invested in loans while Mibanco invested more than 80 per cent of their balance sum in loans. Triodos is the only bank in the sample that reported about additional products like funds and other investment products and cannot be defined as a pure savings and loan bank. Thus we must confess that a significant amount of money that should be channelled as loans into social enterprises, projects or other entities is in fact not used for that. A significant part of that capital is invested in assets of other financial institutions or in public bonds because of liquidity reasons or because there is not a sufficient number of eligible borrowers. Furthermore, compared to conventional banks, such as the German Savings Banks or the Dutch

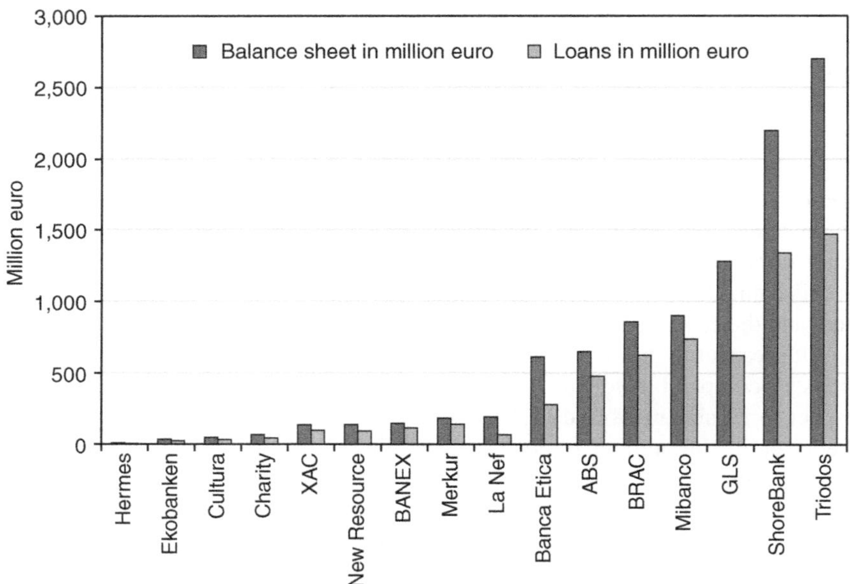

Figure 1.1 Balance sheet and loans of social banks.

Rabobank, which was chosen because of its cooperative character, the amount of loans by balance sheet at social banks is not higher than in conventional banks (see Figure 1.2).

What about the profit of social banks? In Figure 1.3 we present the net profit per balance sheet sum. It shows that the two US based banks and the Charity Bank provided a net loss. All other social banks provided a net profit for the years 2008 or 2009 respectively. Interestingly the microfinance institutions provided the highest net profits. As a second group the smaller Scandinavian social banks provided a net profit per balance sheet that was higher than the bigger German and Swiss banks that are active in the Euro or Swiss region. However, compared to the German Savings Banks and to Rabobank the net profit per balance sheet of the social banks is comparable. Specifically, Triodos, which provides investment products other than loans, reports a high net profit per balance sheet sum. Thus the concentration on the lending business provides two challenges. First, a sufficient selection of potential borrowers must be available to have the opportunity to channel the capital into social enterprises and projects. Second, the net profit is highly dependent on interest rates and especially on the interest margin. Both are relatively small, given the current financial situation in 2010 with low interest rates globally.

After 'setting the scene', in the following we provide a short description of the structure and content of the remainder of this book.

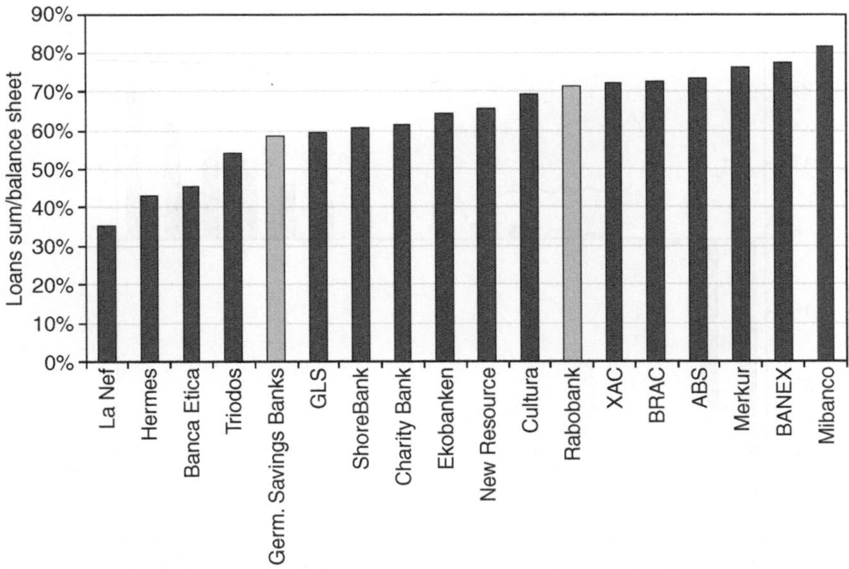

Figure 1.2 Sum of loans outstanding per balance sheet.

How did social banks develop? In Chapter 2, Riccardo Milano presents an overview of the history and the development of the banking system and especially social banks. He states that the present social banks are based on the mission of the Italian banks and the German and Austrian rural banks. These banks were founded to serve clients who did not have access to banking services. He concludes that social banking today tries to build upon the philosophy of these banks that were based on the demand for credit and not on the supply. Milano's chapter closes with the statement that social banking will be able to create a cultural change in the banking business, just like these banks were able to in the past.

Why do we need social banks and social banking? In Chapter 3, Leonardo Becchetti tries to find the answer to this question by illuminating the role of social banks in the economy. He presents social banking as one important example of the development of successful and sustainable models of the creation of economic, social and environmental value. He claims that the ultimate masters of the present economic system are neither the governments nor large corporations. Both of them crucially depend on the vote of citizens, consumers and investors. Social banks allow those citizens who prefer to give more money for solidarity or those who decide to invest their money on the basis of financial return as well as of social and environmental responsibility to act the way they want. Thus social banks are an important part of democracy, giving their clients the opportunity to vote with their wallets.

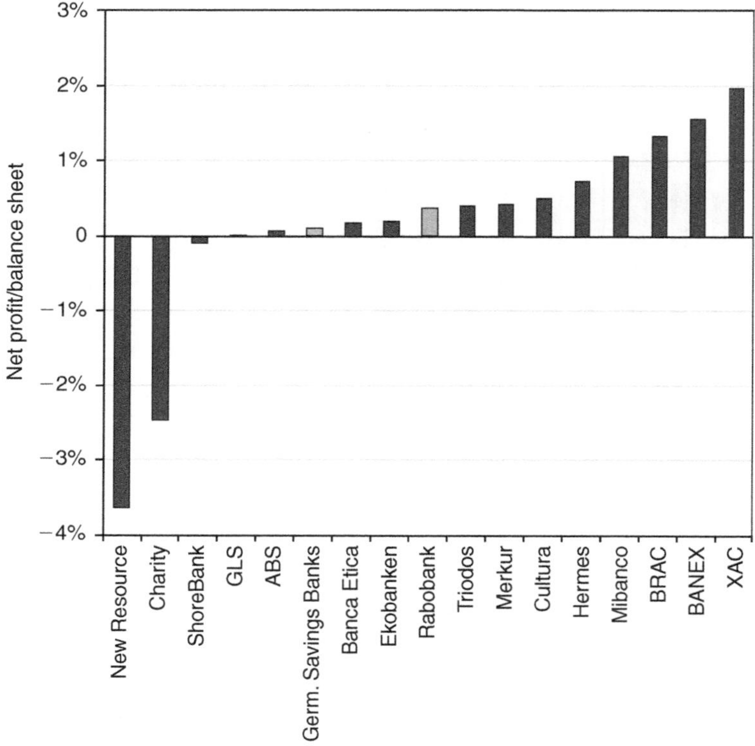

Figure 1.3 Net profit per balance sheet.

In Chapter 4 Christina von Passavant analyses the management in social banking. She describes the specific challenges a social bank's management personnel face and significant issues in human resource management. Furthermore, she raises the question of what it means to see one's customers and clients as partners. Generally she sees social banks as business enterprises and not as social projects. Based on this view guiding principles of managing social banks are developed on the basis of transparency, communication and participation. Christina von Passavant shows that social banks have to use management principles and management systems to fulfil their goals. Furthermore she points out that there are areas of conflicts in personnel recruitment, compensation policies and leadership that have to be solved.

Chapter 5 concentrates on social banking products and services. Olaf Weber concludes that social and environmental banking products and services have become more and more popular. However, most of the social banking products and services are based on conventional products and services and add social, environmental or ethical criteria to them. Additional to financial criteria, often positive or exclusion criteria are used to rate borrowers, company shares or projects. This guarantees transparent financial products and services for those who are willing to invest their money in a social or sustainable way. In the meantime, conventional banks also offer products and services labelled as sustainable or socially responsible, therefore the unique position of social banks is to offer a product portfolio that consists solely of sustainable or socially responsible products and services. Looking on basic differences between conventional and socially responsible products and services, microfinance differs the most from conventional products. Microfinance uses concepts like group lending that are not currently used in conventional banking. This leads to the question of whether social banks should offer more products that differ from the conventional product design, such as loans, mortgages, mutual funds or project finance.

Donations are a very unique social banking service. In Chapter 6, Antje Toennis presents this as a way to fund certain sectors of society. She states that banks can introduce completely new services like consultation for affluent people who want to support non-profit organizations and social businesses. Toennis bases her argumentation on the concept of anthroposophy and points to the important role donations can play towards thinking and acting outside a profit-maximizing economy. She argues that we need to focus on consulting people who want to give, and on education to spread the idea of giving to bring about political and social change in society. While these kinds of social and economic changes will likely take some time, she argues, social banks can already offer services related to giving and donations. Social banks and financial institutions can provide an arena for exploring, trying out and experimenting with the practice of giving as the example of GLS Treuhand shows.

In Chapter 7, Sven Remer finds 'social banking at the crossroads'. He notes that social banking is still a niche phenomenon. Despite growing steadily, social banks never managed to step out of the shadow of their conventional peers, and thus never reached their full potential. This is despite the fact that, given the overall negative economic, social and environmental developments we face today, social banking is needed more than ever. However, Remer argues, in the currents of the recent financial crisis, at least some of today's social banks now have the unique chance to forsake their niche and increase their outreach and impact way beyond what their actual size would suggest. Based on a SWOT analysis of the European social banking sector, Remer identifies and discusses a number of important opportunities and threats along with several key strengths and weaknesses of social banks. From this he concludes that, to make use of the chance at hand, social banks must not be complacent. One of their current key strengths is the weakness of their conventional peers, namely, the lost trust of their customers. But with the memories of the crisis likely to fade in the public consciousness, social banks that want to grow to increase their outreach and impact will have to act swiftly.

The book concludes with Chapter 8, in which *Olaf Weber* develops some specific suggestions for the future direction of social banking based on the previous chapters of this book and on additional interviews with representatives of several social banks. To increase the social and environmental impact, Weber argues, social banks have to keep on growing. But, to do so, they have to advance products and services in a way that stresses their social impact and lowers the financial risk for themselves and for their clients. They have to broaden their product portfolio to become less dependent on interest rates and to differentiate themselves from conventional banks. For this they will have to focus more on (positive) impact finance and less on using (negative) exclusions criteria to exclude non-ethical businesses. In order to address new types of clients social banks have to develop products and services on the one hand, and marketing strategies on the other hand that meet the need of these new clients that are interested in finance with an impact. In order to show this impact social banks will have to develop measurements and indicators that are objective and transparent.

References

Brundtland, G.H. (1987) *Our Common Future*, Oxford and New York: Oxford University Press.

De Clerck, F. (2009) 'Ethical banking', in Zsolnai, L. (ed.) *Ethical Prospects – Economy, Society, and Environment*, Berlin, Heidelberg and New York: Springer, 209–27.

Scheire, C. and de Maertelaere, S. (2009) Banking to make a difference (Preliminary Report), Artevelde: Artevelde University College.

2 Social banking

A brief history

Riccardo Milano

Introduction[1]

What are the social origins of the bank? What are the factors that can account for the historical experience of ethical banks, social banks in general and microcredit?

The path we propose to follow is to demonstrate both the successful Italian experience as well as the Austrian/German one, both of which occurred according to a historical, though not ancient, path (as can be seen from their scope). The former saw the establishment of the first banks, banking methodologies and techniques, and the creation of both public (Banche) and private (Banchi) banks – outwardly similar but in actuality very different – as the world's first aggregated forms of financial intermediation. The latter saw the establishment of the original savings and cooperative banks, which still today continue their operations throughout the world.[2]

Later, a new social awareness and a rethinking of the role of financial intermediation brought about the various forms of ethical banks in Europe and in many parts of the world.

The complexity of this topic is evident and there are innumerable tracks to be followed. Here a simple method of narration is adopted rather than a general, deep interpretive approach.

However, surprises still occur: the economic/social lessons of yesterday were expected to be valid today and tomorrow; given the present financial crisis we hope this to be the case.

The remote historical reality: the construction of the first banks in the Middle Ages

The use of money, banks and usury

The monetary activities of banks and bankers in the Middle Ages were an ancient practice. It was in this period, however, that practices were consolidated and a credit revolution, which would gradually transform the credit history of the world, was initiated. In contrast, bankers' activities were limited by the

Roman Church's law, which regarded those who lent money with the condition of interest to be sinners.[3]

The reason was simple and complex at the same time: time was said to belong to God and the usurer gains profit from time taken for the restitution of the usury loan. The usurer, therefore, speculated on God's property thus he was a sinner, indeed one of the worst ones. This idea is expressed very clearly by the Dominican Fra Remigio de Girolami in his paper 'Determinatio utrum sit licitum vendere mercationes ad terminum' (Capitani 1958) which testifies that the lowest trade among those of the Middle Ages was that of the usurer and that the agents practising this trade were considered to commit the mortal sin of stealing God's time (Andenna 1998: 28–9; Le Goff 1986: 34).

But what was the usury for the Middle Ages? Ambrogio said: 'Usura est plus accipere quam dare'.[4] The usury here means someone who is asked to repay another loan in addition to their original one. By implication these are the highest prices for sale on credit. Tommaso d'Aquino[5] said:

> Pecunia autem ... principaliter est inventa ad commutationes faciendas: et ita proprius et principalis pecuniae usus est ipsius consumptio sive distractio, secundum quod in commutationes expeditur. Et propter hoc secundum se est illicitum pro usu pecuniae mutuatae accipere pretium, quod dicitur usura.[6]

Therefore, usury was a sin and was prohibited by the Christians. This was the reason why the majority of moneylenders were Jewish, whose doctrine allowed lending at interest outside their own community.[7] Since then there exists a dichotomy: while civil society and positive laws do not condemn usury for economic and political opportunity, ecclesiastical law could not tolerate any form of permission for such activities. With the evolution of trade and the development of a new type of capitalist commodity-based society, the meaning of the term usury constantly became more restricted, until the request and the payment of exorbitant rates for loans of money became known as interest.

The population's needs were huge: feudalism and the noble class were not able to either improve quality of life or reduce poverty. The scarcity of agricultural production, the difficulty of the supply of goods, etc. did not permit economic or human growth as the Christians had hoped. 'For the poor there was a reward in the afterlife' exactly because it was too difficult to improve the earthly life.[8] Charity became more and more a practical luxury, so called the charity of crumbs as it could not bring relief to deprivation (Milano 2001: 52). This was typical of great lords and courts (including the Pope of Avignon). These situations and problems could not generate research and reflection from either the civil or the theological points of view, which were expected to provide answers for people's daily lives. These deep issues were tackled with important reflections from the Franciscans.[9]

The Franciscan order, after studying the economic concepts of Benedictine monachism (with its motto *Ora et Labora*) in depth and in order to clarify how the assets of both monks and lay people who wanted to become monks – but were asked to continue living in their families and working in their professions – should be viewed, created an important school of Christian reflection on the economy (well before the ideas of John Calvin). Its purpose was to distinguish between usury and money lending at risk, between luxury and the proper use of property within the horizon of common good which requires not a mere statement of intention but an 'organization', an 'institutionalization' that supports lending and makes it practically possible. In other words, thanks to the choice of voluntary poverty, Franciscans elaborated an economic language that contributed to the formation of basic schools of thought for Western economic ideas. These were aimed at removing the embarrassment of the rich. The civil market was born with the Franciscans, considered a governmental structure of economic transactions.

> Francesco, the founder of an hermitage movement, which was transformed with a brilliant growth in mendicant order, inaugurated by Bernard (of Clairvaux, founder of the Cistercian movement, n.d.r), was not only the principle that made contemplantes become laborantes but also the rule which asked the monks to renounce their common property. However, he left behind a fundamental point: if you want to find an outlet to generate surplus in agriculture and commerce, and then alleviate the embarrassment of the rich, you should expand the area of economic activity by ensuring that everyone can participate. It meant going to the city where the majority of population lived to evangelize and create some precise markets. (Please note the insistent request of J. Le Goff on why the new mendicant orders – the Dominicans and Franciscans – were so attracted by developed cities in Europe since the XI century).
>
> (Zamagni 2008)

An important Italian scholar, G. Todeschini (2007), promised to understand the moral and legal legitimacy of profits derived by merchants who declined to force their counterparts to pay the highest price possible, given by market conditions. The difference between the actual and the highest possible price (one in exigible theory and one in practical life) created a *dono* (gift). This did not mean generous charity, but showed the necessity of defining, within an economic space, subjects who recognized each other as belonging to the same ideological universe. In the same sense charity and profit, representing two sides of the same economic reality, created the appearance of Franciscan masters (Olivi, Duns Scoto, Bernardino da Siena, Bonanventura da Bagnoregio, Ockham and others) and other commentators who focused much attention on urban civilization. This recalls the most famous Franciscans, already well-known in that era, who said that: 'charity helps to survive, but not to live, because to live is to produce, and charity does not help to produce' (Zamagni 2008). This statement, which was an implicit condemnation of welfarism, failed either to give dignity to human life or to promote a path to a social and participative economy which could really provide for itself.

Bankers

In the fifteenth century, Italian wealth blossomed and Italian banks became highly esteemed[10] (not to mention that they were also the biggest): the famous Banco Soranza in Venice, followed by Casa Priuli, then Banco Pisani; the huge Banco di San Giorgio (1407) in Genoa; Sant'Ambrogio (1593) in Milan; and Banco di Napoli in Naples – the oldest credit institute in Europe. The Florentine bankers were the best known due to their perceived ability, initiative and organizational capacity. Large trading families such as the Bardi, the Peruzzi and the Medici created effective family companies, pooling the capital held by each shareholder to form huge companies which, within a few decades, became the arbiters of history not only in commerce, but also often in politics for half of Europe. They had branches throughout Europe, Africa and Asia Minor: they subsidized wars as well as struggles between rival families and businesses in the most distant countries of the Far East.

Their banks' activities initially had three operational sectors:

1 Pawnbroking. However, the collection of interest was in conflict with the prevailing culture, thus it was seen to be unfair to earn money from the loans (the argument had already been supported by Aristotle) which were interest-bearing and usually carried out by Jews.
2 Money exchange. Considering that in Italy alone 270 types of coins were already in existence, this was a basic activity which permitted commerce between different regions.
3 Public banks. Public banks were born in the sixteenth century, from the state's increasing needs for medium- and long-term financial services (armies' maintenance, bureaucratic apparatus). Other financial resources were supplied by land proprietors, who were interested in money injections from the state's budget, to accumulate political power.

Loans were normally guaranteed by Jewish credit banks, Lombard (the term 'Lombard' included all Italian banks), Flemish and gradually French and German families. The interest rate charged was between 30 and 40 per cent, though was reduced considerably when the client was the Commune, the Lordship or the Principality who gave hospitality to the credit institute by dictating the rules of residence in the territory.

Among classic bankers and moneylenders who 'served' people, the development of a civil mercantile economy was impossible. In this way the difference between loans for production and for states (forerunners of today's merchant banks) compared to loans for consumption had been established. This difference justified interest loans granted by big economic operators, while the loans for basic needs and loans for consumption for all the others continued to be persevered with. Subsequently a distinction was made between two financial markets: a legal one, which favoured the development of major banks and of an efficient banking system, and an illegal one, run by the loan sharks, where the most heinous abuses were found.

The Monti di Pietà

Mendicant orders (Dominicans[11] and Franciscans) who were always expressly against the charging of interest and considered moneylenders to be theologically illegal,[12] could not remain silent and had to intervene. In fact, in a society where loans were necessary in order for production and trade to flourish, and sometimes for survival, condemning the charging of interest simply meant driving it underground.[13] The turning point came with the preaching of one Franciscan, Fra Bernardino da Siena, through one of his writings entitled *Tractatus de Contractibus et Usuris* (following also the studies of the characters mentioned earlier), in which he justified private property (with its restrictions), the ethics of trade, the determination of value and price, and finally the possibility of an equitable interest on loans. The theology of Bernardino da Siena states that the enterprising man who is endowed by God should have four qualities: hard work, responsibility, efficiency and the propensity to take risks. These qualities are typical of merchants and artisans. Therefore each of them has the right to earn more to continue in his trade and to reap the rewards of risks.

The mendicant orders of Franciscans and Dominicans set themselves, therefore, the challenges of improving their ability to care for the poor, and offering an alternative to interest loans from Jewish bankers. To meet these demands, taking their cue from Jewish banks and with the intention of replacing them, they started operating credit activities with the purposes of providing support whilst operating on a non-profit basis: the Monti di Pietà. The new doctrine took effect from the convent of Monteripido di Perugia and achieved a universal result: the creation of modern banks based on a revolving monetary fund. The first pawnbroking bank was established on 15 January 1458[14] by Ascoli Piceno in Marche, followed by another in Perugia. In fact, among the monks who attended to Monteripido (which later became the head office of the general Studium in Bernardino da Siena's theology) there was Fra Barnabas Manassei who came from a merchant and administrative family in the city of Terni and involved himself with the contemplative and practical movement, for which he was described as 'an ascetic and economist'. The universal importance of Manassei dated from 1460 to 1462, when he preached in Perugia, together with Fra Michele from Milan, abhorring usury, convincing the city administrators to create a bank where the interest rate was only to preserve the mountain of money necessary to maintain the flow of loans, in accordance with the theology of Bernardino da Siena and applying the rules of the revolving fund.

This bank, which was formed with donations and charitable proceeds, took the name of Monte di Pietà[15] and made loans to merchants and craftsmen whilst excluding loans for luxury expenses.[16] The interest rate was generally not more than 6 per cent. This new bank institute became a symbol of defiance against usury and quickly spread to half of Italy: to Orvieto in 1463, to Foligno in 1465, to Terni in 1467, to Assisi in 1468, to Viterbo in 1471, to Bologna in 1473, to Savona in 1479, to Milan in 1483, to Mantua, Brescia and Ferrara in 1484, to Vicenza in 1486, to Forlì in 1510, and continued further in subsequent years. In Velletri, even before 1477, the first Monte di Pietà was formed without the Franciscans' involvement and was one of the first in central Italy. After that, it expanded throughout Italy and the rest of Europe.[17]

Monte di Pietà is a compound name: Monte meant (in the financial language in Europe) a combination of loans, while Pietà refers to an image of the Passion of Christ. The poor were a real symbol of Christ's suffering: it is the meaning of Pietà. The widest proliferators of the Monti were Bernardino da Feltre (Monti di pietà pecuniari) and Andrea da Faenza (Monti frumentari). The difference between the last two related to the nature of the operations, not to the recipients. The one of Pietà served to control the price of money for the benefit of labourers, while the one of frumentari served to control the price of grain to promote the poorest segment of the agricultural class. The norms which constantly limited the activities of Monti di Pietà were dictated by Pope Leo X on 4 May 1515 with the stamp Inter Multiplices produced in V Lateran Council, confirming at the same time the general condemnation of usury.[18] The Council of Trent put Monti di Pietà among Pii Institutes.

The peculiarities of Monti di Pietà are summarized as follows:

- close regional links, meaning lending money only to residents or those living in neighbouring localities (specifically mentioned in the Statutes);
- granting loans only where sums are relatively proportionate to the guarantee, made up by objects of property value, offered by the borrower;
- oaths of beneficiaries in taking money for necessity and for morally impeccable uses;
- involvement in social activities operated in different ways by different regions;
- acceptance of voluntary deposits, remunerated at an interest rate;
- granting loans to city magistrates during food crises, or transfer of troops;
- promoting private mortgage loans;
- granting dowries to poor women; and
- carrying out treasury functions on behalf of care institutions in communities.[19]

The Monti were also the precursors of saving funds for aristocratic, low and middle classes. In fact, in 1611, in France, Hugues Delestre published a brochure which presented the proposal of adding two new sectors to Monti: one for saving funds for rich classes (aristocratic, high clergy and commercial bourgeoisie) and one for minute saving funds. In Britain, the same proposal was initiated by the writer Daniel Defoe in 1697. An evolution towards the model savings banks started. However, it was interrupted almost everywhere in Italy and in Europe in 1796 by the arrival of Napoleon's French troops who claimed wealth contained in institutions' safes and appropriated it as 'rights of the conquest'. After this, the Monti were grouped in the Congregation of Napoleon's charity instituted by an 1807 provision.

After 1815 the Restoration restored their autonomy. However, at this point the Monti were no longer the protagonists. This role was taken by the savings banks, from the basic Austrian matrix which, as we shall see, had a historic task of developing new ideas for credit and for social commitment.

The conduct of social oriented banks

This historical analysis has shown that the origins of social banking are to be found in the Monte di Pietà, which were also, as the great economist Schumpeter (1954) theorized, local banks that worked as real agents of development. Between the fourteenth and sixteenth centuries they were revolutionary, which in many cases formed the foundations of prosperity, not only in the central northern regions of Italy but also in a significant part of Europe.

Furthermore, the Monti were also civic cultural centres which is not difficult to imagine given their activities and also considering the origins of their assets (the roots of bank foundations in Italy). The service activities of the regions did not actually limit funding or collection. Additionally they supported political, cultural and religious activities and assisted the poor and the sick. We can safely say that the Monti were the equivalent of ethical banks today: this characteristic will not be found in a kind of profit-sharing – however, profit is not the sole objective of the Monti. It is the same approach to banking which configures ethics itself: an interest rate of 5 or 6 per cent is asked compared with a payment of interest on deposits of 4 per cent. A spread of 2 per cent: this is the ethical operation of Monti di Pietà. To this we must refer again today when it comes to ethics, not with respect to the donation of meagre, residual amounts to pious causes, but for a way of banking that has in itself characteristics worthy of consideration. Thus it should be stressed that the Monti were not an example of an ethical business because they distributed gains, but because they conducted banking without usury. Unfortunately, looking at the present banking practice, there are still a lot of lessons to be learned on this point.

It is possible to conclude that in the creation of the first social banks – the Monti di Pietà – the Franciscans had a positive intuition: 'As long as the poor exist – the poor, not by choice but because they have to suffer poverty – the city cannot be fraternal' (Bruni 2006).

The historical reality of social banks in the eighteenth, nineteenth and twentieth centuries

Savings banks

With the Napoleonic era in Europe, the Monti underwent a major change but the substance of their work, especially regarding credit, remained. For a new era, a new business was needed because the deep and creative monopoly of Italian economic reality was over and strong economies had developed elsewhere. The industrial revolution was in its infancy and required new ideas and capacity. The various Monti were forced to transform and re-establish their vitality. Therefore, it was not by accident that the birth of savings banks (Schlesinger 2002) took place in the second half of the eighteenth century, thanks to a philanthropic passion and commitment, especially from the English and French sides. They supported the need for collecting savings from the middle and lower classes in dedicated institutions to support local initiatives from these classes. This was to encourage economic development to be directed to the frame of the incipient industrial revolution. Furthermore, it was strongly informed by the needs of assisting lower classes with care initiatives and promoting both insurance and savings. The realization of this model came about especially in mercantile cities in the north-west of Germany at the end of the century (Sparkasse), and from there spread to Austria and Switzerland and then to the north of Italy – as part of the Austro-Hungarian empire. Similar savings banks were founded in Spain (Caja or Caixa), in France (Caisse d'Epargne), in Great Britain[20] (savings banks), in the United States (savings and loans associations and credit unions)[21] and so on.

More precisely, in 1778, the Savings Bank of Hamburg was established, conventionally considered as the progenitor, in order to provide for 'a more humble, industrious people … the opportunity to set aside something, to deposit savings while earning in a secure way, with some interest' (Clarich 1984: 13).

They were no major problems (apart from ubiquitous poverty) in European countries. The Italian case is interesting precisely because of the presence of several kingdoms within its territory. In fact, in Italy, until 1822 the first savings banks were instituted in the territory of the Austro-Hungarian empire, similar to the spread of Monti di Pietà. In Milan in 1823, Cassa di Risparmio delle Provincie Lombarde was established by the Central Commission of Benefaction,[22] with the solicitation of government authorities. In central Italy – the Grand Duchy of Tuscany and the Papal state – the initiative was taken by citizens' associations, while in the south savings banks were derived from Monti Frumentari and had a very restrained development. The fact that the initiative for the constitution of savings banks was initiated by many actors (governments, communes, Church authorities, citizens' associations) led to a variety of institutional types, including associative and foundation structures.[23] The latter distinction is still applicable to the structure of bank foundations. Savings banks were basically regulated by the Statute, in an eminently private way that determined the organizational structure and the degree of administrative and capital autonomy. The Statute, thanks to its flexibility, allowed timely adjustments for each institute, in order to operate under their specific economic and social realities.

The operation of savings banks

From the beginning, the main function that marked savings banks was the collection of savings from the lower classes paying small providential amounts. This business had no speculative intent. The nature of the deposits can be seen largely by the necessity of ensuring two things:

1 the security of investments through the prudent management of collected money;
2 and a degree of viability as a form of incentive.

These aspects are also inextricably linked to the important pedagogical function that the banks assumed in the view of the poor segment of the population, which changed people's attitudes. With the subsequent emergence of the banking element, savings banks followed separate operational patterns not only with respect to large private banks but also with respect to popular banks, which, as we will see, tended to be at higher risks and therefore played a role in the stabilization of the financial system in periods of economic crisis.

After a few decades, savings banks had already collected the major part of available savings. In 1880, in Italy, there were 183[24] distributed throughout the country.[25] The diffusion and the growth of new institutes led the government to regulate institutions and operations more stringently through a law in 1888 which distinguished and clarified the legal definition of savings banks and put them under the supervision of the Ministry of Agriculture, Industry and Commerce.[26] This law considered them as well defined and distinct institutions, including their social function in comparison with other credit agencies. During this same period, however, they had to face competition in collecting savings with Italian Post[27] and popular banks.

Popular banks and rural banks as cooperative banks: their origins

From the ideological and historical points of view, the idea leading to the formation of cooperatives, which would be the legal explanation of popular banks and rural banks, came from England, from Robert Owen and the pioneers of Rochdale. In France, the first experiments of workers' consortia and cooperatives were set up between 1830 and 1840 in some works by Philippe Bouchez who promoted certain forms of cooperative associations between furniture dealers and goldsmiths, and of Louis Blanc (1848) who presented the government a legal design for constructing operational bodies in cooperative form. Dating back to 1848, including the establishment of an early embryonic form of 'popular' bank in a work by Pierre Joseph Proudhon in the same period in Belgium, François Haeck tried a similar experiment with a cooperative bank. It is important to recall also Charles Gide, founder of the Nîmes School who came to theorize upon a 'cooperative republic', in which profit was completely banished from the economic system (Gide 2001).

There were essentially two grounds upon which these banks were based:

1 to combat usury, which (still) mainly affected the poorest classes; and
2 to give the opportunity to make use of valid organisms of lending, even to those of modest economic means.

Precisely for this reason the cooperative form of credit cooperation was chosen, considered the best suited to collect the modest financial resources of shareholders, to allow better remuneration for small savers and provide capital to small entrepreneurs under more favourable conditions. Thus credit cooperations excluded those classes which could obtain financial capital from other banks. Cooperative banks came in two different forms, one was the popular banks and the other was rural banks, which were found in different sectors of business and immediately diversified strongly.

Popular banks

At around 1850 Germany also began, during a time of deep economic crisis, to give practical effect to the principles of cooperatives. The first attempts of Hermann Schulze-Delitzsch, a Prussian lawyer of liberal beliefs and member of the National Assembly, were geared towards the formation of cooperatives among small employers, for insurance against sickness and death, and for the purchase of raw materials. Subsequently, he chose the path of credit cooperatives which had to be strongly rooted in their own regions with a high level of autonomy, overcoming a rigid and class-conscious individualism of Prussian aristocratic society that retained all levels of political and economic power. This was also in line with the principle of privilege mutuality. Thus many could, collectively, realize more opportunities given the rules of existing credit that constrained the individual. Hence, their entrepreneurial capacity and their desire for economic and social growth were stimulated and rewarded. This economic doctrine was significantly reflected in the urban population. In 1859 there were already 183 banks with 18,000 members in Pomerania and Saxony.[28] In the same year, the first central office was established in order to coordinate, whilst respecting the functional autonomy of individual units and the activity of various credit cooperatives being distant among them. This was the birth of what would later become the Volksbank (Popular Bank).

The pragmatism of Schulze-Delitzsch[29] was expressed in his basic text in 1855. Credit unions that were popular banks, which did not ignore cooperation development and which had already established the first principles of solidarity and support, expanded from the body of work for purchasing goods of consumption and production in 1844 in Manchester. However, Schulze-Delitzsch's liberalism led him to reject the socialist model of Lassalle's 'forced association' which strictly left cooperatives to the control of the state and to financing by public funds. For him, cooperative popular banks had to be based on the capacity of savings and on the security of individual shareholder members, without any contribution from either the state or private charity, as was often practised in savings banks.

The spread in Europe and around the world was enormous and modified everywhere to adapt to different local realities. Cooperative banks tended to be developed mainly within urban areas and to become the banks of merchants, craftsmen and professionals, whilst rural banks were spread in agricultural centres and almost worked exclusively with farmers as clients.

Philosophy and operation of cooperative banks

Savings banks and popular banks traditionally operated regionally or locally.

These banks were developed within an urban environment and constituted a response to the question of funding coming from small entrepreneurs and artisans, who in this way could defend themselves from the danger of being expelled from the market by major manufacturing companies, due to their superior organization and greater concentration. In this sense, institutions of popular credit stood out compared to the existing savings banks, which initially pursued the goal of fighting poverty and of educating the poor to save. Furthermore, the popular banks assumed the structure of a limited liability company, a peculiarity that enabled them to reach larger dimensions than the banks that adopted the system of unlimited liability, which represented a constraint to their dimensional and geographical growth. The larger availability of capital and range of actions of popular banks induced them to offer their services even to non-members, thereby alleviating the exclusive character of these institutions. Although popular banks constituted an extremely heterogeneous category, encompassing both large and small institutions in most of them, the persistence of a strong vocation to regionalism could be detected.

Popular banks, according to Schulze-Delitzsch's project, were provided with capital that was made up of high denomination stocks that less wealthy members could also pay in instalments. They were members who were involved in at least one activity and only in the ones where the bank could grant loans. Capital had to constitute the first operational funds, but banks could also take deposits from non-members by paying interest on them, provided these deposits did not exceed social capital by three or four times. Loans were granted at a low rate of interest for limited amounts and from exclusively personal guarantees. Finally, profits were intended to be, for the most part, set aside as reserves.

The specificity of popular banks was given by their legal/participatory reality:

- the capitation vote was based on each member's vote with each member, regardless of the number and value of shares held, having only one vote;
- the limit of bank ownership, where it was expected that no shareholder may hold shares in excess of 0.50 per cent of social capital;
- the prediction of a minimum number of members that could not be less than 200;
- the institution of satisfaction, for which the Board of Directors may reject an application to become a member based on societal interests, on statutory requirements and on the spirit of cooperative formation.

Through extensive experience and support, popular banks continued to grow and to innovate, while keeping intact their original principles and values. The success of the cooperative system is evidenced by its significant presence in Europe and in the international environment. Further confirmation of this is provided by the establishment of organizations such as the European Association of

Cooperative Banks (EACB) and the International Confederation of Popular Banks (CIBP) based in Brussels which joins the ICBPI (Italian Popular Bank Central Institute) and comprises banking institutions and bodies whose vocation consists of promoting the development of small and medium enterprises and households.

Rural banks

Even though popular banks' activities had expanded, there was still a problem: their growth was urban and it was impossible to reach rural and countryside populations who could not benefit from suitable credit partly because of physical distance and partly due to information asymmetry between the bank and rural areas. A type of bank that could be found in small towns or communities offering to promote fair jobs and profits whilst respecting individuals was needed.

More or less similar to Schulze-Delitzsch, another German social banking character emerged: Friedrich W. Raiffeisen, who had started his activity in the countryside and after a few years of work based on cooperation and charitable foundations, decided to spend his life working on the credit cooperative within the Schulze-Delitzsch model. Therefore, in 1862, the first Raiffeisen Banking Cooperative was established in Anhausen (Ferraresi 2007). However, the spirit which encouraged his work was different (and this established the difference in the operations of popular and rural banks). Raiffeisen, respecting economic principles, favoured the ethical motivations of Christian inspiration. Giving life to credit cooperatives was a precise wording of divine will because they were nothing more than a means to help people to make use of material and spiritual goods which God had given them and which one day they would be accountable for.[30] Externally, the Raiffeisen banks were different from the Schulze-Delitzsch cooperatives with respect to: the extent of the principle of open society, of voting for every single member and of unlimited liability (this has been rectified in a multiple liability, in respect to the subscribed capital and, finally, in limited liability).

After an initial period of low dissemination, a rapid growth in the number of banks began, which in 1888, when Raiffeisen died, stood at 425. In subsequent years, their diffusion created a more sustainable tendency than popular banks. Indeed, on the eve of the First World War there were 16,927 units compared to 980 cooperatives inspired by Schulze-Delitzsch.

In Italy, the symbolic home of banks, the imported model in 1883 allowed the estabishment of the first rural bank in Loreggia (Padua) from the work of Leone Wollemborg. Then, in 1888, the federation between rural banks and related associations was created, involving 51 banks. Shortly after, thanks to a young priest – Don Luigi Cerutti of Venice – the first Catholic rural bank was established. In 1891 the encyclical *Rerum Novarum* of Pope Leo XIII, which urged Catholics to social actions and togetherness to overcome the poorest people's loneliness, became the manifesto of this ample and diffuse movement. An extensive process of emergence and spread of rural banks of Catholic matrix in various Italian regions began. In 1897, there were another 900, of which 775 were Catholic. The federations with diocesan character started to give the first organizational structure. In 1905, the Italian Federation of Rural Banks started working. It was established with the goals of group representation and protection and of promotion and improvement of member banks, within a support structure compatible with the technical and financial tasks of banks.

In the first 15 years of the twentieth century, cooperation continued to grow. It was in line with the overall Italian economy, proving to be a phenomenon destined to stand the test of time as it survived through economic crisis caused by the First World War and the politics of the fascist regime. The latter constrained it noticeably, resulting in a general restructuring: while in 1922 cooperatives had reached a sum of 3,540, they dropped to 986 in 1940 and 804 in 1947.

Subsequently several measures changed their operating characteristics. In 1928, during the fascist period, for understandable political reasons, they were excluded by the exercise of federal agricultural credit. With the laws of 1932–4 and the Banking Law of 1937, credit activities in agriculture and craft were limited, and opportunities of financing for non-members were fixed up to only a maximum of 40 per cent of total credit disbursed. In 1936 the National Institution of Agricultural Rural Banks and Auxiliary Boards was established. The revitalization of rural banks took place in the Republican period with the enactment of Constitutional Cards, which, in Article 45, recognized the role of cooperation with mutual goals. In 1950, the Italian Federation of Rural and Craft Banks was established and, in 1967, it adhered to Confcooperative.

The Raiffeisen model created a reference point for the whole of Europe, with a recent implementation as a result of the transition of Eastern economies after 1989.

Philosophy and operation of rural banks

Economic mutualism and democracy are the specific characteristics of rural banks and cooperative companies. Mutual non-profit enterprises are the ones in which a part of assets are attributed to indivisible reserves. This means that assets are available only to shareholders who invest in the company for reasons of mutual exchange and not in terms of capitalist benefit, namely return on capital. Mutualism, which may be considered as their distinctive element, does not exist in any other bank, even in formal cooperative popular banks. It has an internal character that expresses towards and between the social base, and an external character towards the local community. This final aspect combines togetherness, localism, trust and development and is described in the Social Budget of Mission which is made independently by a group of banks and cooperative credits.[31] It is testimony to the fact that the welfare of the community today is given not only by material wealth, but also by opportunities and by occasions and relationships that are created within regions. The core of a mutualistic cooperative enterprise is represented by the viewing of members as individuals, that is not as shareholders whose value to society is in relation to paid-in capital. The historical roots of cooperative credit are based on the principle that small farmers and craftsmen, combining available scarce resources, built the rural bank and succeeded in surviving in spite of many disadvantages. Their success and their growth coincided with their counterparts in small villages. Hence, today as in the past, cooperation, mutuality and localism are columns of the cooperative system. Through the provision of credit only to members and through charging an interest rate, rural banks aimed at encouraging investment and the modernization of handicrafts, manufacturing and agricultural sectors, characterized by the presence of small and micro enterprises.

Their dynamic, their ability to operate with a social capital lower than that of popular banks, their reinvestment of profits, a tax sufficient to spread prosperity, etc. permitted rural banks to become a significant presence in the European reconstruction after the Second World War. In fact they did not lose their original spirit, and also strengthened their ability to generate wealth and social stability. Subsequently, the financialization of the economy also concerned them, but a return to ethics and the prerogative of new social banks has meant that many banks had a resurgence of consciousness which did not only return them to their core philosophies but also led them to engage in the modality of advanced social finance, as in the case of microcredit.

Rifkin wrote:

> Non-profit local banks care about their region's identity and culture. They may return to finance the means of service to society. Keeping money within a community is an important role. Money which we put in a bank must be reused locally. This is also a way in which local banks can contribute to strengthening the local culture that generates confidence, without which there is no market.
>
> (Rifkin 2000)

The cooperative model that provided the origin for rural banks was echoed by many other social banks, such as ethical banks that were formed during the final decades of the twentieth century. Very often the mission and vision of these banks has been borrowed from rural banks.

Catholic social banks

In this brief excursus on social banks, which were also forerunners in a certain sense, modern ethical banks cannot ignore other types of banks that sprang from the Catholic vision in both Italy and Europe of the newly formed Social Doctrine of the Church due to Pope Leo XIII with his encyclical *Rerum Novarum*.

In Italy, besides many rural banks and popular banks, Catholic social banks were mostly private, often in Italian S.p.A. form (Joint Stock Company – JSC), although many of them were originally created as a Society of Mutual Aid, such as the Banca Cattolica del Veneto which was founded in 1892 with the name of Banca Cattolica Vicentina. Initially the institute was inspired by principles of togetherness and collaboration between citizens and regional productive forces (influential was the religious presence in the Diocese of Vicenza). It is impossible to forget an important work by Joseph Tovini of Brescia who argued for the need to ensure the full financial autonomy of Catholic institutions, especially the educational ones, for example Bank S. Paolo in 1888 in Brescia, and Banco Ambrosiano in 1896 in Milan. On the same wavelength as Ambrosiano were the Catholic leaders of Opera dei congressi which gave birth to many banks: among them, the Piccolo credito bergamasco, Banco San Marco, Banco di Roma, Banca Antoniana, Banca di Desio e Brianza, Banco di San Gimignano, the Credito romagnolo (subsequently Credito Romagnolo) which included among its founders the Catholic John Acquaderni, 120 priests, the Cardinal of Bologna, Domenico Svampa and Bishop of Cesena, monsignor Vespignani.

Three sets of objectives brought about these institutions' birth:

- to help development initiatives that were carried out by entities with no capacity for debt;
- to allocate funds to support charitable works (aid, education, etc.) through targeting a share of the profits (which means partial renouncing of shareholders). A clear precursor of one of the forms in which ethical finance today manifests;
- to meet the needs and interests of local communities.

The distinction between public and private did not have the meaning of confrontation which it was to assume thereafter. These banks had begun very promisingly, but they – after not so long – changed. The conjugation between the moment of wealth production and its immediate distribution, also given by a strong ethical and social spirit, had gradually tapered. However, it did not become a means of poverty alleviation.

Contemporary historical reality of social banks: ethical banks and microcredit

Preliminary problems

A close examination of the birth of elements of banks in the fifteenth century onwards has led to an understanding of how their genesis was more than an idea bound to the human and social development of everyone in their most sacred realities: respect for life and the existence of each person through work. In fact, Monti di Pietà, savings banks, popular banks, rural banks, etc., had this purpose, directed especially towards the poorest and most marginalized people, mostly aggregated/charitable and in cooperative form. For others, the wealthy, there were conventional banks and private banks which tended their investments and had allowed the funding of various 'industrial revolutions' with a considerable profit.[32]

This gradually led a near despondency in ethical/philosophical institutions and to the advent of utilitarianism (started by Jeremy Bentham[33]), which has gradually led the economy, through its finance, to mould individuals to become more *homo oeconomicus* than *homo socialis*. Various economic/financial crises often had their origins in a selfish desire for enrichment and power and the subsequent use of economic instruments in a distorted manner which was certainly not for the benefit of the community. The emergence of some state central banks to give order to the mismanagement of the economy was one testimony of this. In fact until the great crisis of 1929 the banking situation was complex and many problems needed to be addressed; the issuance of currency, the granting of short- and long-term credit, the firsthand commitment to financial activities (which exist even today in the United States with the internal connection between banks and hedge funds), etc. These issues were later answered in the laws and international agreements which had been revisited several times (though not always effectively). In this arena, social banks also had not always respected their vision. The savings banks in the United States with their failures in the late nineteenth century, the problems inherent in many popular banks[34] were already more or less in existence from the beginning. The practical operational difficulties of rural banks,[35] the decline of the social prerogatives, gave birth to Catholic banks. In fact they closed a round of banking activities that was seen at that moment, in their management of production, intimately linked with distribution. The new economic formula after 1929, which hoped that the creation of wealth from its distribution was entrusted to third parties (primarily state and welfare), was a harbinger of another separation. Ethics was no longer a social and common good, but only personal and collective.

The end of the Second World War and the resolutions taken by the winners with the economic policies of the Bretton Woods institutions permitted a robust economic recovery in the world, also thanks to an expansion of welfare policies and the end of colonialism. However, the Cold War between the two superpowers – who embodied two different economic philosophies – and the Middle East conflict with the oil-bearing problem blocked the economic situation which had not yet borne fruit. Subsequently, the beginning of globalization in 1975 with the first G7 at Rambouillet in France laid the foundations for capitalist/liberal politics and started financialization of the economy (also thanks to the creation of information technology). Since then, thanks to a high level of monetary circulation which had no borders, and deriving income from purely financial investments, intermediation activity in finance in general and in banking in particular has been transformed. Household savings started not to be allocated anymore to activities which were becoming productive, but to be invested in a speculative way. The big gains obtained allowed a change of living and working for many people and financial crises, very frequently, resulted in a Darwinian growth that gradually led to the large and unavoidable crisis which began in 2008. This occurred in the almost total absence of ethical thought which had been forgotten and obscured from its original formulations.

The establishment of many 'ethical and alternative' banks after 1975 tried and is still trying to take back the threads of social ideals and consequent ethics which have never been split. This meant finding a third way through economic ideals which have either disappeared (as in matrix collectivism of

Marxist/Leninist) or are undergoing serious theoretical/operational difficulties (such as capitalism and, in particular, liberalism) and give back impetus to the civil economy which underlines the role of social and economic relations in the market and not only in profit maximization.

Various kinds of social banking

In creating these new institutions of social banking many visions and missions were designed by founders relating to criteria of the first banks. In any case, it is possible to divide them into the following sectors:

1 banks (and similar), which continue social banking activities, implement them in a modern way and are dedicated to under-privileged classes of the population (the supposed non-bankables) or to activities outside banking orthodoxy;
2 banks (and similar), which travel a new road from an economic point of view (abolition of interest);
3 banks (and similar), which open new markets (microcredit and microfinance in general); and
4 banks especially engaged in charitable activities (children's banks).

However, in general, unless some distinction was made, these new intermediaries covered all new economic/financial veins that rebuilt financial ethics. The latter had its origins, in a modern style, in the 1920s in the United States in work by Mennonites with the management of ethical funds and applied inclusive or exclusive criteria to portfolios. Due to their worldwide success, a revisiting process of banking credit policy in many schools of thought began and led to the creation of new financial intermediaries.

Ethical and alternative banks

The origin of these intermediaries can be found in individuals who departed from the ideas and motivations which were both of philosophical/theological origin and of economic/social pathway. They now number around 20, among which ten are real banks provided with a bank licence. What unites them is the daily effort to use money as 'a means and not an end', to give credit to national and international cooperation, environmental protection, culture, art, social integration, etc. Most of them are transparent in their management and disclose operational funds, providing the customer with opportunities to choose the interest rate and the sector or project that utilizes his or her savings.

Banks of philosophical/theological nature

These banks were the first to be born and rapidly spread. The concept of reference is from Steiner, who defined his own citizens according to two worlds: the physical and the spiritual. He founded anthroposophy[36] as a science which turned to promote the development of human beings both in physical/material and in inner/spiritual ways.[37] From these ideas, the first ethical bank was born in 1974 and founded in Europe: the GLS-Bank, in Bochum, Germany. GLS denotes Gemeinschaft fuer Leihen und Schenken (community to lend and donate).[38] The new bank's purpose was to allow the carrying out of large projects to promote social cohesion, bringing together many small contributions. 'Initiatives promoted by groups of people and not by anonymous interest in seeking capital or the maximum profit possible', it said in its first informational brochure.[39]

Among the banks' activities were the credit communities (Leihgemeinschaften) allowing the breaking up of large funds into small portions. The GLS was and is a cooperative bank that extended its activities while remaining tied to anthroposophy at the same time. GLS finances wind parks, solar roofs, biological farmers, confinement houses, women-owned businesses and orchestras.

The transformation of GLS was accelerated in 2003 by the acquisition of Ökobank, an environmental bank established in Frankfurt in 1988 by German environmental movements. Born as the bank of movement (Bank der Bewegung), the Ökobank, which no longer exists, was in part operating within the pacifist movement and the Green Party in Germany, offering the opportunity of allocating savings to socio-environmental project funding. Bank shareholders did not want to take the risk of receiving consolidation, even indirectly, by taking deposits from traditional banks, an activity which was essentially aimed at reducing supposed risk.

Gradually, five other Steinerian banks emerged which were created based on the GLS example: in 1980 the Triodos Bank in the Netherlands; in 1982 the Merkur in Denmark; in 1984, the Freie Gemeinschaftsbank BCL in Switzerland; in 1997 the Cultura Bank in Norway and in 1998, the Ekobanken in Sweden. The French cooperative of supportive finance La Nef, which was founded in 1989, should also be added. The reference of anthroposophist values varies from bank to bank. The most faithful to its origins is certainly the BCL of Basel. Triodos, the largest one with headquarters in Zeist, a town near Utrecht, Netherlands, opened offices in Brussels in 1993, in Bristol, England and most recently in Madrid and Frankfurt. The bank's name has its origin in Greek language, meaning 'three ways' or 'crossroads to three ways'.[40] Actually the Dutch bank, which employs nearly 500 people, has grown at a dizzying rate, pointing to a development model which is very similar to that of the traditional bank. It became the largest and the most international ethical bank in Europe very quickly. Unlike GLS and BCL, Triodos is a limited company with an annual dividend for its shareholders, many being large banks, insurance companies and pension funds.

Banks of economic/social nature

Banks (and similar) in this category are definitely numerous and still growing, not only because of difficulties in lending from traditional banks for activities that are not strictly considered to be orthodox in their goals and budgets but also because these traditional banks were (often wrongly) considered risky as a result of several international legislative measures. The space left was logically filled by new players who have a presence, even a cultural or a capillary one, in local regions.

The normal principles of ethical finance are often conjugated in a specific manner according to the reality of each bank (based on a local analysis of needs and history), but still share a general commonality. An example is the Italian Manifesto of Ethical Finance presented in Box 2.1.

Box 2.1 The Manifesto of Ethical Finance

In Italy the basic reference is the Manifesto of Ethical Finance, which was promoted by the Ethical Finance Association at the Conference 'Towards a purpose – paper for Italian ethical finance', Florence 1998. The principles were and are:

1. Belief that credit, in all its forms, is a human right: not discriminate among recipients of loans on the basis of gender, ethnicity or religion, or on the basis of assets but the rights of the poor and marginalized people. Therefore finance activities promote human, social and environmental assessment, projects with the dual criterion of economic viability and social utility. Guarantees on loans are another form with which partners assume responsibility for projects funded. Ethical finance valued the guarantee of asset type, and equally valid forms of guarantees of individual, category or community that provide access to credit also to weaker segments of the population.
2. Consider efficiency as a component of ethical responsibility: it is not a form of charity: it is an economically viable activity which was intended to be socially useful. Taking responsibility, which is not only to make available their savings but also to utilize them in a way which may conserve value, is foundation of a partnership between people with equal dignity.
3. Does not retain wealth which is based on possession and exchange of legitimate money: interest rate in this context is a measure of efficiency in using savings, a measure of commitment to protect resources made by savers and make them blossom in viable projects. Consequently, the interest rate, which is the return on savings, is not zero, but must be kept as low as possible on the basis of economic but also social and ethical issues.
4. It is transparent: the financial intermediary has a duty relating to the treatment of confidential information about investors with which it comes into possession in the course of its business, but transparent relationships with customers requires clarity on aspects of the savings. Depositors are entitled to know the processes of operation of financial institutions and its decisions of employment and investment.
5. Participation in important decisions not only from shareholders but also from savers is foreseen: forms may include both direct mechanisms of preferences of funds' destinations, both democratic mechanisms of participation in decisions. Ethical finance is to bring a strong and courageous message of economic democracy.

6 Has reference criteria for the uses of social and environmental responsibility: identifying areas of employment, and eventually some favoured areas, introducing in economic investigation the reference's criteria based on promoting human development and social and environmental responsibility. Excludes in principle financial relationships with economic activities that hinder human development and contribute to violating fundamental human rights, such as production and trade of weapons, gravely injurious production to health and environment, activities which are based on exploitation of children or repression of civil liberties.

7 Requires a global and consistent adherence from a manager who organizes all activities: however, if the financial asset is only partially ethically oriented, it is necessary to explain in transparent manner, the reasons for restrictions adopted. In any case, the broker is prepared to be monitored by guarantee institutions of savers.

Other institutions, based on unions, have operated with more social than ethical reasons. In any case there is a high attentiveness to service rather than a quest for profit.

In Europe, the archetype of this institution type is the Banca Popolare Etica, which is also the largest one. It was born from the principles of ethical finance whose philosophy can be summarized as follows, premising what it is not:

- it is not specialty finance in non-profit;
- it is not specialty finance in decidedly local interventions;
- it is not finance based on the concept of donations.

Ethical finance means a way of funding which puts the person at the centre of the intervention. As a result the Statute on ethical finance, in Article 5, reveals its Vision and Mission.[41] In fact, everyday experience places the bank at the centre of a series of financial, economic, cultural and social relationships which serve to illuminate the overall design which is being worked. Having to operate within this framework together with complex, sometimes conflicting, relationships, it is fundamentally important to have very clear goals that are deemed necessary to succeed in building, along with many other people and organizations, a new way of economizing. Therefore networking and being loyal to the ethical concepts above which combine theory with operations is crucial. From this, the following slogan was created: 'bank for community, not community for bank'. This new approach is geared towards two objectives. First, the collection of savings where people/depositors can express their views both in deciding where to direct their savings and how much, considering interest and gains, with certainty that their savings will not be involved in any operation related to exploitation: human, environmental or social. For example: not in the commerce of the army, not in various practices against humans, not in anything which directly or indirectly threatens the environment; and to direct employment or funding to: national or international cooperations, to cultural or environmental projects, or to civil society.

The formalities are stringent: the return of savings and the interest rates are equal for all. It is expected that savings are collected for direct funding in their own regions, to connect the surplus of money from employers and the deficit of borrowers in a supportive way at rates as low as possible for all. Therefore they can carry out projects which arise in communities and in which local residents and stakeholders take care of each other's needs. In this way it was possible to finance a number of social projects which do not arrange full securities or sufficient funds.

Therefore Banca Popolare Etica carries out its business in two ways:

1 operating strenuously and dynamically as a financial intermediary with respect to all difficult situations which do not receive help from a classic economic/financial system (thereby seeking to contribute to an integrated regional and environmental development, restoring dignity to the word *credit* and *confidence* in the future of people and also creating jobs where there weren't any);
2 contributing to reflection on the economy and on finance which awaits the citizen of the third millennium. This activity is an indispensable part of its being. The bank creates appropriate structures to talk, understand, listen and discern the way of acting in favour of these who want to live in the way that can be expressed democratically.

Hence, ethical banking may be regarded as a means of construction and development for stakeholders and for the system, but not as an end of pure annuity to satisfy its own financial interest and shareholders.[42]

European economic/social banks

In Europe, besides the Ethical Popular Bank (Italy) there are: Mag (Verona, Milan, Piemonte, Reggio Emilia, Venice) (Italy); Adriatic Ethical Bank (Italy); APS Bank Ltd. (Malta); Bank Für Sozialwirtschaft (Germany); OekoGeno eG (Germany); Alternative Bank Switzerland (Switzerland); Sifa (France); Caisse Solidaire (France); Colonya, Caixa Pollença (Spain); Fiare (Spain); Fets (Spain); Charity Bank (United Kingdom); Cooperative Bank (United Kingdom);[43] Groupe Crédal (Belgium); Réseau FA (Belgium); Soficatra (Belgium); Netwek Vlaanderen (Belgium); Ekobanken Medlemsbank Ekobanken (Sweden); Femu Quì (France); Hefboom (Belgium); Integra Co-operative (Slovenia); Tise (Poland); Takuu Säätiö (Finland); Osuuskunta Eko-Osuusraha (Finland); Clann Credo – The Social Investment Fund (Ireland); Etika – Initiativ fir Alternativ Finanzéierung asbl (Luxemburg).

Added to this, there are a series of banks that do not directly adhere to social and ethical concerns, but in fact operate in the non-profit sector, such as: Banca Prossima (Italy), CFI Compagnia Finanziaria Industriale (Italy), etc.

Economic and social banks globally

A lot of institutions of this general kind have come into existence throughout the world. Many of them belong to FEBEA and INAISE European network (see Box 2.2 and Box 2.3).

Box 2.2 FEBEA

FEBEA (Fédération Européenne de finances et banques ethiques et alternatives) is a non-profit, incorporated under Belgian law, which was founded in 2001 in order to promote and develop ethical and alternative finance in Europe. FEBEA was created by six ethically oriented European financial institutions: Banca Popolare Etica (Italy), Crédit Coopératif (France), Credal (Belgium), Hefboom (Belgium), Caisse Solidaire du Nord Pas de Calais (France) and TISE (Poland). Today there are 24 associates coming from 13 European countries with different origins and sizes. Among these social financial institutions, in fact, some are banking institutions with large dimensions and strong propensities to support the social economy, others are ethical banks and financial companies of ethical finance and microfinance. To participate in FEBEA, they shall adhere to the 'Charte de la FEBEA', a charter of values in which all signatories undertake to operate to put the economy at the service of man, to contribute to solidarity, to social cohesion and to sustainable development, to reject the only objective of financial earnings in its activities and to encourage the realization of high value innovative initiatives from the environmental and social point of view, especially in social areas, sustainable development, international solidarity and fair trade. The birth of FEBEA was dictated from the beginning, not only by representation purposes, but by the concrete and real needs of members to achieve specific financial instruments and services, aimed at supporting institutions which exist or are being created or operating in ethical finance in Europe. Networking is for more support. Then FEBEA formed SEFEA (Societé Européenne de Finance Ethique et Alternative) to provide financial support to European ethical and supportive credit institutions which exist or are being set up, to promote growth and development. SEFEA also finances European projects which promote economic and social development that improves and protects natural, cultural assets and people in all European Union countries.

Box 2.3 INAISE

INAISE (the International Association of Investors in the Social Economy) is an international network of financial institutions that are oriented towards sustainable financial and social development. Formed in 1989, INAISE has grown rapidly, as the movement of social investors in both Europe and non-European countries. Through INAISE, social investors from Norway to South Africa, from Costa Rica to Japan, were able to operate in networks, exchange experiences, spread information and show the world that money can actually be a means to achieve a positive social and environmental change. Its members, through their investment policy, seek to encourage and promote the development of organizations and companies: (i) sustainable environment and development: renewable energy like wind, solar and hydropower, energy efficiency, biological farming, food industry and retail trade, natural conservation, construction of eco-buildings, clean technology, etc. (ii) Social economy: cooperatives, community enterprises, active participation of workers, facilitate the buy-out of employees, creation of micro and small enterprises, particularly among unemployed, migrants and women. (iii) Health: health centres, community care, clinics and hospitals, programmes for the disabled, preventive therapies. (iv) Social development: social housing, community housing, social services, community transport, voluntary, groups of community and volunteering. (v) Education and training: school buildings, training, organizational development, alternative schools. (vi) UPS North–South: Fair Trade, start up small enterprises through microcredit programmes, training and consultancy to small businesses, crafts, agriculture, etc. (vii) Culture and art: art activities with exhibitions, theatre, cinema, dance, local radio.

Also recently (2009) the Global Alliance for Banking on Values was founded. It is a worldwide network of social banking. The new partnership seeks to develop new ways of working, to create suitable organizations to address medium- to long-term the concept of sustainability and new forms of ownership and economic cooperation. In fact it aims to develop an alliance between a number of banks and their affiliates which were formed all over the world to offer innovative products to meet, holistically, the needs of all their communities. In the most recent past, the financial industry has found itself in a crisis of multiple dimensions, among them being the lack of confidence. The Global Alliance for Banking on Values has agreed to use the knowledge of these banks to provide innovative alternatives to address the current crisis, and future times, which strongly influence the overall sustainability of the company. Its members are, therefore, innovative banking institutions whose main purposes are:

1 to provide products of social finance and basic financial services;
2 make community grants to development initiatives based on social entrepreneurs;
3 implement the promotion of sustainable enterprises and environment and fulfil the potential for human development, including poverty reduction;
4 to generate a triple-bottom line 'People, Planet and Profit' (P, P, P).

The shared values among partners are:

1 the use of money as a tool to improve the quality of life for people, social, cultural and environmental development;
2 a co-responsibility for the impact of human activities on 'interdependent environment and communities', especially in the long term;
3 to provide transparency, trust, clarity and inclusiveness to people in the manufacture of products and services.

The common mission is to:

1 provide the joint venture to validate sustainable development, social change and the environment;
2 provide members with strong cultural and scientific thinking and innovative financial management; and

3 to bring together the strengths, characteristics, capabilities and resources to improve the competitive positions of each member.

To conclude, the Global Alliance for Banking on Values wants to play a prominent role in the debate on how to build a sustainable future in finance and the promotion of joint projects among its members to help mankind and the environment.

In history of ethical banks, worthy of mention are two particular examples: the Canadian Caisse d'économie Desjardins Travailleuses et des travailleurs du Quebec and the Japanese National Association of Labour Banks. The Caisse d'économie Desjardins Travailleuses et des travailleurs (Québec) was formed in 1971 by the National Federation of Trade Unions (CSN) in the region of Quebec. It is part of the popular bank network that takes its name from its founder Desjardin (the first was opened in 1900). The network Desjardin is the first financial institution in the province of Quebec and the sixth in Canada. The main reason that prompted the CSN to form the Caisse d'économie was to extend the trade union action into the credit sector, promote greater control in managing savings of workers and directing them towards economic activities that respected people and the environment. The Caisse came about to allow the funding of collective and cooperative projects aimed to improve workers' living conditions and to contribute, with the CSN's action, to a fair growth of Quebec which enhances the development of a supportive and cooperative economy to be a catalyst for a social and collective entrepreneurial culture. In this respect, the Caisse operates mainly in four areas: supportive initiatives, cooperatives and social enterprise of proximity, local communities and culture.

To help entrepreneurs develop their projects, the partnerships with public institutions, local or network funds (Social Investment Network in Quebec, RISQ, the Caisse Centrale Desjardins, FondAction, other local development funds, etc.) were established. Customers can operate by phone, through local branch networks, ATMs and through the Internet. The Caisse has specific products and services for many social needs: programmes for the creation of cooperatives, available solidarity savings for all members, cooperative loans for co-op organizations, emergency loans for cooperatives, supportive and cultural organizations factors which are found in a critical financial situation, etc. Since 1 October 2004, the Caisse changed its name to the Caisse d'économie solidaire Desjardins.

The National Association of Labour Banks was founded in 1950 in Japan. As stated in their informational brochure, the association is a consortium of financial cooperatives which cultivate the dreams and ideals of their workers, their economic promotion, welfare, development and cultural activities and to create, through joint work, a society where all people may live in happiness. From these principles, an operator which is very close to the concepts of social banking arose.

The particular virtue of these banks is their willingness to consolidate in alternative ways compared to ordinary finance, the latter having failed to give satisfactory answers to people, especially in rural areas and cities' large suburbs. The courage and determination of so many supporters is facilitating an unimaginable development in poor and abandoned areas. Thus banking capacity to support credit (which means trust) that has been lost over time is regained. It is hoped that the vitality and the increasing presence of these institutions may then lead to banking diffusion that, by local saving, historically contributes to human and regional growth.

Microfinance institutions

Microfinance and microcredit activity is a proven reality[44] now and is broadly providing a very interesting contribution to the development of nations and of impoverished and poor populations. Not all these activities are ethical. They are ethical only when they satisfy the requirements of ethical finance. Otherwise they are simply banking activities, and in a certain sense, re-propose a capitalist spirit, even if that may be a compassionate one. In any case, their development has been sufficiently rapid that many ordinary banks have started to get involved into microfinance, as they begin to trade with related equities (for products and services of microfinance see pp. 97–122).

The most well-known microfinance institution is Grameen Bank, in Bangladesh. It was founded in 1976, by the 2006 Nobel Peace Prize winner Muhammad Yunus. Based on this initiative, a lot of banks were founded (with many legal specificities) throughout the world. Furthermore they even started to work with microcredit in rich Western countries. Besides Grameen Bank, there are a lot of institutions which are difficult to list throughout the world. Many of them can be found within European consortiums (such as MFM – Micro Finance Network, the Italian Consorzio Etimos, etc). Finally, the majority of big international NGOs have constructed specific associations to deal with microcredit.

Banks which do not take interest

In this group there are many banks that adhere to the ideals of Islamic finance, as well as Western banks that do not operate under an interest rate method. These banks are largely territorial in nature and are funded (mostly) through local, non-speculative activities. In the case of Islamic finance, there are two key concepts that shape its operations:

- the prohibition of interest rates, equated to usury (both terms are translated with *riba*); and
- the prohibition of all uncertainty (*gharar*) which directly affects the insurance market.

These concepts are based on the Prophet Muhammad, a successful businessman, who had said that 'God has permitted trading and forbidden usury'. He juxtaposed these two terms and expressed the predilection for current transactions.

But risk sharing is based on profit and loss sharing. To achieve fairness in distribution, both the losers and the winners share the investment profit. According to this rule, a lender may not impose an interest rate on the debtor (since this does not take into account the actual result of the investment). Islamic banks, which follow these and other concepts of sharia, are rather recent institutions in a long Islamic tradition, but have been spreading a lot over the past ten years. In a certain sense there are many affinities between Islamic finance and ethical finance, especially the ideal of considering money as a means and not as an end.

Another example is the Swedish Jak Bank, which has the peculiarity of not applying active or passive interest rates and considers the charging of interest as the cause of the gradual impoverishment of society and economic instability. The basic premises of Jak's work are:

- income from interest is the enemy of a stable economy;
- interest results in unemployment, inflation and environmental destruction;
- interest moves money from the poor to the rich;
- public interest favours projects which tend to achieve high profits in a short time.

The ultimate goal of Jak is the abolition of speculative interest and the creation of a society free from interest rates. Riding on the wave of this bank, there is an idea of setting up other similar initiatives in European countries (see Box 2.4).

Box 2.4 JAK Bank (see www.feasta.org)

Can a bank operate successfully if it does not charge interest on its loans?

Savings Points

JAK's primary objective is to provide its members with interest-free loans. In order to accomplish this, it must attract interest-free savings. JAK uses a system of 'Savings Points' in order to balance saving and borrowing.

Given the choice of borrowing without interest or saving without interest, most of us would gladly choose borrowing. While people are generally willing to save temporary surpluses of money in current accounts that don't pay interest, few are willing or able to save more significant amounts over a long period of time with no compensation. JAK cannot, of course, lend money without having savings on deposit and so, using an imaginative system of Savings Points, each member who wishes to take out a loan must save money first and, over a lifetime with JAK, every member will have saved roughly as much money and for the same period of time as they will have borrowed. You could almost imagine JAK as allowing its members to borrow (interest-free) from their future selves.

For a new JAK member, the first step towards an interest-free loan is to save and thereby earn Savings Points. These are calculated as the amount saved, multiplied by the number of months for which it is saved, multiplied by a Savings Factor. This factor varies according to the type of savings account the member has selected and is lower (about 0.7) for a demand account from which savings can be withdrawn at any time. For example, assuming a Savings Factor of 0.9, we have:

€100 one month 0.9 = 90 Savings Points

The Savings Factor varies with the type of deposit account and is lowest for demand accounts where savings can be withdrawn at any time (about 0.7).

Example 1: either of these scenarios would earn identical Savings Points.
After saving for a minimum of six months, a member may apply for a loan. In order to borrow €1 for one month, one Savings Point must be redeemed. The amount borrowed and the time taken to repay are entirely up to the member, provided that the appropriate Savings Points are available. For example, borrowing €90 (or €9,000) over one year uses as many Savings Points as borrowing €45 (or €4,500) with repayments spread over two years.

Example 2: a Basic Loan.

Example 3: an alternative Basic Loan, borrowing half as much but repaying it over a longer period.
In addition to a Basic Loan that uses Savings Points already earned, members may apply for an Additional Loan using Savings Points that will be earned in the future. An "Allocation Factor" (currently 14) is multiplied by the member's current Savings Points to determine the number of points available for an Additional Loan.

Each loan repayment includes a savings instalment, and the payments are structured so that when the loan is fully repaid, all necessary Savings Points have been earned. A consequence of this is that upon full repayment of an Additional Loan, the member has built up significant savings. Savings made during the course of repaying a loan are known as Post-Savings, while those that precede the loan are Pre-Savings. Once the loan has been repaid, the balance of the Post-Savings is available to the member to be withdrawn or, as frequently happens, to be used as the start of saving for a new loan.

Example 4: a Basic Loan with an Additional Loan.
There is no interest charged on a loan, of course, but members must place 6 per cent of the value of the loan on deposit for the duration of the loan, and additionally pay a loan fee to cover administration costs. Members also pay 200 SEK (about €22) when they first join JAK and 200 SEK per year as a membership fee.

JAK is a virtual bank in the sense that it has no branches and business cannot be transacted in person. A necessary and prudent decision since the membership of JAK is quite spread out over a large country, and also resulting in no bias against rural members who would have to travel much further to their nearest branch. A result of this 'virtual' status is that JAK members must have an account with another bank with which to conduct their day-to-day financial affairs. Members transfer money into or out of their JAK basic account via post giro, bank giro or Internet. With improvements in technology and the changing financial infrastructure, JAK hopes in the near future to offer direct deposit of paycheques and credit/debit card facilities to its members. For some members, this might negate the need to bank elsewhere.

Credit control

Like any bank, JAK must ensure that loans can and will be repaid. Unlike most banks, however, JAK's system of saving and borrowing has several unique features that combine to give it an enviably low default rate.

A member applying for a loan is given a range of options for the loan size and duration based upon their desired loan amount, desired repayments and available savings points. When they have made their selection, the loan department within JAK must assess the member's ability to repay the desired loan. The member's income and expenses are evaluated with the assistance of computer software that calculates average living expenses for individuals and families based upon age and gender.

Between 20 and 25 applications are processed per week, and 95 per cent are approved. Most loans are secured, either against property or with a personal guarantor. Loans for up to 37,000 SEK (about €4,000) with 2–5 years' duration can be unsecured, but these are limited to 5 per cent of JAK's turnover and so surplus applications must be held in a queue until funds are available. The most common reason for borrowing is to refinance a conventional bank loan obtained to buy a house followed by purchasing a car and making home improvements.

In general, people who can save regularly are good performers when it comes to loan repayments. The JAK system where saving must precede borrowing is therefore ideally suited to attracting these regular savers. In addition, around halfway through repayment of a loan there is a break-even point where the Post-Savings on deposit are equal to the balance outstanding on the loan, and from this point forward the loan is fully secured by the member's savings.

Very few JAK loans end in default. Borrowers are decidedly involved 'members' as opposed to disinterested 'customers'. Many feel quite strongly about the idea of interest-free banking and this common bond goes a long way towards encouraging good behaviour. Personal guarantors rarely need to be asked to make good on their guarantee.

Liquidity

At the simplest level, a bank takes one person's savings and lends them to someone else. Ideological arguments aside, this presents some practical difficulties. First, what if a saver wants their money back before the borrower has finished with it? Second, what if there are not enough or too many borrowers relative to savers?

The first point is generally dealt with in the banking system by having a reasonably large number of savers and making sure that enough money is set aside to cope with those who, on any given day, want some of their money back. While individuals might withdraw their savings in a random manner, a large group of savers will tend to be stable and predictable.

It is JAK's policy to keep a minimum of 20 per cent of Pre-Savings available in either a bank account or in government bonds, either of which can be made available almost immediately. Too much liquidity means that money is lying idle rather than being lent out to members, so it is not seen as desirable to have much more than 20 per cent on reserve. Post-Savings do not need to have a component on reserve since these can only be withdrawn at specified times.

JAK also encourages stability from its savers by offering a higher Savings Factor in long-term deposit accounts. JAK members can choose from six-, 12- and 24-month deposit accounts which represent the advance notice required to make a withdrawal.

With regard to the second point, JAK has a more difficult balancing act between saving and borrowing than other banks, due to the fact that the two are intimately linked by Savings Points. Most people save with the intention of borrowing in the future. An excess of saving today could indicate too much demand for borrowing next year.

The Allocation Factor has a central role in the relationship between supply of savings and demand for loans. In general, the JAK board sets the Allocation Factor to reflect the current level of liquidity within the bank. The greater the pool of excess savings, the higher the Allocation Factor to encourage members to take out loans and reduce the excess. Unfortunately for JAK, the relationship between the Allocation Factor and the demand for loans is not as simple as this. In the short term, increasing the Allocation Factor can actually make things worse, as members decide to increase their Savings Points with a view to taking out a larger loan in the future. Excess demand for loans would be particularly problematic for JAK. Reducing the Allocation Factor would likely lead to an outcry from members who had made financial plans based on a higher factor. The alternatives, however, would be to refuse more loans or to introduce a waiting list. The dynamics of this saving/borrowing relationship are likely to be a constant challenge to JAK's management as the membership grows and the range of banking services offered by JAK expands.

JAK culture

A significant amount of JAK's energy is devoted to communicating with its 21,000-strong membership. JAK is a cooperative, fully owned by its members. In addition to a quarterly newsletter, 24 regional offices staffed by trained volunteers keep in touch with members through study groups and exhibitions. While JAK's primary function is to provide interest-free banking, it is also viewed by the membership as a vehicle for economic reform.

A recent innovation in support of economic reform is the Local Enterprise Bank. Community members save in a special JAK account and, rather than earning points themselves, their savings are used to provide an interest-free loan for a local enterprise. Savings are fully guaranteed, so members are not exposed to any financial risk. The first two projects to be funded in this way are an ecological slaughterhouse and a replica Viking village. It is an interesting experiment in local finance for local projects, and so far has been very warmly received by local media and participants. While savers don't, of course, receive any interest on their savings, they benefit both economically and otherwise from the improvements in their local economy and infrastructure as a result of the projects.

Children's banks

A very special institute working for poor people is the Children's Development Bank. It is the first bank in the world created to meet the needs of working children in India. It operates according to banking and cooperative principles, and it aims to protect the savings of younger workers and also to play an educational function. This bank was founded in 2004 by the Butterflies Association in New Delhi, an organization which operates in India for the benefit of working children, under the belief that every child has the right to enjoy childhood care, characterized by respect of people. The awareness of the harsh reality prompted Butterflies to launch initiatives which may protect small earnings of young children and, at the same time, educate them in the culture of savings which are needed to deal with daily adversities. Before the experiment of the Bank for Children, children did not see that it was useful to save their earnings. Given their life expectancy is very low, they preferred to spend it immediately. Initially, in the early 1990s, Butterflies had initiated a programme of savings and credit that guaranteed high interest to children who deposited their money without withdrawing it for 11 months. However, children thought that the period was too long. Thus, following a meeting, it was reduced to six months. The subsequent development was the establishment of the credit union, with a social capital grown by the daily deposits. They aim to provide various services to their members: education, training, medical care and loans to start business activities. The Children's Development Bank (Bal Vikas Bank) was the natural continuation of the Credit Union. Formally launched in 2004 with capital provided by the Indian National Foundation, it is entirely run by children, while operators of Butterflies play a role as facilitators. Each child was provided a personal record and, as for savings programmes, whoever deposits a sum and does not pick it up for six months receives an interest premium. Also, in addition to ensuring a safe place to keep money, the Bank pursues its objective of creating a culture of savings in children. Children older than 15 may borrow small amounts of cash to start small businesses. Until now, all loans requested were repaid. This initiative has expanded rapidly in many parts of India, and later also into other countries such as Nepal, Afghanistan and Sri Lanka.

The current state of the art of banks of ethical and social finance in Europe and the world

There is no doubt, from this analysis, that the social banking sector is vibrant and vital and it has an extremely bright future on the horizon. Savers and people in general are approaching a fail-safe surrounding that these banks are able to deliver a renewed social consciousness, in which money must contribute to achieving a concrete economy and not a 'paper' one which has characterized the last 30 years of financial assets worldwide. Additionally, these institutions provide a strong demand for transparency on the use of the means which are at their disposal.

But there is also a need for developing new technologies, respecting the environment and nature in general. Conventional banks show a marginal interest in these concerns, hence a sustainable and supportive future is a ubiquitous ideal. Many serious analyses of market statistics have shown that there is a 'desire for ethics' and only scarce knowledge of financial modalities blocks an even bigger growth (Demos and PI 2009). There are also new opportunities on the horizon. The imminent activity of the Banca Etica Europea (BEE) – between the Italian

Ethical Popular Bank, the French La Nef and the Spanish Fiare with the first realization of a Cooperative Company according to the European law[45] – will certainly mark the start of aggregations and agreements of European ethical/social financial entities, to give practical answers more quickly, to improve the diffusion of the idea of ethical finance and the supply of adequate and social operational tools to shareholders and stakeholders.

Is everything at its best? Not yet. There are still many problems to tackle and to solve, especially at the level of economic/financial/social theory. Some of these are important and urgent and need to be solved as soon as possible in a 'high and appropriate' way.

Hence, a few points can be highlighted:

1 While conventional finance travels on well-known platforms, social banking is still in training and not without substantial differences between different representatives. It is not enough to want to 'do good' and to fund 'non-bankables' to qualify the theoretical reality of this new discipline. It requires also the formulation of a new common economic, ethical or social thought that leads to change in those situations that economic doctrine offers to its customers. In other words, the underlying thought of social banking should not be niche, but should aim to correct the deformity of the whole economic system.
2 The network between different European and global entities is leading to new economic/financial activities, including the involvement of political and financial institutions of stature. However, there is a need to work in a legislative context for new regulations that make the policy-maker recognize new opportunities of extremely attractive instruments (with the meaning of *oikonomiké*[46]), such as microfinance, microcredit, social housing, etc. which are not present in many legislative contexts.
3 It is necessary that the economic concepts of civil economy, ethical (or social or supportive) finance, common good, etc. are better researched, justified and discussed as the path which has been travelled so far is insufficient for their widespread diffusion. The involvement of universities and academies in general is indispensable, as is the formulation of a strong thought that must not only be theoretically sound, but also theoretically deep and stringent. The point of view must always be of means and of service and not of the end. It is necessary to involve current economic activities which led to the financial crisis in a fundamental transformation in an ethical sense. At that point there is no need of two parallel economic directions (the so-called ethics and the classical canonical/orthodox), but only one that can respond comprehensively to the real demands of mankind for adequate and supportive growth.
4 It is impossible to imagine that the ideals and the activities of social banking would become characteristics of traditional banking. Hence, it undergoes 'bankarization' and may fall back into a peaceful operation which silences consciences but does not solve the problems, which lead people to be members

and customers of social banks. In fact, the banks should be constantly listening and receptive, also from a practical/operational point of view, for new ideas and dynamics given by the reflections above. In the long run, moreover, the non-application of these concepts is likely to invalidate these banks, as historically happened to the banks created with high ideals which soon turned into completely commercial institutes.

5 New frontiers given by the network of social banking must be always in contact with their community bases and should never disengage 'from below'. Inevitable differences are always dutifully present, because the cultures of origin are various and different, but it should not ever fall into the problem of information asymmetry (deliberately given and exacerbated by the economic system) and misunderstanding.

Ultimately, if the current state of social banking is good, it is necessary to keep its guard and not assume that this will be the case in the future. Too many people put faith in these banks and institutions with respect not only to their money but also to their own present and futures; and they rely completely, but not blindly, on those who carry forward the framework of a new economy.

Conclusion

The historical excursus showed certain common considerations: a historical and social continuance between old and new banks, though there was a break of a rather long time, especially in facing basic problems given by a lack of credit supply.[47] It is quite apparent that during the Middle Ages, the Monti di Pietà – the first banks – did constitute a novelty with the creation of new intermediaries. In the following centuries the supply of credit was expanded to new areas which were still marginalized and not fully served by bourgeois and business banks. The twentieth century saw a mix of all banking practices with the creation of legislative ordinations with a more operational philosophy that respects collective welfare.

Social banking, which is still young, from when it was born until the last 30 years, tried and is still trying, to re-take an important philosophy based more on the demand of credit (even as a social relation) than on the supply. Can conventional banks be defined as 'canonical/orthodox' while the concept that is promoted by social banking is defined as 'alternative?'. Probably not, since current finance itself is not a descendant from classical economic theory, but only subject to a desire for the enrichment of a few that are creating poverty for many. Therefore, is it not completely canonical finance, but truly 'alternative', though in a less appealing sense of the term?

In any case it will be the quality of response, both theoretical and practical, that social banking will give which will determine if an economic cultural change is possible, though it has still not yet arrived. Studying the past has told us that it is possible.

References

Andenna, G. (1998) 'Riflessioni canonistiche in materia economica dal XII al XV secolo', in *Chiesa, usura e debito estero*, study day on church and lending at interest, yesterday and today: on the occasion of the 50th anniversary of Faculty of Economics, 19 December 1997, Milan, Italy.

Bruni, L. (2006) *Il prezzo della gratuità*, Rome: Ed. IdeEconomia Città Nuova.

Capitani, O. (1958) 'La venditio ad terminum nella valutazione morale di san Tommaso d'Aquino e di Remigio de' Girolami', *Bullettino dell'Istituto storico italiano per il Medio Evo e Archivio Muratoriano*, 70: 298–355.

Clarich, M. (1984) *Le Casse di risparmio verso un nuovo modello*, Bologna: Ed. Il Mulino.

Demos and PI (2009) *Voglia di etica. Cittadini, banche e finanza in tempi d'incertezza. Indagine Demos per Banca Etica*. Online, available at: www.demos.it.

Ferraresi G. (2007) *La filiera corta come strumento di sviluppo locale*, Iniziativa Comunitaria Equal/NuoviStilidiVita: Laboratorio di Progettazione del Politecnico di Milano, Macrofase 2/Individuazione dei modelli condivisibili e degli indicatori territoriali: rapporto di ricerca.

Giacchero, M. (1981) 'L'atteggiamento dei concili in materia d'usura dal IV al IX secolo', in Costantiniana Romance Academy, 4: Proceedings of the IV International Conference in Honor of M. De Dominicis (Perugia, 1–4 October 1979), Perugia: Library Universitaria.

Gide, C. (2001) *Coopération et économie sociale 1886–1904*, Paris, Budapest and Turin: l'Harmattan; Paris, Comité pour l'édition des oeuvres de Charles Gide, [présenté et annoté par Patrice Devillers].

Le Goff, J. (1986) *La bourse et la vie. Economie et religion au Moyen Age*, Paris: Hachette.

Matteucci, N. (1998) 'L'origine storica delle casse di risparmio', in Roversi Monaco, F.A. (ed.) *Le Fondazioni Casse di Risparmio*, Rimini: Ed. Maggioli.

Milano, R. (2001) *La finanza e la banca etica. Economia e solidarietà*, Milan: Ed Paoline.

Schlesinger, P. (2002) 'Riforma o controriforma della disciplina sulle Fondazioni bancarie? Considerazioni di un civilista', Conference Cesifin 'Le fondazioni bancarie dopo la legge finanziaria 2002', Florence, Italy.

Schumpeter, J.A. (1954) *History of Economic Analysis*, New York: Oxford University Press.

Todeschini, G. (2007) 'Credibilità, fiducia, ricchezza: il credito caritativo come forma della modernizzazione economica europea', in Avallone, P. (ed.) *Prestare ai poveri*, Rome: CNR.

Zamagni, S. (2008) 'L'emergenza dell'Economia Civile', in Zabbini, E., Dallari, F. and Sala, A.M. (eds) *Emilia-Romagna. Regione della coesione e dell'ospitalità. La didattica della geografia. Metodi ed esperienze innovative*, Pàtron Editore.

3 Why do we need social banking?

Leonardo Becchetti

Introduction: stylized facts

At the beginning of the third millennium mankind is plagued by a three-sided problem:

1 the persistence of a large share of individuals suffering malnutrition and/or living below or slightly above absolute poverty standards;
2 the incapacity of the economic system to take care of environmental public goods, in the standard interaction among private enterprises, domestic rules and global institutions;
3 the lack of long-run correlation between increases in per capita income and increases in life satisfaction at aggregate level which is associated with a large and increasing share of psychological disease in high-income countries (Easterlin and Angelescu 2009; Bartolini *et al.* 2010).

With regard to point 1 the problem is essentially related to the distribution of both productive capacity and bargaining power along product and service value chains. More specifically, there seem to be some barriers that prevent the 'trickle down' of the creation of economic value which, according to the most optimistic view, should bring economic affluence from the high to the low end of the income distribution.

The optimistic trickle down perspective proved once again to be ineffective in the global financial crisis where previous progress in fighting poverty bounced back with an estimated increase of 200 million suffering from malnutrition. The main reason for this defeat is that equal opportunities, which should be the prerequisite for redistribution in productive capacities, are prevented by barriers to access to education and finance. The vicious circle of misery and lack of opportunities produces a degradation which depletes the other fundamental factors for life flourishing, that is, access to good (family and non-family) human relationships.

On the environmental side the main problem is global warming with the (almost lost) challenge of keeping the increase of the average earth temperature below two degrees Celsius from the pre-revolution era to today. When looking at the environmental side, beyond the global warming issue, we must not forget the large impact of pollution on human health, even though its exact consequences have not yet been fully assessed. As well summarized by the concept of 'climate justice' the environmental and poverty problems are not unrelated: almost 95 per cent of the victims of climate change in the 1990s were poor[1] since they had no resources to insure and defend themselves against environmental catastrophes and lived in countries which depend on agriculture and are most affected by global warming.

Final and third, the Easterlin (1995) paradox has seriously challenged the belief that the pursuit of economic growth would automatically coincide with an increase in wellbeing. The paradox shows that in the United States, in the post-Second World War period, a steady increase in per capita income was paralleled with a stationary or slightly decreasing share of individuals declaring themselves very happy. The paradox generated a wide debate which is still ongoing.[2] An important finding in this debate is that the short-run positive effect of money on life satisfaction is dampened by phenomena like hedonic adaptation (Frey and Stutzer 2002a) and peer effects (Ferrer-i-Carbonell 2005), that is, comparisons with others and oneself in the past. In addition to it, the quest for economic well-being and the race for status may crowd out other goods (such as relational goods) which have a much steadier positive effect on life flourishing.

To sum up, according to a famous image of Paul Samuelson, an alien landing from Mars would be astonished observing how, in spite of the miraculous technological progress, which creates enough economic value to rescue from need and produce good living conditions for more than six billion people living on earth, mankind is plagued by the above described three-sided problem.

In order to explain to the alien how this could happen we need to consider three main factors, which are both cultural and structural and then explain in the rest of the chapter how social banking may have a crucial role in creating virtuous circles which may address these issues.

The three obstacles

The first problem behind the social and environmental sustainability is the inversion in the scale of values. For several cultural and organizational reasons our economy is dominated by productive organizations, in which one of the stakeholders (the shareholder) dominates all the others (workers, customers, suppliers, local communities).

The rationale for the dictatorship of shareholders originates from the fact that this peculiar type of stakeholder possesses one of the most important resources (equity capital) for the life and activity of enterprises. The superior risk, taken by shareholders, is an additional justification for it. The power of shareholders is reinforced by takeover and stock exchange mechanisms by which any deviation from the maximization of shareholder value of listed firms de facto endangers management leadership. This point, however, neglects the fact that workers (and suppliers) take a high risk for the enterprise by investing in firm-specific human (physical) capital.

The fact that the maximization of shareholder value becomes the dominant value is not without consequences for other stakeholders and the simplistic view that such ranking of values creates benefits for all other actors is simply untenable.

Without focusing just on the shareholder/worker conflicts the problem affects consumers as well. Reputational incentives hold only in repeated interactions between producers and consumers who are perfectly able to evaluate the consequences of their choices in the short run. The consequence is that in most economic relationships the maximization of shareholders' wealth may occur at the expenses of consumers (a main example is exactly that of financial and banking scandals).

The observable consequence of this conflict is that we live to see the exploitation of one 'accidental' part of ourselves (our being shareholders) over two more substantial parts (our being workers and holders of relationships). The inversion of the ranking of values is such that we are still not distant from an Aztec economy that asks us to make 'human sacrifices' for shareholders.

There seems to be no way out from it under the dismal outlook of economic culture which is plagued by anthropological reductionism (human beings are only driven by self-interest without sympathy and commitment) and corporate reductionism (all productive organizations are profit maximizing since only this kind of organization can survive in the Darwinian selection of market competition). This is also because the actors, who should take care of redistribution in this grim scenario (domestic governments and international institutions setting the rules and defining economic policies), are weakened by shirking budget constraints, lack of enforcement power and risk of regulatory capture.

The inversion in the ranking of values has a clear cultural counterpart and support in the two (anthropological and corporate) reductionisms of the mainstream economic culture. Back to the anthropological reductionism, individuals are 100 per cent self-interested (rational fools who lack sympathy and commitment as acutely remarked by Amartya Sen in 1977), or, better, myopically self-interested given that a healthy 'longsighted self-interest' understands that passions for others are the main part of our own life satisfaction. According to the second, only profit-maximizing productive organizations may survive in the Darwinian selection of competitive markets (Frank 2007).[3]

In this dramatic scenario a potential solution is looming on the horizon: a change, which does not originate from a sudden conversion of benevolent planners but by the alliance between 'concerned' socially responsible consumers and investors, on the one side, and socially oriented, non-profit-maximizing enterprises on the other side (Calveras *et al.* 2006), of which social banks form the lion's share.

The role of social banking in devising the solutions

The solution to the three-sided problem requires an integrated vision with the goal of increasing our capacity of producing economic value in a socially and environmentally sustainable framework.

A promising way to that is the alliance between socially concerned citizens willing to 'vote with their wallet' for social and environmental value incorporated in the products and corporate pioneers in social responsibility, such as fair traders or social bankers. They assume the creation of socially and environmentally responsible economic value 'retail public goods' (Besley and Ghatak 2008) as their main goal, conquer market shares and thereby trigger imitation of traditional corporate actors by transforming social and environmental responsibility into a competitive factor.

In this scenario social banks, with their activity and financing priorities, play a pivotal role in allocating financing resources to these urgent needs, helping to move towards a new scenario of 'integrated general economic equilibrium', in which the multifarious impact of entrepreneurial activities will be properly taken into account. In the standard approach firms produce material output and the question of social and environmental externalities is tackled by governmental and regulatory authorities. In the new integrated approach looming on the horizon it will be understood that entrepreneurial activities, beyond traditional output, produce other kinds of output (waste, social values, etc.) by modifying the environment and the society, in which they operate. The ambitious goal of social banks in prioritizing financing to social enterprises (fair trade, microfinance, ethical tourism, solidarity purchasing groups, social cooperatives, socially responsible for-profit firms) is to go beyond the dichotomy of the two moments of production and distribution by creating economic value already in a socially and environmentally sustainable way (Becchetti and Borzaga 2010). These initiatives fully acknowledge that productive activities, beyond what is considered their standard output, generate (or destroy) natural resources, human relationships, self-esteem and social capital. However, in many paradoxical cases, the strive for profit maximization may disregard the fact that destruction of the above-mentioned immaterial resources may create social and environmental problems, which must be addressed by public authorities at great cost. The problem may then be alternatively handled by anonymous bureaucracies or by grassroot organizations, which take advantage from closer proximity to the problem, attract voluntary work and develop specific skills to address the social issues at stake.

In extreme synthesis, the three-sided problem we face does not depend on ignorance about its potential solutions. We know the problems and even the rules and institutions, which might help us to solve them. We can think of solving it with the Archimedes or with the Baron Munchausen approach.

The idea that the knowledge of such rules automatically implies that we can implement the solutions is similar to the Baron Munchausen approach, who thinks he can lift himself up by his bootstraps. In response to it, the solution brought forth by the alliance of socially responsible citizens voting with their portfolio for social banks is more similar to the Archimedes lever.[4] In order to activate a socio-political process, which can lead to the creation of consensus for new rules and institutions, we need a fulcrum and a lever. The first is the role of savings and consumption on which all the economic system depends. The second is represented by the action of socially responsible pioneers such as social banks, which challenge anthropological and corporate reductionism and, by competing with traditional intermediaries in terms of social responsibilities, create the premises for contagion and transformation of the economic system.

The structure of the chapter

After the introductory reflection on the socio-economic scenario and the role of social banks in providing solutions, the chapter includes five other sections. In the second section we illustrate the goals and challenges of social banks. In the third section we discuss the microfinance phenomenon as a successful example of social banking. In the fourth section we look at the crucial role of socially responsible citizens in the success of social banking. In the fifth section we outline an extended general equilibrium framework, which allows for non-reductionist behaviour of firms and economic agents and, as such, ensures a socially and environmentally sustainable outcome and illustrates the crucial impact of social banks on it. In the sixth section we discuss the potential role of domestic and international policy and regulation for promoting the role of social banks. The seventh section concludes.

Goals of social banking

The history of the financial systems is characterized by three generations of financial intermediaries. The first generation is represented by village moneylenders and goes back to the pre-industrial era even though this type of intermediary has not disappeared and is still working and operating in poor villages of low-income countries.

Moneylenders usually enjoyed monopolistic operative and informational positions and could extract all the willingness to pay from borrowers, thereby creating permanent vicious circles of indebtedness and preventing their capacity to move beyond subsistence levels. In many cases moneylenders owned lands close to those that borrowers used as collateral to obtain the loan and were therefore more interested in failures (and in the land) of their clients than in their solvency (Ray 1998).

These characteristics of the activity of moneylenders were in some sense the cause of the aversion towards them, well expressed in the Bible and in the Koran, which ultimately led to the bad reputation of interest-bearing loans.

The creation of the first banks dates back to the Italian cities of the Renaissance. Following and developing these historical ancestors, modern banks in the industrial system perform some crucial roles for the economic system. They pool savings and lend them to investors, reducing the transaction costs that investors would have if they should collect such sums by themselves. They allocate efficiently funds to the most promising projects thereby increasing their productivity. They transform financial assets across time by modifying their risk and duration. Last but not least, they provide essential liquidity services to the system by accepting to hold liquid liabilities (deposits) against illiquid assets (loans) (Bhattacharya and Thakor 1994).

Even though this second generation of financial intermediaries plays a much more relevant social role, it does not solve the problem of the 'unbankables' or of these who have no collateral to pledge and thereby have significantly limited access to credit. In addition, the most recent experience of the financial crisis and the inversion in the ranking of values (see pp. 49–53) is such that banks, driving the profit maximization goal to the extreme, realize that financial activities promise higher returns than traditional loan intermediation and therefore progressively depart from their traditional social functions, moving from the 'originate-to-hold' to the 'originate-to-distribute' lending approaches.[5]

This is the historical scenario, in which a third generation of social banks starts operating. Social banks recover the goals that most of second-generation financial intermediaries originally held and go beyond them.

The examples of Banca Etica, Triodos, Grameen Bank and others (see the next section) well illustrate that social banking entails first and foremost a change in corporate goals. The first aim of social banks is not profit maximization but the creation of social and environmental value together with economic value. If the goal of Grameen and other microfinance intermediaries is to promote access to credit for the unbankables, the goal of high-income countries' social banks such as Banca Etica and Triodos is that of using their portfolio of loans strategically to finance projects of the highest social and environmental value under the obvious constraint of their economic viability.

The declared goal of social banks has strong effects on their depositors and shareholders. In the same way as consumers, buying fair trade products even at higher prices than their non-fair trade equivalents, express their willingness to pay for the social and environmental intangibles contained in the products, depositors and shareholders of social banks accept lower returns in exchange for the value of contributing to social and environmental sustainability.

The matching between socially responsible depositors and social financial intermediaries represents the best (non-experimental) proof that anthropological and corporate reductionisms (pp. 64–65) are false. First, individuals are not 100 per cent self-interested and (at least a relevant part of them) aim to satisfy something deeper and look for something more than the best bargain when they go on the market. Second, not all economic organizations originate and develop to pursue profit maximization and the vast number of them aiming at different goals may survive and prosper even in highly competitive markets.

With the above-mentioned specific characteristics, social banks distinguish from traditional cooperative banks, which are generally deemed as the most socially oriented second generation of financial intermediaries. Cooperative banks, which still represent an important share of the banking system,[6] pursue by their one share/one vote governance the goal of satisfying the needs of their associates, the local entrepreneurs and of future generations. To do so they have constraints in distribution of profits, which are mainly accumulated into reserves. Traditional cooperative banks, which find their origin in the pre-globalization era, do not have the ambition of enlarging the set of beneficiaries to other stakeholders and do not share with social banks the extremely ambitious goal of changing the economic system in order to make it socially and environmentally sustainable. While traditional cooperative firms are local, the new generation of social banks is eminently global and retains the additional merit of creating contagion and transforming social responsibility into a competitive feature of globalized financial markets.

Challenges of social banking

The life of social banks is fascinating but not easy. Some of the main challenges are related to the traditional issues of cooperative firms such as:

1 the comparatively higher difficulty in raising equity financing; and
2 the trade-off between democratic stakeholder participation and the need to take rapid decisions in a highly competitive environment.

With respect to the first point the problem depends on the relative scarcity of long-term and socially responsible equity capital. Socially responsible depositors are much easier to find than socially responsible shareholders since multi-stakeholder social banks not only remunerate their intrinsic motivation and willingness to pay for the social and environmental intangible but also build trust and satisfy their risk aversion by promising that they will not set shareholder value before the safeguard of their deposits.

A second open issue is that of coordination between participation and management (see Chapter 4 in this book). Grassroots engagement and participation is an important resource for social banks. The downside of it is that banking activity requires rapid decisions and social bank shareholders often have limited information and education to understand the constraints that the economic activity may pose to the satisfaction of their ideals. The typical solution of social banks in this respect is to discuss wide-ranging strategic issues while delegating day-to-day decisions to the management.

In the perspective of social responsibility the main dilemma of social banks remains in cruising between the Scylla and Charybdis. On the one side, the risk is that of an uncompromising and extremely severe stance, which severely limits the operational activities in order to preserve some kind of non-contamination. This bears the risk of significantly reducing the capacity of being a factor of transformation for the market. On the other side the opposite risk of 'compromising too much', fully amalgamating with traditional intermediaries, exists and therefore the potential of social banks to transform current economic structures decreases.

A representative sample of social banks: the Global Alliance for Banking on Values

What are the most relevant examples of social banks in the world and what is their performance and relative weight in terms of intermediated funds?

A very good source of information on this issue is the evidence collected by the GABV, the Global Alliance for Banking on Values, an organization that gathers some of the most relevant social banks in the world (see www.gabv.org). The mission statement of GABV and of its members may be summarized in two points:

1 the main goal of serving the un(der)served and, related to it,
2 the abandonment of the traditional priority of profit maximization.

An original characteristic of the Alliance is that it gathers banks from high-income and emerging or low-income countries, making it clear that the models of social banks in the two areas are quite dissimilar (see Table 3.1).

The Alliance partners operating in high-income countries are defined as ethical banks: they are generally smaller banks, having easier access to deposits from ethically concerned investors than financing loans, which satisfy the ethical requirement demanded by such investors. The partners operating in emerging or low-income countries are defined as *poverty alleviation banks*, which have the opposite problem, that is, the amount of loans outstanding is much higher than the amount of customer deposits. That makes them much more dependent on the interbank market (see Table 3.2).

As a consequence poverty alleviation banks are mainly financed by borrowed funds and equity while ethical banks are financed mainly by deposits (see Table 3.3).

Overall the 12 institutions of the GABV totalled at end of 2008 a volume of almost 6.5 billion dollars of outstanding loans (with a 20.7 per cent growth with respect to the previous year) (see Table 3.4).

The rate of non-performing loans was extremely low for all of them, ranging from 0.3 to 4.6 per cent (see Table 3.5).

Microfinance as a successful form of social banking

Microfinance[7] (one of the main branches of social banking) represents a significant advancement in banking activities due to its superior capacity to fulfil one of the main roles of banks in the economic system, that is, matching individuals

Table 3.1 Distinction of the GABV banks in clusters based on their main mission focus

Poverty alleviation banks	*Ethical banks*
Banex (Nicaragua)	ABS Bank (Switzerland)
BRAC Bank (Bangladesh)	Banca Etica (Italy)
BRAC Microfinance (Bangladesh)	GLS Bank (Germany)
Mibanco (Peru)	Merkur Bank (Denmark)
ShoreBank (United States)	New Resource Bank (United States)
XAC Bank (Mongolia)	Triodos Bank (the Netherlands)

Source: Scheire and de Maertelaere (2009).

Table 3.2 Deposits–loan relationship 2008

Bank	*Volume of customer deposits (US$ M)*	*Volume of loans outstanding (US$ M)*	*Conversion rate of deposits into loans (%)*
ABS Bank	678.60	574.20	84.6
Banca Etica	786.80	394.60	50.1
Banex	37.72	133.14	353.0
BRAC Microfinance	231.83	660.34	284.8
BRAC Bank	841.50	764.20	90.8
GLS Bank	1,170.20	850.90	72.7
Merkur Bank	166.60	170.00	100.2
Mibanco	490.70	781.20	159.2
New Resource Bank	143.00	112.50	78.7
ShoreBank	1,683.20	1,639.30	97.4
Triodos Bank	2,927.60	1,790.10	61.1
XAC Bank	60.30	118.10	195.9

Source: Scheire and de Maertelaere (2009).

with ideas with those who have the financial resources to support them, even when the former cannot financially back the required loan (see also Chapter 5 in this book). Traditionally, the banking system has successfully performed some fundamental roles (quality asset transformation, liquidity services,[8] pooling of savers' financial resources, project selection) but it has been incapable of lending to poor uncollateralized borrowers. This is because, in the anthropological reductionist perspective, borrowers are looked at with suspicion and are assumed to behave like *homines oeconomici*.[9] This strand of thought explains that asymmetric information between borrowers and lenders in three crucial phases of the lending relationship (*ex ante* selection of projects, interim monitoring of

Table 3.3 Financing of GABV banks at the end of 2008

Bank	*Poverty alleviation (P)/Ethical (E)*	*Financing by equity (%)*	*Financing by deposits (%)*	*Financing by borrowed funds (%)*
ABS	E	7.0	91.1	0.0
Banca Etica	E	4.3	91.2	0.6
Banex	P	9.4	21.0	69.8
BRAC Microfinance	P	21.0	34.3	45.2
BRAC Bank	P	7.5	80.1	3.2
GLS Bank	E	5.4	81.9	0.0
Merkur Bank	E	13.1	75.3	2.3
Mibanco	P	8.5	51.2	24.7
New Resource Bank	E	15.2	84.0	0.0
ShoreBank	P	6.4	64.0	30.2
Triodos Bank	E	8.6	87.9	1.0
XAC Bank	P	10.6	36.7	51.0

Source: Scheire and de Maertelaere (2009).

Table 3.4 Balance sheet total and growth

Bank	*Balance sheet total 2007 (in M US$)*	*Balance sheet total 2008 (in M US$)*	*Growth 2006–7 (%)*	*Growth 2007–8 (%)*
ABS	686.3	744.8	6.6	8.5
Banca Etica	773.7	862.8	16.1	11.5
Banex	162.6	179.7	47.8	10.5
BRAC Microfinance	630.3	675.2	56.0	7.1
BRAC Bank	691.1	1,050.9	54.5	52.1
GLS Bank	1,171.0	1,428.4	20.8	22.0
Merkur Bank	195.6	221.3	17.5	13.1
Mibanco	611.8	958.7	4.7	56.7
New Resource Bank	126.4	170.2	211.5	34.7
ShoreBank	2,377.8	2,671.8	11.0	12.4
Triodos Bank	2,774.5	3,330.7	22.5	20.0
XAC Bank	122.9	164.4		33.8
TOTAL	*10,324.0*	*12,458.9*		*20.7%*

Source: Scheire and de Maertelaere (2009).

borrower's effort and *ex post* verification of results) generates the three well-known pathologies of adverse selection (higher lending rates are likely to select worse quality/higher risk borrowers), moral hazard (borrowers may shirk if they are not fully monitored) and strategic default (borrowers may declare at the end of the project that they are unable to pay even if this is not the case). In this mainstream line of thought the collateral is the fundamental deterrent, which prevents the three pathologies and, more generally, '*homo oeconomicus*' borrowers from taking actions, which are against the interest of the bank.

Table 3.5 Bad loans

Bank	*Provisions for bad loans as percentage of outstanding loans 2007*	*Provisions for bad loans as percentage of outstanding loans 2008*
ABS	2.2	2.0
Banca Etica	0.0	N/A
Banex	3.4	4.3
BRAC Microfinance	2.0	3.5
BRAC Bank	2.1	4.6
GLS Bank	0.5	1.2
Merkur Bank	0.1	0.3
Mibanco	4.3	N/A
New Resource Bank	1.6	3.6
ShoreBank	0.4	1.8
Triodos Bank	0.0	0.3
XAC Bank	0.7	1.1

Source: Scheire and de Maertelaere (2009).a

The success of microfinance is leading theoreticians to revise such ideas on the lender–borrower relationship. One of the main rationales advanced to explain the success of microfinance (and its low rate of non-performing loans in spite of the widespread absence of formal collateral) is the mechanism of group lending with joint liability. If group members are economically responsible in case of failure of one of their mates they have the incentive to match with good borrowers (assortative matching) and to monitor them accurately during the investment period. In this way the bank can solve the asymmetric information problem relying on the capacity of local borrowers of knowing and selecting each other.

However, large parts of microfinance experience do not rely on group lending and the same Grameen Bank (the leading microfinance institution funded by Muhammad Yunus who was awarded with the Nobel Peace Prize in 2006) in the second and current phase of its activity (Grameen II) is no longer based on such lending practice. As a consequence, reasons for microfinance success go beyond group lending and cannot be understood if we are not ready to modify our anthropological view of the *homo oeconomicus*. What microfinance adds to our anthropological concepts is that there are immaterial factors (dignity, social capital, self-esteem), which are crucial for individual wellbeing and that a borrower's delinquent behaviour would endanger. Poor marginalized individuals having a chance of inclusion through a microfinance loan and experiencing an increase in dignity and self-esteem do not want to lose what they have conquered on a social point of view.[10] In addition, a good system of incentives to avoid non-restitution may also abstract from group lending and joint liability and be based on progressive lending since failure to repay current instalments may prevent the possibility of receiving another loan.

We have reasons to include microfinance within the realm of ethical and solidarity initiatives as it directly aims at providing opportunities to individuals to escape poverty. It is also a grassroots initiative since it has been historically 'subsidized' by socially responsible savers who accepted a lower return on their deposits in exchange for the moral 'satisfaction' of financing the poor (we may express the same concept by saying that microfinance institution (MFIs) have conquered an ethical premium when they collect financial resources, which allows them to pay a rate below the equilibrium market in such circumstance).[11] In this respect, the international pattern of assets and liabilities of social banks participating in the GABV well illustrates that savings collected by ethical banks in high-income countries may be channelled into microfinance investment vehicles, which fund microfinance loans in poverty alleviation banks in the South.

It is also important to avoid the idealization of microfinance. The wide range of experiences around the world includes many different approaches and methodologies. On the one hand there are MFIs that sacrifice their profits and whose primary goal is inclusion of the poor. On the other hand there are others that are standard profit maximizers and therefore charge significantly higher loan rates to their borrowers but still do microfinance.[12] An interesting work by Cull *et al.* (2009) discusses the opposite models of Grameen (low lending rates, non-profit-maximizing goal) and Banco Compartamos in Mexico (high lending rates and profit-maximizing goal). The two microfinance institutions are just two archetypes (or the two extremes) of a continuum of corporate behaviours, which highlight a trade-off between shareholders and microfinance borrowers (the more a MFI is oriented towards profit the higher will be, *ceteris paribus*, the lending rate charged to customers). This trade-off may obviously be eased by innovation in scoring methods and by an improvement in operational efficiency.

It is very difficult to have an overview of the microfinance phenomenon given that this industry is characterized by a large number of small institutions. One of the most interesting attempts is that of the Microfinance Information Exchange (2008), which created a representative sample of 231 MFIs, consistently monitored over a period of years. A large proportion of these MFIs (134) are NGOs and a majority (174) are not financial intermediaries. The most interesting end-of-2008 data shows that:

1 the gender effect is not only a Grameen characteristic: 62 per cent of borrowers in its sample MFIs are women, with the notable peaks of 94 and 92 per cent for the village and all-Asian MFI subsamples;
2 even non-profit-maximizing MFIs make profits with an average profit margin of 4.9 per cent;
3 the trade-off between profitability and outreach is evident. The subgroup of MFIs providing loans to low-end beneficiaries has a 2.1 per cent rate of profits against an average 9.8 per cent rate of those serving small businesses;
4 factors of conditional convergence (Temple 1999; Durlauf and Quah 1998) (quality of infrastructure and institutions) matter since the worst regional performance is that of African MFIs (a negative 5 per cent profit rate) and, within this group, of small African MFIs (a negative 20.5 per cent rate);
5 there are no significant differences in efficiency between profit and non-profit institutions. The ratio between personnel expenses and the loan portfolio is quite similar ($10 for for-profits versus $10.20 for non-profits) and the same is true for the ratio between operating expenses and the loan portfolio (19.3 versus 19.1 per cent) (Becchetti and Borzaga 2010).

The experience of microfinance in Europe is far more dispersed and fragmented since it is harder to identify targets of potential customers in such context. The most promising fields of action seem to be these of consumption loans to liquidity constrained borrowers, of small loans for start-ups of small entrepreneurial activities, of loans tailored for immigrants starting activities in Europe and, finally, of student loans.

In general, the main problem that microfinance must tackle is its capacity to enable borrowers to scale up, that is, to give borrowers the opportunity of access to high added value entrepreneurial activities instead of trapping them permanently into low productive activities around the subsistence level.[13] Among the thousands of experiences in the field some are, and some are not, successful from this point of view. However, we cannot be too severe with microfinance on this specific point by demanding a degree of vertical mobility for low-end classes, which is never observed in reality. A reasonable performance indicator on which we may agree is that of 'intergenerational mobility'. At minimum we should require that microfinance must be effective in allowing borrowers' children to invest in their human capital and in giving them more opportunities than would have occurred in the counterfactual situation.

Social banking and the crucial role of responsible citizens

The Eizenberg principle of indeterminacy, which prevents in 'hard sciences' to maintain stable features across time, due to changes generated by the interaction of the same factors and systems under observation, can be applied all the more so to social sciences where the 'basic object' of investigation is the human being who reacts to social, economic and political factors and modifies his behaviour across time.[14]

The indeterminacy principle applies even more to the question of the survival and growth of ethically responsible enterprises such as social banks. Their success crucially depends in fact not just on internal factors such as employees' motivation but also on the support of socially responsible consumers and savers. Even in the most optimistic scenarios, in which such enterprises can compete in price and quality with standard firms, the acknowledgement of an ethical premium by the public may dramatically increase their chances of success.

In this respect recent empirical advances and results from lab experiments reject the reductionist hypothesis of individuals only moved by self-interest and fully support Sen's (1979) idea that sympathy and commitment are important elements in the picture. More specifically, experiments on trust, dictator and public good games fully reveal that, even though self-interest obviously remains a dominant factor, players are also moved by reciprocity, inequity aversion, strategic or pure altruism and 'warm glow' preferences (i.e. they get satisfaction from the pure pleasure of giving).[15]

These additional motivations of human action help us to understand why the willingness to pay for socially and environmentally responsible features of products is growing significantly. Several consumer surveys run in different OECD countries show that the share of those who would prefer a socially responsible product for the same level of quality, even at a higher price, is not insignificant.[16] The driver of this desire is not just altruism: enlightened (or longsighted) self-interest may be enough. In the environmental field the link between the public and private good elements of the issue is absolutely evident. Care for environmental sustainability is not only good per se but for the positive consequences providing directly to any individual as well. This is particularly clear in two directions. First, the deterioration of a non-reproducible and non-appropriable resource such as climate is clearly perceived as affecting every individual even though the consequences are not the same for everyone and the poor are always less capable than the rich to protect themselves from environmental calamities. Second, green products are extremely appreciated by consumers since the latter clearly perceive that tracking the productive chain will reduce the uncertainty about the origin and productive process of the product, and the health problems that may arise from it.

Even though the link between private and public good elements for fair trade or socially responsible banking products is slightly more difficult to perceive, such link remains robust and should be more effectively explained to consumers. As is well known from the economic literature, the main source of (illegal) migration is the difference in per capita income between country of origin and country of destination. Moreover, in globalized labour markets poor standard of living of unskilled workers in less developed countries is the main source of wage competition, which endangers work rights of equally low skilled employees in industrialized countries.

Once these links are properly acknowledged it should be absolutely clear that socially responsible consumption and saving are 'natural' economic actions, which reconcile the dichotomy between our worker and consumer selves. As consumers our welfare depends directly on the difference between our maximum willingness to pay and the market price and therefore lower prices increase it. However, too low prices may create pressure on workers' rights of a given industry, contribute to a more general climate of pressure on workers' wellbeing and therefore may end up being in contrast with our interest as workers.

To sum up, the 'wallet vote' attributed via socially responsible consumption and saving primarily represents an increase in participation and economic democracy. We vote once every four or five years for coalitions with articulated political programmes of which we appreciate some, but inevitably not all, aspects. With socially responsible consumption we can vote everyday and more precisely by evaluating, not just price and quality, but also the social and environmental production of a given corporation.

A final intriguing element of this new phenomenon of grassroots action matched with the action of corporate pioneers (such as social banks) is that they jointly contribute to increase market dignity. As is well known, the market has some important qualities:

- it generates spontaneously a decentralized price clearing equilibrium, which reconciles the interests of a large number of anonymous consumers and producers;
- it provides correct signals with prices about relative scarcity and tastes for a given product;
- it is a mechanism, which, from the starting point of endowments of transacting parties, can generate a deal, which is advantageous to both parties.

What the market cannot do (or could not do so far) is a social intervention aimed at affecting the endowments or starting conditions of individuals, that is, the distributional problem, which is at the origin of some market exchanges, which we may not consider fair. To make a cruel example, an extremely deprived individual in need of financial resources may decide to sell voluntarily his kidneys to a rich consumer. The market allows both of them to realize the transactions but cannot do anything to solve the social problem, which is at the core of such a transaction.

The novelty of socially responsible consumption and savings is that, for the first time, it is possible to use the market mechanism to address directly social issues. By financing microfinance or buying fair trade products we can at the same time vote and contribute to the inclusion of the poor and improvement of their economic conditions with a simple market action. What is absolutely obvious and cannot be neglected is that illustrating the potential of the alliance between 'concerned' individuals and ethical corporations such as social banks does not imply arguing at the same time that institutions and rules are no more important, just because we discovered market mechanisms, which may be used to address social issues. Such mechanisms only want to emphasize that, given the characteristics of the current economic system, there are new synergies between grassroots and institutional action, which may be exploited to reinforce the effectiveness of actions aimed at improving societal wellbeing.

The role of social banks towards a model of 'integrated general economic equilibrium'

In this section we want to generalize the characteristics of the interaction between 'ethical pioneers' and socially responsible savers and consumers, illustrating the crucial role of social banks in this scenario. We will use an example accessible to non-technical readers as well to illustrate what we mean by 'multi-product' firms and what the advantage of having firms who reconcile creation of economic value with social and environmental sustainability can be.

The standard textbook approach conceives a firm production function in the following way:

$$Y = f(K, L, H) \tag{1}$$

with the firm producing the material output Y (goods or services sold on the market) with its production function $f(.)$ by using as inputs physical capital (K), labour force (L) and human capital (H), that is, workers' knowledge accumulated through schooling years and learning on the job.

This approach completely neglects that corporate activity is more than just producing material output. What we mean here is that 'immaterial' variables such as 'relational goods',[17] workers' self-esteem,[18] interpersonal trust and social capital[19] are not the same before and after productive activity. In the same way corporate production significantly modifies the environment by producing waste, consuming resources and producing polluting emissions. An integrated approach to corporate activity should therefore take into account all these correlated effects and conceive the production function as follows

$$h(y, SE, EN, MO, REL, SC) = f(L(MO, SE, REL), K, H, SC) \tag{2}$$

where, on the left-hand side, it is acknowledged that firms 'produce' (modify the existing level of), not only material output (*Y*), but also workers' self-esteem (*SE*), relational goods (*REL*), social capital (*SC*) and morale (*MO*) plus several by-products, which have strong environmental consequences (*EN*). An important difference arises on the left-hand side as well where it is acknowledged that 'immaterial factors' such as self-esteem, morale and relational goods are fundamental components of workers' productivity. To make just some examples on this point consider that modern corporations may be conceived as 'trust game corporations' (Becchetti and Pace 2006) where productive output depends crucially on team-working and on a series of complex tasks, which require joint application of workers with specific non-overlapping skills (a lawyer, an economist, an engineer, etc.). The most important feature of productive activity in trust game corporations is the creation of superadditivity (a result that is more than the sum of the individual contributions of its participants). Superadditivity has two fundamental rationales. First, by explaining things to others we learn better what we think we know. Second, only by joining different pieces of the puzzle represented by individual specific know-how, we may reconstruct the overall picture and increase our knowledge in a given field.

In this framework low quality of relational goods among co-workers may seriously harm such processes. The basic ingredient of it is in fact, as in the standard game theoretic literature of trust games, the decision to share information with teammates, a decision that implies the risk of abuse and exploitation of such information. In working environments, in which the quality of relationships among workers is lower, there will be less information sharing and no superadditivity with negative effects on corporate productivity.

In this integrated general equilibrium model individuals maximize their utility/happiness functions

$$MaxU(C, MO, REL, SE) \tag{3}$$

with not just consumption (*C*) but also the same immaterial variables (morale (*MO*), relational goods (*REL*), self-esteem (*SE*)), which are both determinant of their productivity and affected by their corporate life.

The maximization is subject to the standard constraint

$$(1 - t)M - PX + S \tag{4}$$

which equals (after tax) personal disposable income $(1-t)M$[20] to the value of consumption (price (*P*) time quantity (*X*)) and individual savings (*S*).

$$S = I \tag{5}$$

Finally, relation (5) simply acknowledges that investment equals aggregate savings ($S = \Sigma s$) in equilibrium.

The anthropological framework we assume for the approach proposed above rejects the reductionism in the conception of the individual happiness function (consumption is not the only driver of life satisfaction!) but, at the same time, accepts a principle of rationality (individual behaviour responds to a strategy, which maximizes individual goals given time and budget constraints), which we consider a reasonable approximation of what on average happens in reality.

Note that some of the factors determining individual life satisfaction (relational goods, self-esteem) are not subject to the budget constraint and may be increased at no cost. The question here is that their satisfaction does not depend only on the individuals but also on the social environment in which they live, the corporate climate and the individuals with whom they have relationships. To put it simply, the main constraint here is not just money but also others, that is, the disposition of partners in the production and consumption of the relational good to invest in it together with the individual at stake.

Finally, as in standard economic models we acknowledge that physical capital, a fundamental input in productive activity, follows the standard law of motion

$$\dot{K} = I - dK \tag{6}$$

in which the instantaneous rate of change of capital stock $\dot{K}$ is determined by investment (I) minus depreciation (conventionally calculated by applying the depreciation rate d to the stock of capital investment).

In this rudimentary model we have a standard budget constraint as well (in which we assume for simplicity that the budget clears every period with no generation of debt).

$$tY = G(EN, SEC, REL, SE) \tag{7}$$

On the left-hand side of (7) we have tax inflow from aggregate output and, on the right-hand side, government expenditure. What we want to emphasize here is that such expenditure is a positive function of the negative social and environmental externalities (all arguments in parentheses already explained in equation (2)) created by corporations into their activities. More specifically, the volume of government expenditure is a positive function of environmental and social problems.

Imagine now we have two types of firms. The first one is the standard type of profit-maximizing entity, which does not care about social and environmental externalities. This firm produces material output and contributes to economic growth but, at the same time, may generate negative social and environmental externalities. On the first point (negative social externalities) we may assume that a negative corporate climate may reduce quality of relational life of their workers, their morale and self-esteem. Furthermore, layoffs may produce marginalization, which needs to be tackled by government policies aimed at unemployed rehabilitation, etc. Obviously things can go the other way round but what we want to underline here is that, in order to evaluate companies' contribution to the creation of economic value at aggregate level, we must consider not just the direct productive effects but also the indirect effect on the social and environmental dimension of their activities, consistently with the concept of the multiproduct production function.

In this respect the role of social enterprises can be very important here. Firms with different rankings of priorities, which consider their main goal environmental sustainability and creation of social value, compatibly with their capacity of creating economic value, may maximize their positive social and environmental contribution by alleviating instead of worsening government budgets. Practical examples of this are mentioned in the previous sections and, among them, microfinance or ethical banks, which contribute to the solution of social problems with their lending schemes to unbankables or energy saving companies who restructure houses in order to improve their environmental efficiency and therefore create economic value by reducing environmental degradation.

Several crucial questions arise here. Are socially responsible firms able to survive in the competitive race with the conventional type of firms (standard profit-maximizing companies)? How may citizens and institutions contribute to the picture?

The synthetic suggestion, which comes from the model, tells us that these firms survive because:

1 they compensate superior costs (required by the fulfilment of more severe social and environmental standards) with potential benefits (higher worker productivity due to the high levels of immaterial factors such as morale, self-esteem and relational goods);
2 a minority of socially and environmentally concerned citizens vote with their wallets in favour of these companies;
3 institutions support them with both non-costly (regulation) and costly (tax allowances, etc.) intervention.

In the next section we will enter further into the details of this picture by analysing the role of institutions in the proposed framework.

The role of the government

Microfinance and social banking were born and have grown without any direct government support, even it could have been of great help to them. To provide an example in microfinance, profitability and outreach are inversely correlated and those microfinance (MF) initiatives more directly targeted to the poor required subsidies to survive. However, such subsidies come from foundations, socially responsible investors (accepting lower returns on their deposits to finance MFIs) and private donors and, generally, not from the government. The above-mentioned features and the history of these initiatives demonstrated that their businesses are sustainable and pushed profit-maximizing players to enter in these fields.

In the present state of affairs, the role of the state could be of great importance, in spite of its almost neutral stance adopted so far, to foster these initiatives and contribute to the edification of an economic system in which creation of economic value may be reconciled with social and environmental sustainability. We must not forget that competition does not occur in a rule-free environment. On the contrary, success of one or another player does not depend only on its intrinsic quality but also on the rules of the game. This is absolutely evident, for instance, in environmental regulation where new pro-environment rules (such as limited access or access charges to large metropolitan areas based on environmental quality of cars) or simply expectations of their implementation may be crucial to tilt the competitive race in favour of the more environmentally friendly producers. In the field of social banking effective government intervention should be related to all these policy measures, which acknowledge the capacity of social banks to internalize negative (social and environmental) externalities of producing public goods in a subsidiary action with respect to the public institutions. The delicate point here is to devise measures (i.e. tax allowances), which create incentives for the internalization of externalities and the production of public goods without falling under the accusation of unfair competition (or unfair support to only one of the competitive players in a given industry).

More in detail, we believe that, if the government cares about redressing economic activity in a more socially and environmentally sustainable direction, and if it understands that failure to do so would imply high welfare costs, it should take two types of cost-free and costly initiatives.

The cost-free initiatives involve regulation on social rating and pro-socially responsible players' procurement rules. The costly initiative concerns various forms of tax allowances, once the contribution of social responsibility to societal wellbeing and its positive effect on government budget is properly taken into account.

On the first point it must be considered that consumers' and investors' willingness to pay for socially and environmentally responsible features of products is extremely high according to surveys run in different parts of the worlds.

These large numbers do not often become market shares because they are based on a 'virtual' choice (availability on each shelf of the CSR and non-CSR products and full information on their characteristics), which is not what happens in the reality. A compulsory norm on the disclosure of the social ratings of companies selling products would greatly help. Such a norm would not create any distortion or discrimination at country or industry level, since it would pose the same obligations on all producers selling in a given country. Furthermore, it would contribute significantly to an increase in information and in the capacity of the 'wallet vote' of consumers and investors who would remain free to use or not use the new information. As it occurs in the industry of financial rating (with S&P, Moody and Fitch), competition among the most important players should ensure that social rating information comes from a variety of independent sources (in our case they may be the well-established KLD, Ethibel, Eiris, etc. already selling their services to ethical investment funds and the general public).

Social rating would tackle some problems that are very close to those of financial rating. Conflicts of interests between rating agencies and corporate customers (who would have to pay for the rating) could be reduced by the creation of a multi-stakeholder authority. Fixed costs of social rating would be an unsustainable burden for small firms and banks and a different treatment for them should be allowed. In spite of all the inevitable limits and problems, a compulsory social rating system would greatly contribute to spur the debate on the issue and provide firms with the right market incentives to adopt socially responsible strategies.

The second field of (cost-free?) intervention is procurement rules. It is true that, by prizing socially and environmentally responsible features of competitors, the public sector could be ultimately led to purchase goods and services at slightly higher prices. On the other hand, a blind application of the minimum price rule would seem nonsensical given the overall public (and Lisbon) goal of matching creation of economic value with social cohesion and environmental sustainability.

With regard to costly intervention with tax and subsidies promoting social and environmental responsibility, the clear link to a specific behaviour would eliminate the suspicion of unfair competition or support of one actor versus the other, opening the opportunity of fiscal benefit for all economic players conditional on the assumption of such behaviour.

Conclusions

No one denies that macroeconomics, institutional reforms and infrastructures are fundamental to promote economic development and social cohesion. In the traditional Western democracies grassroot voice on this issue was mainly limited to the participation in political life and, for most people, participation is limited to the electoral vote. However, global integration of market economies, the weakness of international institutions that are not directly elected and the lack of global governance rules aimed to address the issues of global public goods is making it ever more obvious that an economic system may not work by just waiting for such 'top down' interventions.

In addition, a longstanding tradition of participated action of non-governmental organizations has often demonstrated that local community organizations, which are closer to social problems and are composed of motivated members, may tackle more effectively social and environmental problems. Such organizations have proven that they can do better than the molochs of traditional welfare systems, which often deal anonymously with beneficiaries providing scarce contribution to the frequently mentioned immaterial factors (trust, self-esteem, dignity), which we showed to be so important in promoting social inclusion.

These are the reasons why quality and effectiveness of intervention in social and environmental issues in the future will crucially depend also on bottom-up participation as well as on the synergies between participation of the civil society and local, national governments and regulatory authorities.

In this chapter we presented social banking as the main example of this approach, which has developed successful and sustainable models of creation of economic, social and environmental value. In presenting them we are fully aware of their limits as well as their great potential. Microfinance and social banks (together with fair trade, solidarity purchasing groups, ethical tourism) are only examples of a more general principle, which will inspire new historical realizations, which we still do not see on the horizon today. The principle is that the ultimate masters of the present economic system are neither the governments nor large corporations. Both of them crucially depend on the vote of citizens, consumers and investors. This implies that we cannot complain when we see something that we do not like since the ultimate responsibility for change is on us and on our decisions on the market.

To understand why the potential of these initiatives (which are there to remind us about our power) is enormous when supported by citizens we may imagine what could happen if, say, 60 per cent of the individuals decided to give more money for solidarity or if they alternatively decided to invest their money on the basis of price and quality as well as on social and environmental responsibility of the economic players. In the second case the additional advantage would be an unprecedented dramatic incentive for all corporations to modify their productive systems in the direction of a 'three-dimensional' integrated target of society wellbeing, with increased consistency between the creation of economic value and the pursuit of social goals.

The existence of a potential does not mean that we have already reached it, nor it is a guarantee that we will definitely be there one day in the future. It only reminds us of an incredible opportunity to solve global imbalances with simple everyday life choices. We generally complain about the changes we would like to see in politics and economics without being aware that we may be the main actors of that change.

References

Andreoni, J. and Miller, J. (2002) 'Giving according to GARP: an experimental test of the consistency of preferences for altruism', *Econometrica*, 70: 737–53

Armendariz de Aghion, B. (1999) 'On the design of credit agreement with peer monitoring', *Journal of Development Economics*, 60: 79–104.

Bartolini, S., Bilancini, E. and Sarracino, F. (2010) 'Social capital predicts happiness: world-wide evidence from time series', paper presented at the 31st General Conference of the International Association for Research in Income and Wealth, St. Gallen, Switzerland, 22–28 August 2010.

Bhattacharya, S. and Thakor, A.V. (1994) 'Contemporary banking theory', *Journal of Financial Intermediation*, 3(1): 2–50

Becchetti, L. and Borzaga, C. (eds) (2010) *The Economics of Social Responsibility: the World of Social Responsibility*, London: Routledge.

Becchetti, L. and Pace, N. (2006) 'The economics of the "trust game corporation" ', CEIS Working Paper 233.

Berg, J., Dickhaut, J. and McCabe, K. (1995) 'Trust, reciprocity, and social history', *Games and Economic Behavior*, 10: 122–42.

Berger, A.N. and Udell, G.F. (2002) 'Small business credit availability and relationship lending: the importance of bank organizational structure', *Economic Journal*, 112(477): 32–53.

Besley, T. and Ghatak, M. (2008) 'Retailing public goods: the economics of corporate social responsibility', *Journal of Public Economics*, 91: 1645–63.

Bird, K. and Hughes, D. (1997) 'Ethical consumerism: the case of "fairly-traded" coffee', *Business Ethics: An European Review*, 6(3): 159–67.

Blanchflower, D.G. and Oswald, A.J. (2004) 'Well-being over time in Britain and the USA', *Journal of Public Economics*, 887(8): 1359–86.

Bongini, P. and Ferri, G. (2007) 'Governance, diversification and performance: the case of Italy's Banche Popolari', paper presented at the conference *Corporate Governance in Financial Institutions*, Nicosia.

Calveras, A., Ganuza, J.J. and Llobet, G. (2006) 'Regulation, corporate social responsibility and activism', *Journal of Economics and Management Strategy*, 16: 719–40.

Camerer, C. and Thaler, R. (1995) 'Ultimatums, dictators, and manners', *Journal of Economic Perspectives*, 9: 209–19.

Castriota, S. (2006) *Education and Happiness: a Further Explanation to the Easterlin Paradox?* Mimeo.

Cull, R., Demirguc-Kunt, A. and Morduch, J. (2009) 'Microfinance meets the market', *Journal of Economic Perspectives*, 23(1): 167–92.

Durlauf, S.N. and Quah, D.T. (1998) 'The new empirics of economic growth', in Taylor, J.B. and Woodford, M. (eds) *Handbook of Macroeconomics*, Amsterdam: Elsevier, 235–308.

Easterlin, R.A. (1995) 'Will raising the incomes of all increase the happiness of all?', *Journal of Economic Behavior and Organization*, 27(1): 35–48.

Easterlin, R.A. and Angelescu, L. (2009) 'Happiness and growth the world over: time series evidence on the happiness-income paradox', IZA Discussion Paper (4060).

Fehr, E. and Gächter, S. (2000) 'Cooperation and punishment in public goods experiments', *American Economic Review*, 90(4): 980–94.

Fehr, E., Kirchler, E., Weichbold, A. and Gächter, S. (1998) 'When social forces overpower competition – gift exchange in experimental labor markets', *Journal of Labor Economics*, 16: 324–51.

Fehr, E., Kirchsteiger, G. and Riedl, A. (1993) 'Gift exchange and ultimatum in experimental markets', *Vienna Economics Papers*, vie9301.

Ferrer-i-Carbonell, A. (2005) 'Income and well-being: an empirical analysis of the comparison income effect', *Journal of Public Economics*, 89: 997–1019.

Fischbacher, U., Gächter, S. and Fehr, E. (2001) 'Are people conditionally cooperative? Evidence from a public goods experiment', *Economics Letters*, 71: 397–404.

Frank, R. (2007) *Microeconomics*, New York: McGraw-Hill.

Frey, B. and Stutzer, A. (2002a) 'What can economists learn from happiness research', *Journal of Economic Literature*, 40: 402–35.

Frey, B. and Stutzer, A. (2002b) *Happiness and Economics: How the Economy and Institutions Affect Well-being*, Princeton: Princeton University Press.

Ghatak, M. (2000) 'Screening by the company you keep: joint liability lending and the peer selection effect', *The Economic Journal*, 110: 601–31.

Gui, B. (2000) 'Beyond transaction: on the interpersonal dimension of economic reality', *Annals of Public and Cooperative Economics*, 71(2): 139–69.

Gui, B. and Sugden, M. (2005) *Economics and Social Interactions, Accounting for Interpersonal Relations*, Cambridge: Cambridge University Press.

Knack, S. and Keefer, P. (1997) 'Does social capital have an economic payoff? A cross country investigation', *The Quarterly Journal of Economics*, CXII: 1251–87.

Microfinance Information Exchange (2008) Online, available at: www.themix.org (accessed 12 November 2010).

Putnam, R. (1993) *Making Democracy Work: Civic Traditions in Modern Italy*, Princeton: Princeton University Press

Ray, D. (1998) *Development Economics*, Princeton: Princeton University Press.

Scheire, C. and de Maertelaere, S. (2009) 'Banking to make a difference', Preliminary Report, Artevelde: Artevelde University College.

Sen, A. (1977) 'Rational fools: a critique of the behavioural foundations of economic theory', *Philosophy and Public Affairs*, 6: 317–32.

Stiglitz, J. (1990) 'Peer monitoring and credit markets', *World Bank Economic Review*, 4: 351–66.

Tafarodi, R. and Swann, W. (2001) 'Two-dimensional self-esteem: theory and measurement', *Personality and Individual Differences*, 31: 653–73.

Temple, J. (1999) 'The new growth evidence', *Journal of Economic Literature*, 37(1): 112–56.

Uhlaner, C.J. (1989) 'Relationa', *Public Choice*, 62: 253–85.

Veenhoven, R. (1993) *Happiness in Nations: Subjective Appreciation of Life in 56 Nations 1946–1992*. Rotterdam: RISBO, Erasmus University, Rotterdam.

Zak, P.J. and Knack, S. (2001) 'Trust and growth', *The Economic Journal*, 111: 295–321.

4 Inside social banks

Christina von Passavant

Introduction

Scene 1: spring 2009, on the sidelines of a meeting at a social bank. The topic of discussion is investments. An executive suggests buying UBS shares on the grounds that they have plummeted significantly and the company's gross misconduct is, after all, legally irrelevant under Swiss criminal law. Thanks to the government money thrown at it, he says, its shares are likely to rise rapidly fairly soon. The initial response is incredulous silence – a taboo has been broken. It is followed by vehement protest from some and expressions of approval and interest from others. Finally somebody asks: would any of you buy UBS shares privately? Or have you? Once again, silence all around.

Scene 2: the application process for an administrative position is underway. The main responsibilities, as set out in the job advertisement, include answering and fielding initial contact phone calls and emails. In the course of an interview for the position, an applicant is asked whether there are any specific tasks she dislikes. Her reply is: 'Making phone calls.' Asked why she applied for the position in the first place, given that phone communication is an essential part of the job description, her answer is: 'Well, you're presenting yourself as a social organisation, so obviously you're not like the others who only think of the bottom line. So surely this kind of thing is negotiable.'

These are two scenes that illuminate the field of tension that management and human resource management in social banking operate in.

The topic of this chapter is management in social banking. What are the specific challenges a social bank's management personnel faces? What are significant issues in human resource management? What does it mean to view one's customers and clients as partners? In many regards, the answers to these questions apply to the management of every bank and every SME – still, certain aspects are specific to social banking.

The dual approach of ethics and profitability

It is not your typical banker who works in a social bank. And the customers and clients who decide to conduct their business with a social bank are not your typical banking customers either. Two things, however, are indisputable: like any other bank, a social bank needs solid banking expertise, and it has to compete in the free market. Customers, however, choose a social bank not primarily for its banking expertise, but for the values it offers and embodies: a social bank guarantees its customers that their money will be managed ethically; the customers, in turn, trust the bank and are relieved of the responsibility to examine its products individually. In other words, strong banking expertise is not enough to win customers who consider socio-ecological responsibility a priority. But it is certainly possible to lose customers with insufficient banking expertise and bad customer relations. A high degree of professionalism, excellent expertise in the field and strong customer orientation do not guarantee a social bank's success, but they are necessary prerequisites for long-term success.

Social banks have become the true centres of expertise for ethical financial management. 'Ethical' here denotes not just an abstract philosophy of life but 'ethics as free action whose aims are a world where life is cherished and coexistence in fairness and solidarity' (Ulrich 2008). These aspirations need to be put into practice – in the form of ethical products, but also in the form of corresponding business practices, i.e. designs for action that are consistently in line with the basic ethical values underlying them. Ethical products, transparency and fairness in business processes, a clear commitment on the part of the owners, and a dialogue with the customer that is guided by socio-ecological values: these are success factors a social bank can and must pay attention to in order to establish itself in the marketplace and distinguish itself from the competition. A social bank becomes successful not just by virtue of offering different products but mainly because its profile differs from that of traditional banks.

Only by virtue of this dual profile – strong banking expertise and a high level of ethical competence – can social banks operate professionally. Ultimately, the decisive factor is how well a bank manages to establish credibility among its customers and staff and within its environment in general: its conduct has to be in line with the promises it makes in its entire internal and external communication (mission statement, public relations, etc.). But credibility can only be achieved if the bank as a whole is seen as an ethical business – in its business operations, but also in its organizational structure, its decision-making and implementation processes, and its communication. This overall picture also includes its locations, the ecological and social balance sheet of its facilities and tools, and its use of materials and energy. And it also includes, as an essential element, the bank's relations with its customers and employees.

Moreover, social banks see themselves as having a social mandate. Ethical financial management does not exhaust itself in providing customers and employees with a clear conscience: it aspires to contributing to a fairer society.

All this creates particular challenges for management. It requires management personnel who are convinced that profitability and ethics can complement and inform each other in a constructive way and that surplus is generated in the interaction between the two.

Managing a social bank as a business enterprise

So how is it possible to manage a bank in such a way that it lives up to its ethical values and acquires credibility? How can these values be put into practice in actual business processes and the actions of all employees?

Guiding principles for management

A social bank distinguishes itself from its competition not just through what it does, but also through how it does it. A social bank's values are easiest to put into practice if management is guided in its decisions and actions by the following three principles:

- the principle of transparency;
- the principle of communication;
- the principle of participation.

These principles should be implemented in all areas of a bank's routine operations: in its product development and palette, in its business processes, in its relations with customers and owners, in marketing and public relations, and – last but not least – in its human resource management. However, this is only possible if both management and owners are guided in their actions and decisions by ethical values.

The principle of transparency

This principle follows from the company's ethical standards: ethical action needs to be open to scrutiny and public debate. Customers, owners and staff have a right to know where the money comes from and where it goes, what actually happens with the depositors' investments and what these investments' long-term effects are. The bank's lending and investment criteria, its exclusion criteria, etc. need to be transparent. And of course social banks need to make their compensation system and annual financial statements transparent.

The following example illustrates how the transparency principle can be put into practice. A certain bank has always made it a policy for prospective borrowers to consent to the publication of a credit list that contains the names of all debtors. It has also always asked for a declaration from its clients stating that taxes have been paid on all money brought in. Both policies have been regarded by other banks as completely untenable and harmful to business. But they have turned out to actually help build trust in the bank and garnered it a lot of goodwill; they have also become effective marketing arguments.

The principle of communication

This principle arises first from the need to balance economic interests against socio-ecological ones. Wherever different interests need to be weighed against each other, dialogue and making convincing arguments for one's case are essential. Second, social banks are committed to promoting the idea of ethical banking as a contribution to a fairer society. Both require extensive professional communication, and not just internally. Where other banks hold events on home financing, retirement plans or faster asset growth, social banks organize panels on the social ramifications of particular financial transactions, the risks and potential of ethical investment, and new developments in the ecological sector. They also initiate public discourse on important socio-political issues. In other words, one respect in which social banks differ markedly from traditional ones is the high visibility of their socio-political stance.

The principle of participation

People who work in social banks generally put a high value on fairness and meaningful work. Consequently, they engage more critically with their employer and working conditions than employees of traditional companies do. Something similar is true of a social bank's customers: their primary rationale for putting their money with a social bank is not the maximization of their returns, although the recoverability of their deposits and investments and a fair lending policy are, of course, of central importance. But these customers also want to handle their financial matters in a way that ensures social and ecological sustainability. This means that social banks, more so than traditional banks, 'live in a glass house': both their employees and their customers watch closely whether they actually walk the talk. Bearing this in mind, it is advisable to involve staff and customers in the bank's product-development and decision-making processes. However, participation should not be limited to these two groups. Social banks, more so than traditional ones, rely on stakeholders in their environment. Environmental associations and groups that share its social aims are indispensable partners for a social bank seeking to gain socio-political clout; they also provide necessary expert input into the development of new products and the evaluation of financial transactions. To ensure the participation of important stakeholders, however, formal structures need to be in place. These can take the form of advisers giving their opinion on the investment universe, feedback groups composed of representatives of relevant groups that keep a critical eye on the bank's operating activities, or an ethics board that monitors the bank's ethical performance. They can also entail the involvement of external key persons, or the mandatory involvement of pertinent organizations in teams that develop ratings or new products. Some social banks can rely on a solid network of volunteers committed to the bank's interests and socio-political activities.

Elements of managing a social bank

Ethical leadership

What holds true for other companies applies to social banks as well: it is crucial to have good people at the top. Like any other bank, a social bank needs management personnel with professional expertise and leadership skills, but beyond that, it needs managers who are ethically motivated. It is not enough for a manager to merely adopt a few of the company's values when assuming his or her position – they need to have truly ethical core beliefs accompanied by the firm conviction that entrepreneurship guided by ethical values and sound professional expertise can be economically successful. In addition, they need to have a high degree of integrity and communication skills. In this regard, social banks have particularly high standards. The highest-ranking executives are important identification figures not just for the staff, but for the bank's clients and environment as well. Ethical leadership needs to make an impact both internally and externally.

Holistic business management

Generally speaking, business management manifests itself on three levels (Steiger and Lippmann 2003):

- structure;
- tools;
- personal contact.

These three levels have to be kept in mind both with regard to internal processes, in the way the company is managed, and externally, with regard to the dynamics of the market and the interaction with the company's environment. In this respect, managing a social bank is no different from managing any other company. One factor to be considered is that social banks are often pioneering enterprises with the tendency typical of such businesses to focus too much on the personal level. It is particularly important for these banks to create structures and instruments that will enable them in the long run to organize their financial operations in a manner that is not just professional and ethical but efficient as well.

Management by structure

The first aspect to be considered is the bank's organizational structure: what and how many units should it have? What hierarchy levels, and how many, best suit its needs? With regard to structure, there is not much leeway: there are banking standards and legal regulations to observe. There is, however, some leeway with regard to special departments (e.g. legal services, equal opportunity office, corporate communications office, sustainability monitoring office, etc.). These can either be integrated into a supporting unit or directly attached to the Executive Board. It is strongly advised that any special department with a strong supervisory and legitimizing function be directly attached to the Executive Board.

With regard to hierarchies, there is a certain danger of approaching the question dogmatically rather than pragmatically. There is a widely held belief in the traditional business world that a stringent hierarchy with a distinct top and bottom is an essential prerequisite for business success. Socio-ecological circles, on the other hand, tend to hold that flat hierarchies are the *non plus ultra*. The rule that should apply in social banking, as in any other business, is: the structure of a company's hierarchy should be determined by the most effective way of running it. Spans of control that are too wide make effective leadership impossible; by contrast, any management level that is not strictly necessary creates unnecessary expense.

Whatever the organizational structure, it is imperative that roles are clearly defined and that the tasks, competencies and responsibilities of each function are properly coordinated. A clearly defined role in combination with the corresponding competencies and a consistent assignment of responsibilities is the best prerequisite for high employee motivation.

Along with the organizational structure, a bank's process structure is a key element. Core processes, management processes and important support processes should be identified, delineated and laid down in binding standards and process steps. Not only is this conducive to the company's efficiency, it also ensures equal treatment of all employees and customers in all matters of discussion. Third, it facilitates the induction and integration of new employees. And last but not least, clear processes and standards increase transparency and prepare the ground for good knowledge management. But efficient process organization requires keeping sight of the big picture. Employees need to be aware that they are responsible to the organization as a whole, that they are part of a process chain of tasks, in which each function makes a specific contribution. Self-serving interests need to take a back seat, and no process steps should be skipped.

A third area of management by structure concerns forums and methods of communication and information. As mentioned earlier, communication is a core principle of social banking, and information is just as vital. By the level of information they have access to employees gauge whether they are being taken seriously and whether independent thinking and participation are encouraged. But often information is exclusively taken to mean the 'downward' flow of information from the Executive Board through management to all employees. The flow of information from the bottom to the top of a company is just as important, but it is much harder to achieve. Top management has to make sure not only that goals and objectives are communicated to the staff but also that it gets the information it needs from the employee base. Horizontal information is also important, mainly because it facilitates cooperation at interfaces, informal support among co-workers, and knowledge transfer. Procedures need to be in place to ensure that there is efficient information flow in all directions – established forums for communication, exchange and the forming of opinions. This runs up against two concerns: for one, the advance scheduling and planning of forums like team, department and staff meetings is sometimes dismissed as pointless formalism; holding meetings as the need arises is favoured instead. But this approach severely decreases participation and transparency: who gets to decide what is needed when? And how are staff members supposed to know where they stand? A second concern is the fear of wasting too much time with unproductive meetings. This, however, is a matter of meeting organization and chairing skills. The ability to chair meetings in a professional manner is an indispensable skill for the management personnel of a company that is guided by participation, communication and transparency.

The final central aspect of management by structure concerns decision-making structures. Participatory organizations in particular need clear and binding decision-making processes. Where they are missing, people easily feel entitled to have their say in everything, regardless of qualification. Decision-making responsibilities need to be defined properly and in line with the employee's organizational level and function: it needs to be clear who has a say in what, and who has decision-making responsibilities, in which area. Broad input can contribute significantly to a constructive opinion-formation process and potentially constitutes an important factor in the quality of decision-making; nonetheless, decision-making authority needs to be clearly defined. And staff members in turn need to reliably take on and exercise their decision-making responsibilities.

But value-based companies often aim for a high degree of consensus. There is a strong assumption that a commonly held set of values means by implication that differences of opinion in important matters simply do not occur. The fact that clearly delineated roles are particularly important in decision-making processes is often overlooked. A strong desire for harmony is a potential pitfall that can lead to much confusion and dissatisfaction. When this happens, people try to establish consensus by downplaying differences of opinion, or a faux consensus is reached just because everybody involved in a particular discussion is worn out and nods assent to everything just to bring the discussion to a close. But decisions of high quality are reached precisely through taking in and carefully analysing the participants' input and differing opinions.

Management through tools

The use of professional management tools is an important factor in achieving efficiency, ensuring consistent quality and implementing goals in an effective and measurable way. Like many value-based companies, however, social banks have a hard time with the idea of actually employing these tools: after all, their effective use requires a certain degree of standardization, whereas these companies' culture sets great store by tailor-made responses – the specific is considered more important than the general. Just to give an example: in one particular social bank, it turned out to be extremely difficult to define function groups as part of devising a new compensation system. In a first round, the participants came up with almost as many function descriptions as there were staff members and could not easily be convinced to let go of this overly detailed classification system. There is also a widespread myth according to which anything standardized is of inferior quality. This belief is often rooted in a deep-seated suspicion of the collection of measurable data and the establishment of set procedures – both of which create transparency and, with it, measurability. There is often a noticeable fear of control, not only on the part of staff members, who do not want to be 'standardized', but also on the part of members of management who shy away from implementing their objectives and tackling possible deficiencies. These motivations, however, are not openly expressed; instead, they are hidden behind smokescreen arguments of a humane working environment, employee self-responsibility, etc. And sometimes, attempts to introduce management tools are roundly rejected with the argument that it just wouldn't be worth the trouble.

Another not uncommon problem in social banks concerns management personnel who are highly committed to good banking and the company's ethical values, but considerably less interested in professional management. But management means implementing the company's goals. In ethics-based companies, as in any other company, management is held to use the company's goals as guidelines. That is the bottom line. The disinterested and, in some cases, suspicious attitude of management personnel of social banks towards management theories may stem from an uncomfortable association of management theories with large corporations, profit maximization, and employee exploitation. Whatever the reason, it carries with it a danger that information on new management optimization tools and new developments in management is not taken on board. It also leads to a lack of networking with other management professionals, which means no information exchange on what works and what doesn't and no exchange of tips and tricks of business management. The following is not intended to be a comprehensive overview of available management tools but a look at some of the tried-and-true ones specifically with regard to their use in social banks.

Management by objectives

Management by objectives (MbO) has become an established and widely used tool in companies around the world. The two major components of this tool are, first, strategic objectives, and second, clearly defined target agreements. MbO has found its way into social banking as well, where it faces particular challenges. For one, it does not work without clear strategies that can be operationalized. But social banks are ideological organizations, and as such prone to putting their mission at the centre and sticking with it without translating their vision into strategies that can be operationalized and clearly communicated. This is a potential weakness. In businesses whose sole aim is profit maximization, economic considerations – i.e. the goal of profitability – act as a strong integrating factor that shapes actions, decisions and the coordination of interests. But ethics-based companies have to constantly strive for integration in the area of tension between economic efficiency and the values of sustainability. This means that for a social bank, a clear strategy and the strategic goals derived from it are of crucial importance. They are an indispensable prerequisite for staff members to know where they stand and get clear objectives.

One particular feature of target agreements in social banks arises from the dual approach discussed above: these agreements need to include not just economic objectives but, by definition, ethical ones as well. All employees need to know what is expected of them within a given time frame: which tasks need to be performed? What are the economic objectives? But also: which values and attitudes are supposed to guide the staff member's behaviour and actions? What kind of knowledge is the employee expected to acquire – banking knowledge, socio-ecological knowledge, knowledge in the field of ethics, or general knowledge? Ethics, attitude and competency targets need to be subject to the same criteria that apply as a matter of course to economic performance targets: they need to be clearly defined and measurable. Moral appeals are not targets, and they do not create a constructive working atmosphere.

The evaluation of ethical targets should be taken just as seriously as the evaluation of economic ones, and staff members should receive recognition in both areas. This can be taken quite literally: where employee recognition systems (involving bonuses, awards, etc.) are in place, they need to take into account both areas; otherwise management will swiftly lose credibility with the employees. Both areas need to be kept in view with regard to deficiencies as well, and appropriate and consistent action must be taken where necessary.

Mission statement

A mission statement is an integrative management tool whose purpose it is to align the people and trends within a company with its values and goals by giving a succinct overview of the cornerstones of the company's philosophy. Companies whose sole aim is profit maximization do not need a mission statement; for them, the rationale of profitability is enough of an integrating force. If they have one anyway, it often serves to foster a clan mentality – 'we are a sworn band; our aim is to conquer and win' – or to put the reader at ease: 'see, we only have your best interests at heart'. Ethics-based companies, by contrast, need a mission statement that lays out their vision and values and sets out the attitudes and behaviour that are to be employed to put them into practice. This means that a social bank's mission statement has to be far more than a promotional brochure: it lays out the nature, range and limits of the bank's commitment without making false promises.

Reports and management information systems

Members of management face three central questions:

1 How can I be certain that not just my immediate co-workers but all staff members in my management area perform up to standard?
2 How can I make sure I get the data and information I need to manage business operations well and identify both risks and opportunities early on?
3 How can I be sure that my superiors or, respectively, the owners, have the data and information they need for informed decisions and management actions?

During a company's pioneering days, it may be sufficient to rely on intuition or personal contact with all staff members: in this phase, trust arises from a sense of personal connection. But once the business becomes larger and more complex, this is no longer enough. At this point, it becomes necessary to request reports. One problem that can arise at this point is that staff may interpret the introduction of a reporting system as a sign of suspicion. Also, the additional administrative effort may meet with resistance. In this situation, good communication is paramount. Employees need to accept that there are instances where the company's needs and their own do not coincide.

Management, in turn, needs to be clear on what information it needs to be able to make informed decisions and have sufficient trust in the staff to perform their functions. And it needs to consistently insist on getting this information. This requires the development of procedures that make it possible to compare data over longer periods of time while taking as little additional effort as possible. There are a variety of IT-based management information systems available these days, but they need to be adapted to the specific requirements of a social bank. It is not enough for a report of activities to just contain key figures and data; it also needs to capture the ethical component and express it in quantifiable terms, i.e. in figures and data.

Risk management systems

As a rule, banks are heavily regulated organizations. As such, they are subject to legal regulations on risk management that mostly cover the standard financial and organizational risks. However, there is a multitude of other risks that need to be identified, assessed and dealt with swiftly and effectively, should they arise.

The common categories of business risk apply to social banks as well. They include the basic business risks (earnings risk, market risk, margin risk, organizational risk and – an increasingly important one – IT risk), as well as the risks specific to a particular industry (i.e. industry risks; in banking, these entail, for example, credit risk, investment risk, currency risk, interest rate risk, etc.). However, there are other risk areas that are either of particular significance for social banks or take on a different character in social banking.

Ethical risks

Ethics is not a fixed set of rules. An assessment once made can later become problematic, and often, new questions will arise: is it ethical to charge interest? Banks in the Islamic world take a different view on this than those in the Western world. Is it ethical to grant credit to a business that sells condoms in a Catholic country? Is it ethical to give a loan on preferential terms to a sectarian evangelical community? Is genetic engineering ethical? What about genetic seed modification or the genetic treatment of hereditary diseases? And so on and so forth.

Image or credibility risks

As mentioned previously, credibility is extremely important for a social bank. A mistake in daily business operations, bad business partners, unacceptable employee conduct, problematic clients, an ill-advised addition to the bank's investment universe, a controversial personnel decision – all these things and many more can damage a social bank's image and quickly set off ramifications that are completely out of proportion to the original incident or situation.

Personnel risks

Personnel risk is inherent in all businesses. In social banking, it is a particularly significant factor because employees need to be doubly qualified, both professionally and ethically. As a consequence, social banks have to put particular effort into recruiting good staff or, if new employees don't come with this dual qualification, providing the necessary training measures. The departure of good staff members is a big loss, and they are hard to replace. One aspect of personnel risk is motivation risk: staff members of social banks are, for the most part, intrinsically motivated by the knowledge that their work is meaningful and that they are making a contribution to society. Accordingly, loss of motivation due to a bad working atmosphere, differences of opinion in ethical matters, or loss of credibility are all the more serious. Such crises have far more severe consequences in value-based enterprises than they do in traditional companies.

Risks related to customer demographics

Social banks often have their origins in social movements, which have provided them with a stable of loyal customers. Social banks clearly appeal to a specific segment of the population: the overall impression at many customer events is one of strong homogeneity. Once in a while, a particular socio-political event will gain social banks new customers; the financial crisis, for example, brought them a wave of new customers. But both the narrow customer segment and the occasional surge have their risks. Social banks are well advised to have a thorough knowledge of their customer demographics and the attendant risks.

Adaptation risks

All companies have to keep adapting. Social banks, with their strong emphasis on discussion and their culture of participation, run the risk of being somewhat sluggish. They may make too much of a production of introducing simple and/or necessary adaptation measures or take too long in implementing them.

Innovation risk

Social banks are practically the embodiment of innovation in the banking industry. This has led some social banks to underestimate the need for innovation in business practices and product development: they more or less assume that their ethical stance will protect them from the dynamics of the market, including the pressure to innovate. But social banks are facing a situation today where social banking has become a trend among banks of all stripes: the innovative products originally developed by social banks have by now been adopted by other banks as well. As a consequence, social banks are under huge pressure to innovate.

Knowing these risks is important, but so is systematic risk analysis. One useful tool for this purpose is a risk assessment chart (see Figure 4.1), a simple tool that should be used periodically to capture and assess the risk situation. In addition, predetermined risk management procedures should be developed in advance – one crucial aspect of good crisis management is outlining important steps and assigning key responsibilities while things are running smoothly. If and when a damaging event occurs and quick, effective action is called for, such predetermined crisis management procedures can be crucial for a company's survival.

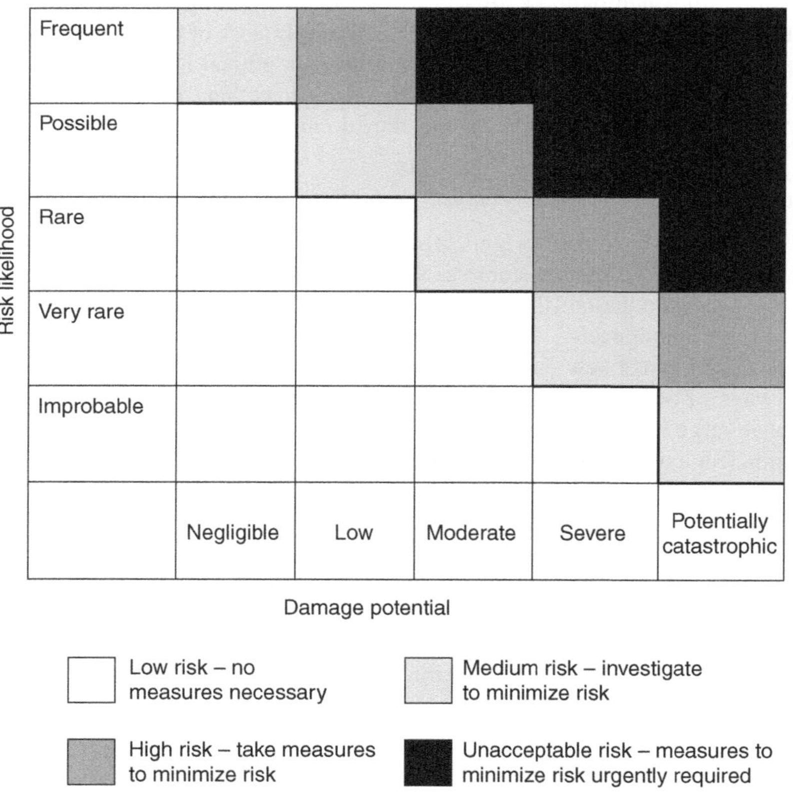

Figure 4.1 Risk assessment chart.

Ratings

Ratings are an important tool in the banking industry. Their purpose is to capture situations in a systematic manner, quantify assessments and create measurability. More so than traditional banks, social banks deal with unconventional business situations: loan applications for new businesses, businesses with uncertain economic prospects, investors seeking to invest their money in accordance with their ethical values, financing requests for alternative residential housing or ecologically innovative buildings, etc. Clients often have a hard time understanding that a social bank's unconventional character does not automatically entitle them to a business relationship with this bank; they expect social banks to be more open-handed and less hung up on formal business procedures than their traditional counterparts. Staff members, on the other hand, often get vicariously excited about a customer's ideas and aspirations or simply see how urgently a customer needs a proposal to be approved, and find it hard to critically evaluate or turn down an application. Against this background, it is important to have tools in place that allow for competent and fair assessment and also ensure equal treatment of all customers. This is where ratings provide a good indication. They also enable banks to operationalize their ethical values by way of quantifying social and ecological factors, thus providing a basis for pricing that is in accordance with the bank's values. There are a number of social banks today that have developed values-based rating systems in the areas of (among others) mortgage credit, business credit and investment.

Still, the development of rating scales is a complex endeavour. Moreover, it is essential that the criteria applied be measurable and ensure a high degree of transparency. It is therefore advisable to develop such ratings in a participatory process involving internal and external stakeholders. Involving experts and representatives of accredited organizations ensures that the criteria selected are pertinent, ethically relevant and objective. Such carefully developed rating scales make it easier for staff members to assess business proposals and particularly to communicate with clients. They also add decisively to a social bank's credibility and hence are an important means of raising its profile. This aspect also makes them effective marketing strategy tools.

Knowledge management systems

The systematic capture of professional and company knowledge is as essential for social banks as it is for other companies. In social banking, however, it plays a particularly important role because here the amount of informal knowledge is proportionately higher than it is in traditional banking. In addition, in social banks informal knowledge is not relegated to the periphery but plays a highly significant part in core processes and management. Knowledge about what ethical business means and how socio-ecological responsibility can be successfully put into practice is still being accumulated. While the ecological sector has a growing pool of verifiable data at its disposal, the social sector has, as yet, considerably fewer hard facts to work with. Ethical issues are influenced by a variety of ever-changing factors, and the answers to ethical questions depend very much on attitude and opinion. It is therefore vitally important to capture and evaluate developments, approaches and experiences. Social banks are faced with the necessity of accumulating specific knowledge, and if this knowledge is to be consistently expanded and – a key point – transferred, a knowledge management system is indispensable. And if social banks are serious about their social commitment and want to establish themselves as players in the world of financial management, they also have to pursue the accumulation of industry knowledge beyond the pools of knowledge accumulated by individual companies. This requires cooperation between banks: it requires official international associations willing to further the accumulation of knowledge in this area and to provide specific tools for knowledge management in social banks.

Management through personal contact

Direct staff management will be discussed in more detail in the third section. What follows here are just a few general observations.

Management through personal contact means first and foremost to unambiguously assume one's role as a member of management. It also requires presence – not primarily in the physical sense but in the sense of making one's presence felt, of being clearly and evidently committed to the company's goals. Owners, customers and employees want to know who is in charge of managing the bank. They want the management team to assume responsibility, to communicate openly in difficult situations, and to represent the company's strategy. Another particularly significant aspect in social banking is that members of management are expected to lead by example: they are primarily seen as representatives of certain values who stand for the bank's ethical stance and the possibility of reconciling ethical conduct with success in business. More so than the staff of traditional organizations, staff members of social banks expect their superiors' professed values to be in keeping with their actions; discrepancies are not looked upon kindly and quickly lead to an erosion of trust and a deteriorating working atmosphere.

Management through personal contact also entails a visible interest in all stakeholders. Management needs to maintain good relations with important partners in the company's environment, but it also needs to create dialogue with customer groups. And it needs to take an interest in the employees' thoughts and concerns. 'Knowing one's business' does not end with sound professional expertise and knowledge of procedures; only a person who is in dialogue with all stakeholders can be said to truly know their business.

Human resource management in social banking

Management philosophy

A bank's ethical commitment also needs to manifest itself in its human resource management. A social bank's management culture should be characterized by dialogue, absence of discrimination, and an emphasis on trust. It should be a matter of course – just like the equal treatment of men and women – that staff members of all levels are involved in decisions that affect their working conditions and area of work and that all staff, regardless of their position, treat each other with fairness and respect.

In a company that operates on the principles of dialogue- and trust-based leadership, it is particularly important for roles to be clearly defined and taken on responsibly. Staff members need to exercise a high degree of self-responsibility in taking on tasks, make full use of their competencies and reliably meet their responsibilities. Where roles are vaguely defined, effective participation is difficult to achieve. This easily leads to directives not being clearly communicated, decisions not being made effectively, and long, meandering discussions without clear outcomes – in other words, to a situation that confirms all stereotypes about social organizations.

One phenomenon that can be observed quite frequently in social banks and similar organizations is a certain tendency, both on the part of executive and staff, to have an ambiguous attitude towards leadership. The idea of leadership tends to be regarded as being at odds with the idea of a staff member as a responsible, committed and competent human being. At the same time, staff members have high standards for their superiors, who are expected to be infallible people with natural authority. As a result, there is often a certain amount of veering between over- and underestimating the value of leadership: a dismissive attitude towards it in day-to-day business may quickly give way to calls for strong leadership once a difficult situation arises.

This makes leadership culture a key factor in social banking. Personnel management needs to reflect the three core principles discussed in the previous section: transparency, communication, participation. Staff members will hold their superiors to these principles.

Transparency is an important trust-building factor. Just as business decisions need to be transparent, so do matters of salaries, fringe benefits, working hours, tasks assigned, etc. But the crux of transparency is that it is generally not measured by the amount of information imparted but by a subjective sense of 'being in on things'. 'Not transparent enough' can become a killer phrase. The ability to create a high degree of transparency and dealing constructively with staff members' misgivings and dissatisfactions in this regard while at the same time refusing demands that cannot be met is an important leadership quality in social banking.

There can be no doubt that social banks need a participatory leadership culture. But putting participation into practice in a way that works is a challenging endeavour. Members of management need to be clear on which issues and topics they want staff members to have input and decision-making authority on. It is problematic if staff members are involved in every single discussion and management then goes on to make unclear decisions on the basis of these discussions that they don't take full responsibility for: 'What can you do; that's what they want'. Equally problematic is a situation in which staff members are encouraged to discuss whatever they feel is important but management entirely disregards these discussions in their decision-making. It is the management's responsibility to decide, with a high degree of sensitivity to the employees' concerns and motivations, how and at which points they are to be involved in decisions and new developments. These considerations need to be guided by two questions: first, how can staff motivation and commitment be fostered, and second, how can staff members contribute with their knowledge and experience to economically sound solutions or instigate new developments. This means by implication that staff members cannot just give their input where their own interests are concerned and withdraw from decision-making and problem-solving processes in other areas. In social banking, participation cannot be regarded as just an aspect of employee interest representation, nor can it be limited to mere compliance with statutory regulations. It is also a resource that contributes to a business's conceptual and organizational development and hence entails taking on shared responsibility for the entire company.

The third principle of leadership, direct communication, also needs to manifest itself in human resource management. Organizations whose employees expect their job to be not just a means of making a living but a source of meaning in their lives typically have a much higher communication density than other companies. Consequently, communication plays an important role in human resource management. In addition to the aforementioned communication with stakeholders and staff in general, personal communication between members of management and individual staff members is key. Clear communication of directives and expectations and conversations about work planning and procedures are important. One particularly important element of communication is feedback – this entails recognition of good performance, but also constructive criticism where deficiencies have been noticed. Employees are often very clear on what, in their eyes, characterizes motivating communication with their superiors: they are interested not just in the work but in the person as well, they are approachable and pay attention in conversation, they are appreciative, respectful in their criticism, and you know where you stand with them.

Staff identification with the company

Identification with the company plays an important role in staff motivation. In social banks, this aspect often takes on a particular form. Most of their staff members derive their motivation in large part from a conviction that their work is meaningful and part of a larger whole and that it contributes to positive changes in society. While they identify strongly with the values the bank stands for, they often have a much lower level of identification with the company's business side, placing more importance on pursuing these values than on actual output. What is important to them is making a contribution to a better society, and they tend to regard economic efficiency and professional organizational structures as annoying, if necessary, side issues. This makes leadership difficult. But it is one of management's most important tasks to foster employee identification with the company, to bring them closer to the company and to get them on board for its goals. The staff members' work needs to be a constructive contribution to the company's goals. This presupposes that staff members take an interest in the business side of things, that they take the company's concrete organizational and economic concerns seriously and accept that these are key factors for the company's success. Many mission statements issued by social banks reflect this dilemma: they lay out the company's socio-political stance and ethical values and provide guidelines for its business operations, but they are quite short on organizational matters and on what is expected of staff and management with regard to the actual business operations.

Personnel recruitment

The assumption that there are no good bankers with an ethical conscience is just as mistaken as the one that economic success and ethical values do not go together. As for any other company, it is imperative for social banks to get the best people they can. In social banking, this means hiring people with both expertise and a high level of ethical competence. This dual qualification is a must, at least for managerial staff, employees in key positions, and employees with direct customer contact. These prerequisites make personnel selection a challenging process that requires a thoroughly professional approach. There is often a tendency in social banking to hire personal acquaintances: people one knows from past political activities, from a citizens' action group or an ecological association, or simply housemates – in any case, people who share one's values. This may work during a company's early stages; after all, early social banking initiatives had a certain spirit of 'manning the barricades together'. But the demands and expectations placed on professional banking institutions have grown, and fulfilling them has become a crucial success factor for social banks. Job advertisements need to highlight professional qualifications and specifically call for a banking specialist, a person with leadership expertise, a marketing specialist, a communications specialist – whatever the position in question requires. These qualified professionals need to share the bank's values and – in the case of management personnel and employees in key functions – have ethical action and decision-making skills as well. Social banks need to have instruments and techniques at their disposal that enable them to assess an applicant's ethical suitability for a particular position in a professional manner.

What if, in spite of the bank's best efforts, people with the requisite dual qualification cannot be found? In this case, some social banks will follow a policy of hiring a person whose values match the company's and give them the opportunity to acquire the necessary professional competence on the job – the rationale being that, from a sustainability point of view, it makes a lot more sense to convey expertise to people who share the company's values than it does to convey these values to experts with no prior interest in them.

One difficult aspect of personnel selection in social banks is that they get more applications from people without industry experience than other banks do.

They also frequently get applications from people who cannot, or do not want to, work to full capacity. There is a widespread assumption that social banks are more flexible in their hiring policies and less demanding of their staff than other banks. This makes it all the more important for a social bank to have clear personnel policies in place. Well-qualified, highly motivated employees are an important asset. The bank can, of course, offer employment opportunities for people with reduced working capacity, but the hiring procedures for these positions should be kept separate from the regular personnel recruitment and management processes.

Social banks, too, compete amongst each other for the best people. People with integrity, excellent knowledge of the field and high social competence are sought after. In addition, a social bank will not pay these outstanding people the salaries they would draw in a traditional company. But social banks should not be discouraged too much by these difficulties. There are good qualified people out there who have made a conscious decision to work in a socially and ecologically conscious environment. Employers in the values-based sector confirm that their culture is an asset in staff recruitment: for example, they keep getting speculative applications from interesting professionals (Christen Jakob and von Passavant 2009). Why should people in the banking industry be any different in this regard from engineers, business economists, carpenters or food chemists? With the meaningful work and room for creativity they offer, social banks are attractive employers for people who do not base their decisions exclusively on financial considerations.

As anywhere, the less-qualified positions are easier to fill in social banking. For the most part, social banks offer employees on this level better-than-average working conditions. As a consequence, there is a certain risk of these employees losing their labour market mobility because they are very unlikely to find similar working conditions elsewhere. This occasionally leads to functions that have become obsolete – e.g. as a result of streamlining – being preserved and becoming an economic liability. It is therefore an important responsibility of ethics-based companies to foster the employability of all, including low qualified, staff.

Inducting new employees, assigning tasks and setting goals

The induction of new employees is a distinctly different process in a social bank than it is in traditional banks. As in any company, new staff members need to familiarize themselves with the pertinent processes, tools and documents, build relations with their customers, and establish cooperation with superiors and co-workers. But in addition, they have to be introduced from day one to the bank's culture and values. Any induction programme for new employees should include an introduction to these values and culture, and new staff members need to be coached on them. However, this can only be done successfully if the bank has laid down its values in a clear and unambiguous way that communicates well.

Another component of personnel management is the allocation of staff capacity, or task assignment. Managerial staff has to make sure that employees are assigned clearly delineated and properly coordinated tasks that contribute to the company's goals. This does not just entail deciding which staff member is assigned to which tasks but also how much capacity is allocated to each task. However, it is a well-known fact that employees generally spend a considerably smaller proportion of their working time on the important tasks they have been assigned than one would think (Malik 2006). It is safe to assume that problems of capacity management are more prevalent in social banks than they are in other companies. Hence they require particular attention. This is first because of the previously mentioned high communication density, and second, because ethical companies are committed to providing a working environment that enables their staff to perform their work in good health and with a good work–life balance over many years, which implies that the work can be accomplished with the capacities allocated to it.

The topic of target setting has been addressed above; the section on management through tools in particular discussed the significance of management through target setting and clear strategies. Based on clearly communicated goals, individual targets should be set for all staff members in keeping with their tasks, competencies and skills. These should include not just performance targets (What is the objective?) but also ethics/attitude targets (What values should it be based on?) and development targets (What experiences can be drawn from it? What are the knowledge and skills supposed to be acquired?).

While performance targets are easy to quantify, this is not always the case with development targets, and attitude targets are particularly difficult to quantify. In this regard, it is advisable for management and employees to work together to develop a set of indicators that allow the objective evaluation of target achievement.

Consequently, progress on tasks and the evaluation of target achievement should be the main focus of employee performance reviews. These should be conducted at regular intervals and should contain an element of two-way feedback as well. For managers, they are an important source of information about staff concerns, the company's day-to-day operations, and optimization ideas from staff members; for employees, they provide direction and the knowledge that they are being acknowledged and that their input is heard. These periodic performance review talks also provide good opportunities for employee coaching.

Human resource development

Human resource development is an essential part of human resource management. Fostering employee advancement through systematic human resource development has three rationales:

- supporting employees in staying current in their function and professional development;
- bringing new knowledge into the organization;
- furthering employees' personal development.

The dual approach that characterizes social banks should also be applied to providing continuing education for employees: it should advance and expand both professional expertise in the narrower sense of the term and socio-ecological and ethical competencies. And staff members' personal development – especially in the areas of self-management, social competence and demeanour – should, of course, be fostered as well. So far, social banks have been fairly conservative where their employees' further education is concerned: courses and educational events are the most common formats. But such off-the-job events are not always the most sustainable and effective training tools. Moreover, there is often not enough emphasis on transferring knowledge back into the organization. Employees who take training courses or classes should be obliged to make their newly acquired knowledge available to the organization.

One effective training tool for employees are 'near-the-job' activities like quality circles, intervision groups, critical incident analyses, groups working on specific topics, etc. This format has the advantage of bringing employees together in a common learning experience. The exchange not just of knowledge and experience but of views and opinions on particular topics creates a synergistic learning effect.

One kind of professional development activity that is not very common yet in social banking but very much worth looking into is on-the-job training. This includes mentoring and coaching, but also formats like reflective project work, reflecting teams, etc. Individual employee development can also take the form of job enrichment, job enlargement or job rotation. These are means of exposing staff members to new work experiences, thus enabling them to expand their perspective and competencies.

For social banks in particular, near-the-job or on-the-job development activities offer good opportunities for personnel development. Especially with regard to soft factors like attitude, values and experience, these formats are more effective than courses and seminars.

To systematically further an employee's professional development, however, it is necessary to discuss their development needs in periodic performance reviews or, at the very least, in an annual career development discussion. The employee's wishes and preferences cannot be the only factor considered here; management personnel needs to get a clear picture of what the company needs and set targets accordingly. But this does not mean that employees should just be signed up for courses; rather, management and employees should discuss the most useful development activities together.

Career design and planning

Career design, and especially career planning, is a challenging aspect in social banking. Like many SMEs, social banks are faced with the problem of offering few prospects for promotion: not only are there few managerial positions available to begin with, there is also not a lot of turnover at this level, partly because comparable positions are scarce. This can be frustrating for good staff members.

Nevertheless, superiors should keep an eye on staff members' career development and periodically discuss it with them. They need to have the generosity of spirit to support staff members in their professional development even if this means that their next career step may take them outside the company. On the other hand, a productive discussion with a good employee about their career plans and prospects can help keep them in the company. After all, social banks in particular offer not just promotion in status but job enrichment possibilities as well – an important means of keeping good, established staff members and giving them the opportunity to further expand their potential. This is an area that calls for creativity on the part of superiors.

Terminations/dismissals and resignations

Another important aspect of human resource management is employment termination. How do staff members terminate their employment? How does a social bank terminate a staff member's employment?

Ethics-based companies generally have a hard time handling terminations (Christen Jakob and von Passavant 2009). There is a tendency to see employees who leave the company as disloyal, especially if they move on to another company or, worse, to an employer who is considered 'less ethical'. This is regrettable. For one, this attitude makes it harder for staff members to rejoin the company at a later date, and second, the bank loses an external stakeholder whose knowledge will be lost to them – not to mention the hurt feelings and damaged relationships that ensue.

Dismissals are a particularly thorny issue for social banks. They do not deal easily with staff reductions for economic reasons or with the termination of employees who do not perform up to the expected standard or have serious conduct problems. As a result, employees are often let go too late and, occasionally, the legal requirements are not met. This results in elaborate procedures and huge costs that often have a detrimental effect on the affected team and the entire company. Also, it should not be underestimated that badly handled terminations constitute a huge image risk for an ethics-based company. Ethical standards must be maintained, regardless of whether or not an employee termination is difficult. Fairness and transparency must be ensured. This entails clearly communicating points of criticism to the staff member in question and – unless the employment is terminated without notice because of grave misconduct – giving them a chance to improve their behaviour and/or performance. This requires clear target agreements in conjunction with follow-up performance reviews on set dates. But the principle of fairness also obliges the company to involve an independent third party (e.g. a HR officer or a mediator) in difficult discussions and to let the staff member in question bring a support person they trust.

Regardless of whether or not a termination occurs by mutual agreement, it is important for management to shape the process. For example, there should always be an exit interview and if possible – even if the circumstances of the termination are difficult – a goodbye meeting with the entire team.

Handling disagreements and conflict

Professional human resource management also necessarily involves dealing with disagreements and conflict. In social banking, this aspect is particularly important. For one, a concern for fairness in conflict is part of a company culture based on the principles of dialogue and trust. Second, the staff, customers and environment of social banks have high standards when it comes to their bank's ethical handling of difficult situations. Conflict can quickly damage a social bank's image. Disagreements and conflict occur wherever people work together, and they are not necessary a bad thing – neither for the staff nor for management nor for the company as a whole. On the contrary, they can reveal areas in need of improvement and trigger important learning processes. But a critical point is reached when a conflict begins to tie up too much energy, when the normal course of operations is disrupted or important work is left undone. At this point, management should intervene quickly and decisively, with the rationale of resolving the disagreement in such a way that the company's smooth operation is ensured and similar crises can be resolved better in the future. Managerial staff often has a tendency to ignore disagreements for too long or, at best, to appeal to the goodwill of everybody involved. Managers in social banks are no exception in this regard. Moreover, they tend to emphasize the question of who is to blame over a constructive look at how to work towards better cooperation. This attitude carries the risk that what begins as slight tension eventually turns into a chronic conflict that ends up causing huge friction and loss of productivity. A key competency required of managerial staff is the ability to identify and tackle collaboration problems early on. This approach also contributes hugely to building trust with employees.

Compensation and profit sharing in social banking: an attempt to square the circle?

While the discussions of recent years surrounding bankers' excessive salaries and bonuses have gained social banks new customers, they have had little bearing on internal discussions about adequate salaries. Anybody applying for a job at a social bank knows that they are not going to draw a top salary in comparison with other banks. But obviously social bank employees will not work for a song either.

The matter of remuneration in social banking is by no means a trivial one. A low wage structure can make a bank appear unprofessional and economically unsound; a high one, on the other hand, creates a different kind of image problem: is this company still serious about its ethics? These considerations apart, what it comes down to is: what wage level can the company afford to pay, given its profit situation, and what wage level does it want to pay, given its personnel policies?

This chapter is not the place for a discussion of salary figures. There are, however, certain cornerstones that are essential to the establishment of compensation systems in ethics-based companies:[1]

- a fair and transparent compensation system;
- a fixed maximum wage range between the lowest- and the highest-paid position in the company;
- a clear, transparent long-term policy with regard to bonuses and awards.

A fair and transparent compensation system is a system based on clearly defined functional levels. Functions should be categorized solely on the basis of requirements and level of responsibility, with professional, economic and ethical factors being given equal weight. A clearly defined compensation system is meant to ensure equal treatment of all staff and facilitate the induction of new staff members. But it also allows a high degree of transparency and can be communicated clearly both internally and externally. Social banks also need to pay attention to the increasingly louder calls for owners to decide on companies' compensation systems and sizes of payouts.

A fixed maximum range between the lowest and the highest salary is an important feature of ethics-based companies. A number of social banks have expanded this range in the course of their history in order to be more competitive in the recruitment of management. These days, the maximum wage ranges in the social banking sector are set between 1:5 and 1:8, although in reality there are narrower ranges as well (1:3–1:5). In a survey among ethics-based companies, a ratio of 1:12 was mentioned, in a different context, as the absolute limit (Christen Jakob and von Passavant 2009).

The controversial discussion over bonuses and awards has extended to social banks as well. Traditional banks hold to the view that bonuses are the main driving force for motivation, but a number of studies in the field of labour psychology question this assumption. According to one significant theory, bonuses destroy intrinsic motivation while overemphasizing extrinsic motivation, thus stimulating addictive behaviour. Against the background of this discussion, the use of bonus pay systems in social banking appears justified, although most social banks operate without them. However, the following points are essential:

- Bonuses should be based on clear target agreements. This creates transparency and makes it possible to communicate clearly what they are paid for.
- A bonus system cannot just be a reward system. It should also contain a malus component that comes into effect in case of bad business results or bad performance.
- The bonus amount can under no circumstances exceed the fixed salary.
- The size of bonuses should be linked to long-term performance, based on a time period of at least three, ideally five, years.

Another important question is whether bonuses, and particularly awards, should be contingent on individual or on team performance. Since individual bonuses and awards encourage competition between employees, where an individual reward system is in place, target agreements should include cooperative goals. Group or team bonuses contribute to the credibility of a company's team-based philosophy.

The customer as partner

As mentioned above, a social bank's customers are no 'ordinary' bank customers. First, there are those who are not just looking to conduct their banking transactions but also want to put their money to use in a socially responsible way. What attracts these customers is the opportunity to contribute with their banking to positive developments in society. One thing many staff members, owners and customers of social banks have in common is a deep-seated suspicion of the money economy. Is it possible to make money and still be a decent person? Is great wealth not always acquired through exploitation of resources and/or other human beings or through criminal activities? This ambiguous attitude towards wealth and property often takes on strange forms. Wealthy social bank customers almost feel compelled to defend themselves to their bank for having money and often act as if they were embarrassed about it. And employees occasionally treat well-off customers like spoiled people of privilege who it wouldn't hurt to wait their turn once in a while.

Then there are the customers who apply for a loan assuming that they will get better loan conditions with a social bank than they would with a traditional one. In the best-case scenario, what they are seeking financing for is an economically and ethically promising business idea or an economically and socio-ecologically interesting piece of property in which case bank and client will quickly come to an agreement and, as a rule, end up being proud of their business relationship.

Things get tricky when the project in question has social and/or ecological potential but little economic potential, or when attempts are made to bolster a loan application that has been rejected by a number of other banks with ethical arguments. In such cases, many customers will vehemently appeal to the bank's moral obligation of putting ethics before profit – a situation that invites bitter disappointment and not infrequently leads to reputational damage for the bank as well.

Put differently, a social bank's customers see themselves not merely as business partners but also – perhaps primarily – as partners on the basis of shared values. This brings with it opportunities, but it also presents challenges that need to be addressed creatively. Emphasis should be placed on the following measures:

- Developing more products aimed at well-off customers beyond ethical funds or development loans at reduced interest rates – products that allow customers to make effective use of their money through supporting socially/ecologically oriented initiatives or becoming shareholders in a company with an excellent business idea in the socio-ecological sector.
- Training staff to enable them to integrate both the aspect of profitability and the dialogue on values into their customer relations, to interact with customers in a competent and approachable way, and to represent the company's interests in a professional manner.

- Developing a marketing strategy that conveys not just ethical values in general but ethical financial management in particular and specifically targets interesting companies and well-off customers.
- Holding events aimed at strengthening customer relations that cater to the customers' interest in social and ecological issues and promote knowledge and discussion of ethical issues.
- Offering a range of advisory and consultancy services for customers who have a business idea worth supporting but insufficient business skills, as well as for existing business clients who have run into economic difficulties.

As discussed above, social banks are well advised to know their customer base, but they need to do more. They need to work on maintaining it and on shaping its future development. Social banks, too, need to secure their future!

References

Christen Jakob, M. and von Passavant, C.H. (2009) *Corporate Social Responsibility*, Frauenfeld: Huber.

Malik, F. (2006) *Führen, leisten, leben*, Frankfurt and New York: Campus.

Steiger, T.H. and Lippmann, E. (eds) (2003) *Handbuch angewandte Psychologie für Führungskräfte*, Berlin, Heidelberg and New York: Springer.

Ulrich, P. (2008) *Integrative Wirtschaftsethik*, Bern, Stuttgart and Wien: Paul Haupt.

5 Products and services

Olaf Weber

Introduction

This chapter presents products and services that are connected to social, environmental, ethical or sustainable finance. On the one hand there are products and services that integrate sustainability risks and options in order to create a positive financial impact. These products and services are offered by both social and conventional banks. Their main drivers are financial returns and clients' needs. On the other hand there are products and services striving to reach a positive social, environmental or sustainability impact. These are mostly offered by specialized social or ethical banks. Their main driver is the fulfilment of social, environmental or sustainability needs by channelling capital into respective projects. Thus products and services can be structured by their financial and social impact. While sustainable credit management mainly integrates social and environmental indicators to improve the credit risk prediction and therefore mainly has a financial impact, sustainability loans and mortgages are created to foster projects and other borrowers that have a positive impact on social, environmental or sustainability aspects.

Socially responsible investment (SRI) products could have both positive financial and social impacts. There is a great range of different products in this field covering both financial and social impact. The same is valid for carbon finance. In this field conventional banks create new financial products based on the Kyoto Protocol Mechanisms. On the other hands there are products and services striving to mitigate climate change by investing in projects that reduce CO_2 emissions.

With sustainability savings accounts and certificates of deposits savings can be connected with social loans or other investments. They are the link between socially oriented people and institutions and those that need capital to create a social impact.

Microfinance is maybe the most known social banking product. It provides both a financial risk rating structure that differs from conventional loan products and services and high social impacts.

Project finance is connected to social banking since the launch of the Equator Principles for project finance. These provide guidelines to take social and environmental aspects into account in project finance. In contrast to big universal banks, social banks are often financing smaller projects like renewable energy projects.

Sustainable credit management, sustainable loans and mortgages

Environmental risks that caused credit defaults in the past were often linked to real estate collateral. In the beginning of the 1990s the first European and North American commercial banks were confronted by environmental risks. Under the US Comprehensive Environmental Response, Compensation and Liability Act of 1980 (CERCLA), the owner of a contaminated site was responsible for the decontamination and redevelopment of the site. Though Superfund specifically exempts lenders from being classified as owners, some banks were held liable under CERCLA because they owned or participated in the management of a contaminating business (Bacow 1998). Probably the best-known case of lender liability is the Fleet Factors case in Providence, Rhode Island. In 1990 Fleet Factors was made responsible for the costs of the site remediation of a borrower, because they were, as a lender, in a position to influence the borrowers' compliance with environmental laws (Labatt and White 2002). There were a number of cases in Germany as well that were documented by Scholz *et al.* (1995). Reasons for credit default were (Case 1996; Thompson and Cowton 2004; Weber 2005):

- contaminated sites used as collateral;
- changes in environmental regulations that result in costs for environmental technologies or other costs; and
- market changes caused by environmental awareness and attitudes of clients.

Furthermore banks could suffer from a negative reputation if they were connected to debtors that had a negative environmental image or were known to have negative environmental impacts. Looking at the case of Asian Pulp and Paper (Noor and Syumanda 2006) there was both a credit default caused by the non-sustainable use of the forest and a negative reputation for the banks financing the company (www.evb.ch, www.banktrack.org).

Let us have a look at the risk caused by contaminated sites used as collateral: if lenders accept a site as loan security they generally estimate the value of that collateral. In case of a credit default the lender has the chance to sell the collateral to back up the credit default. However, if the value of the security decreases because of costs of decontamination the lender will not be able to generate the expected revenue. As a consequence literature indicates that most banks consider environmental risks as part of the credit appraisal process (Coulson and Dixon 1995; Wanless 1995; Weber *et al.* 2008b). The World Bank and the International Finance Corporation (IFC) published detailed guidelines for integrating environmental assessment into the credit risk assessment (International Finance Corporation (IFC) 1998) as well. These guidelines found entrance to environmental assessment strategies of commercial banks and multilateral development banks

(Annandale *et al.* 2001). Consequently a number of banks are integrating environmental and sustainability risks into their credit risk management operations as Weber *et al.* (2008a) show.

A list of sustainability indicators that were used in the study of Weber *et al.* (2010) is presented in Table 5.1. However that list is not exhaustive and could be modified taking newer findings into account.

The integration of environmental risks does not only produce costs because of a more costly process of credit rating, but it increases the quality of the credit risk rating. Weber *et al.* (2010) demonstrated that the rate of correct credit default predictions improves about 7.7 per cent if sustainability criteria are added to conventional credit risk indicators. This improvement will be material for any portfolio of a lender. The AUROC as standard measurement for the validity of a credit risk rating instrument improved significantly from 0.92 for traditional rating indicators to 0.94 for the combination of traditional and sustainability indicators as well (see Figure 5.1).

The results of some studies suggest that the incorporation of sustainability indicators in the credit risk rating process has some positive impacts for the lender, especially by reducing the costs of credit defaults. Furthermore, if higher risks are connected to higher interest rates, debtors being rated well with respect to their corporate social performance have better access to better priced credit and mortgages. This will foster companies with better corporate social performance given that other risk factors are constant.

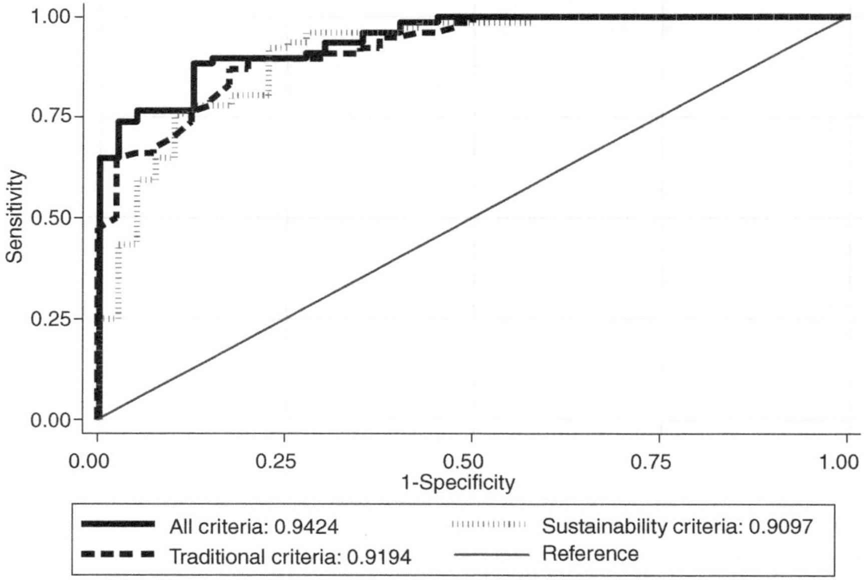

Figure 5.1 AUROC of traditional, sustainability, and both groups of criteria used for credit risk prediction.

Table 5.1 Sustainability criteria in credit risk management

Economical sustainability criteria	*Environmental sustainability criteria*	*Social sustainability criteria*
Net debt service	Costs of environmental measures	Wage policy
Sustained growth	Emissions	Health policy
Quality of growth	Environmentally friendly construction	Social security of the employees
Sector development	Consideration of nature and landscape	Workers' participation
Integration of environmental aspect in economic decision-making	Soil erosion	Conservation of workplaces
Robustness against crises	Sealing of soil	Flexible working conditions and working hours
Personal resources	Sewage emission	
Community relations	Sewage quality	
Risk of accidents	Air emission	
Job creation	Noise emission	
Adequate firm size	Resource protection	
Eco-efficiency	Material use	
Information and communication	Ratio of renewable resources	
Material productivity	Use of non-renewable energy sources	
Spatial relation	Use of renewable energy	
Commuter mobility	Use of water (amount)	
Fleet		
Energy efficiency		
Technical update of power plants and machines		
Amount of waste		
Waste management		
Toxic waste		
Contaminated sites		
Technology management		
Material substitution		
Longevity		
Recycling capacity		
Redemption of used products		
Miniaturization of products		
Ecological product design		
Contracting		

Sustainability loans

In contrary to sustainable credit management aiming at improving the financial risk for lenders, sustainability loans and mortgages are provided for borrowers that have a positive impact on sustainable development. Sometimes these loans and mortgages are connected with different interest rates depending on the sustainability performance of the debtor. These products and services support 'sustainable' debtors and may have a positive influence on sustainable development as well. An example is described in the Box 5.1.

Box 5.1 CO_2 emission of loans: the case of Alternative Bank Switzerland

As one of the first banks Alternative Bank ABS calculates the CO_2 emissions of their loans and for the clients' assets. By financing 73 projects that produce renewable energy in 2008 3,700 tons of CO_2 could be avoided. If a client invested 100,000 Swiss francs in ABS deposits for renewable energy about nine tons of CO_2 emissions per year are avoided compared to an investment in a conventional energy project.

Though there are many sustainable mortgage products on the market (see below, pp. 102–103) specialized sustainability loans are not frequently offered. Mostly, the so-called ethical, social or alternative banks are offering these products and services. Banca Etica offers loans in the following areas (see www.bancaetica.com):

- Social cooperation: social, sanitary and educational services; fight against social exclusion and integration of disadvantaged people in the community.
- International cooperation: social and economic development of the poorest areas of our planet, supporting fair trade, training and educating, promoting micro-enterprises, assisting and supporting immigrants, and aiding partnerships between solidarity organizations from the South and from the North of the world.
- Environment: promoting research, experiments and use of: alternative and renewable energy sources; non-polluting production techniques; waste disposal services; ecological public transport; productive and distributive processes with a positive impact on man and his environment; management of natural heritage; development of biological and bio-dynamic agriculture; promotion of ecological awareness and culture.
- Culture and civil society: management and protection of artistic and cultural heritage, promoting social-cultural animation in areas most affected by social decline, and helping develop non-profit-making associations, artistic and cultural initiatives, aiding access to sport activities for the most disadvantaged categories.

The German GLS lists the following sectors as eligible for loans (www.gls.de):

- alternative, 'free' schools
- organic sector and organic agriculture
- facilities for the handicapped
- the elderly
- housing projects
- renewable energy
- cultural projects and facilities
- health sector.

Another social bank, Triodos Bank, describes the sectors that are provided with loans as follows (www.triodos.com):

- charities and social enterprises
- organics
- renewable energy
- environment
- fair trade.

Generally these loans are not only rated with respect to their financial acceptability, but with respect to ethical, social or environmental criteria as well. These criteria encompass both positive and negative criteria. As an example for a list of exclusion criteria we present the list of Alternative Bank Switzerland that excludes potential borrowers due to the following criteria (see www.abs.ch):

- nuclear power
- chemical large-scale industry
- armaments industry (including suppliers)
- genetic engineering
- non-renewable large-scale energy production
- resource-intensive products and those that are harmful to the environment and humans
- conventional agriculture using harmful chemicals and fertilizers
- large-scale animal farms
- highways
- parking docks
- infrastructure projects that are harmful to pedestrians and bicycle riders
- non-sustainable tourism
- conventional medicine
- public relation and print products for products that violate the negative criteria
- consumer loans
- debtors that violate gender equality
- debtors that discriminate against certain groups
- debtors that violate the right of unionization and workers' organization

- debtors that violate workplace security regulations
- socially harmful large-scale building projects
- luxury buildings
- non-energy-efficient buildings
- environmentally harmful construction materials
- speculative businesses
- firms and subjects that behave exploitatively.

Thus by directing loans to preferred sectors and denying loans for sectors rated as non-sustainable or non-ethical, social banks take the responsibility to foster sustainable development as defined by Schmidheiny and Zorraquin (1996).

Sustainability mortgages

In contrast to credits and loans, mortgages are secured by real property. They are used to finance private or commercial real estate. Additionally to the strong economic effect of mortgages that led to some financial crises, i.e. the recession starting in 2008, the impact on sustainable development is important as well. There are estimations that about 30 per cent of the CO_2 emissions of industrialized countries are caused by housing (Johnston *et al.* 2005). Furthermore, because of long lifetimes of buildings, their energy efficiency cannot be changed on a short-term basis. Therefore some regulative bodies started programmes to foster sustainable construction and renovation of buildings (Bizer *et al.* 2003) that are supported by state-owned banks like the German Kreditanstalt fuer Wiederaufbau KfW (www.kfw-foerderbank.de).

In addition to the environmental aspect of sustainable development there is a social aspect as well. Providing affordable homes that foster social structures is an important factor in designing a sustainable society. Thus creating and providing mortgages for social housing is an efficient way to foster sustainable development. The Alternative Bank Schweiz AG developed a programme that connects the sustainability performance of a building with the interest rate for the mortgage (Alternative Bank Schweiz AG 2009). In contrast to other programmes the Alternative Bank does not only take energy aspects into account, but social and economic criteria as well. They use the following criteria to rate a mortgage:

- environment
  - environmental impact of the building process
  - energy efficiency of housing
- society
  - location and type of use
- economy
  - costs.

Depending on the sustainability rating consisting of 13 indicators, clients can reach a reduction of the interest rate up to 0.625 per cent.

Other banks connect economic, social and environmental aspects as well. Thus the Chicago-based ShoreBank finances urban development projects where borrowers convert deteriorated apartment buildings into income-producing properties (Scheire and de Maertelaere 2009). Furthermore ShoreBank offers the so-called rescue loan programme that is presented in the following business case (see Box 5.2).

Box 5.2 Rescue Loan Program of ShoreBank

Rescue Loan Program (see www.sbk.com)
ShoreBank's nationally acclaimed Rescue Loan Program fights foreclosure. It helps homeowners with sub-prime or adjustable rate mortgages by refinancing their original loans from other institutions with new fixed rate mortgages with affordable payments from ShoreBank. The program has already helped hundreds of people in Chicago, Detroit and Cleveland, and it may be able to help you too.

If you are trapped in an adjustable rate or sub-prime loan, the Rescue Loan Program may be able to help you save hundreds of dollars a month on your mortgage, and also make you eligible for home improvements that reduce energy costs.

Thus, the Rescue Loan Program is one of the few examples of social banking that concentrates on the consequences of the sub-prime crisis and thus has a valuable social impact.

Summary and conclusions: loans and mortgages

The integration of environmental and social aspects into credit risk management started in the 1980s caused by the introduction of regulations due to the liability for environmental damages. Lenders tried to predict and manage the financial impact of environmental risks on their borrowers and their loans by taking environmental indicators into account in their credit rating systems.

In contrast to that, social banks concentrated on three aspects:

1 Lending to firms or projects that contribute positively to the environmental or social development, such as firms from the renewable energy sector, organizations providing services for social needs, or community improvement projects.
2 Providing mortgages for green or sustainable housing and construction.
3 Excluding sectors with negative impacts on sustainable development, i.e. conventional agriculture or non-renewable energies.

What is missing are products and services that are specially designed for the clients of social banks with respect to their financial structure and are not based on using real estate or sites as collateral. Frequently, social banks use standard products and services like their conventional counterparts and apply them to their clients. However, we will present innovations with respect to the product design in microfinance section of this chapter.

Socially responsible investment

More and more investors integrate social and environmental criteria into their investment decisions (Kasemir *et al.* 2001). Thus the number of investment funds in the socially responsible investment (SRI) sector has increased correspondingly. In 2007 there were 313 SRI funds available in Europe (Eurosif 2007). These funds strive to satisfy the needs of their investors with respect to social and environmental impacts (Köllner *et al.* 2007).

But how can funds contribute to sustainable development, the environment or social needs? Generally the influence is indirect. Through sustainability rating and communication with companies fund managers can directly influence the company management towards more sustainable practice. Second, by representing shareholders at shareholder meetings, the fund managers of representatives of socially responsible investors could influence companies' strategies and operations by proxy voting on sustainability issues. Third, SRI portfolios consist of stocks and bonds based on negative or positive screenings (Jayne and Skerratt 2003). Thus companies that do not pass the negative screening are less likely to be invested in while those that commit to positive screening are more attractive for SRI portfolio managers.

However the criteria to rate the social, CSR or sustainability performance of assets are varying. On the one hand there are investment strategies based on negative criteria like the production of and trade with alcohol, armaments, the nuclear power sector or human rights violations. Sometimes even the negative screening results only result in exclusion if the main business or a big part of the business of a company is connected with the exclusion criteria. On the other hand there are complex systems of positive and negative criteria striving to invest in companies that have a positive impact on the environment, the society and sustainable development.

At present there are a number of strategies for socially responsible investment. They may be characterized as the following (however combinations of the different strategies exist as well):

- Negative screening: investments are screened with respect to the violation of criteria based on ethical, social, environmental or sustainability standards. Among the criteria for negative screening are alcohol, arms makers and sellers, breaches of human rights of employees or local residents, gambling, nuclear power, polluters, supporters of oppressive regimes, pornography and adult entertainment, tobacco or users of pesticides in farming. However the list can be extended depending on the ethical background of the investors.

- Positive screening: investments are screened with respect to their ethical, environmental, social or sustainability performance. These criteria can vary as well from these, filtering the best investments relative to all possible investments to others, labelling companies that provide a positive impact on the environment, the society or sustainable development.
- Best-in-class screening: this strategy often combines the first two strategies and filters the best performer of the respective sector, service or region. It is used to be able to invest in companies in problematic sectors as well if they provide a better performance than their peers from the same sector.
- Thematic screening: this relatively new field of socially responsible investment concentrates on themes or topics that are seen as decisive for the environment or future sustainable development. At present especially investments in companies connected to water, renewable energies or environmental technologies are attractive from a SRI point of view.
- Shareholder advocacy: this strategy strives to influence strategic decisions of firms by representing shareholders' opinions on how a firm should behave with respect to ethical, environmental or sustainability criteria.
- Engagement: many investors engage with the companies they have screened or invested in to maintain or positively influence their strategies and operations towards ethical, environmental, social or sustainability criteria. Especially if firms are interested to be listed in SRI products the impact of investors or analysts on the company is significant and may lead to a change to more ethical business strategies.
- Donations: some funds solely or additionally provide donations to organizations or projects supporting societal needs or the environment. There are also funds that provide a certain amount of the return for these donations.

The investment screening of a social bank (Alternative Bank Schweiz) is presented in Box 5.3. It consists of social, environmental and economic exclusion and positive criteria. The application of these criteria leads to an exclusion of a high number of companies and concentrates on a small portfolio of social and environmental leaders. It shows that social banks use a high number of social, environmental and other criteria before they integrate a company into their portfolio of recommended assets.

Box 5.3 Investment screening of Alternative Bank Switzerland

Business case: investment screening of the Alternative Bank Switzerland AG

Sector-specific environmental exclusion criteria

- Energy and water: nuclear power, non-renewable energy production, etc.
- Agriculture, forestry and fishery: conventional agriculture, non-certified fishery, non-certified forestry, etc.
- Genetic technology: research and use of genetic technology to manipulate plants, seed and animals, food production using genetic technology, etc.

Sector-specific social exclusion criteria

- Armament sector, tobacco products, gambling, etc.

General exclusion criteria

- Competition: violating competition guidelines, corruption, money laundering, etc.
- Remuneration: inadequately high remuneration of the management, non-transparent remuneration policy, remuneration independent from management performance, etc.
- Corporate governance: non-transparent corporate governance policies, no independent members in the board of directors, no diversity in the board of directors.
- Reporting: no social and environmental reporting, no accepted financial reporting guidelines.
- Environment: destruction of protected nature areas and protected species.
- Employees: discrimination at the workplace, no diversity policy, no free unions, child labour, etc.
- Political: cooperation with dictatorial regimes.

Sector-specific environmental positive criteria

- Materials: organic fertilizers, recycling of packaging, etc.
- Construction: environmentally friendly building materials, sustainable renovation, etc.
- Industrial production: production of parts for photovoltaics, solar-energy or other renewable energy products, etc.
- Trade: trade with goods that are positive with respect to the environmental positive criteria.
- Textile: use of organic commodities.
- Tourism: fostering environmental awareness.
- Restaurants, hotels, etc. Use of organic food, etc.
- Training: training in environment and nature protection.
- Marketing: green marketing.
- Agriculture, fisheries: organic and certified agriculture and fisheries.
- Food trade: organic food markets.
- Finance, insurance, real estate: taking environmental criteria into account in all businesses and services.
- Information technology: soft- and hardware for environmental technology.
- Energy, water: renewable, water treatment, etc.

Sector-specific social positive criteria

- Services: consulting on sustainability, environment, social integration, services for children, services for elderly, etc.
- Real estate: affordable housing.
- Tourism: fostering social interaction, integrative tourism, etc.
- Research and education: socio-environmental research and education, sustainability research.
- Marketing: social marketing.
- Media: high-quality offers, information on sustainability, nature and environmental protection.

- Trade: fair trade exclusively.
- Health: low-priced medicines.
- Finance: taking social criteria into account in all businesses and services.
- Information technology: technology for training in sustainability and environmental protection.

General environmental positive criteria

- Zero-emission firms.
- No waste firms.
- Firms that produce at least as much renewable energy as their energy use.

General social positive criteria

- Offering flexible workplaces.
- Offering workplaces for disadvantaged people.
- Offering services for disadvantaged people.
- Offering integrative workplaces.

General economic positive criteria

- Start-ups planning capital increase and meeting the positive criteria.
- IPO of companies that meet the positive criteria.

When it comes to socially responsible mutual funds, there are probably no products on the market that meet all the criteria listed in the business case. To tackle that problem and to be able to offer socially responsible financial products that meet their and their clients' needs, ethical banks could construct their own investment products that meet all their ethical criteria. Therefore, financial and regulatory criteria have to be taken into account as well.

Nevertheless, there are some special fund products of ethical banks. Examples are the funds of Triodos Bank. But these portfolios contain companies that are criticized with respect to their sustainability performance as well. Triodos Bank argues that they tackle these companies with company dialogue and shareholder advocacy.

However, from all social banks Triodos Bank offers the most comprehensive set of funds based on principles of social investing. These funds are presented in Box 5.4 (see www.triodos.com).

Box 5.4 Triodos funds

1 Triodos–Doen Fund: the fund strives to make the world a livable place. It funds organizations and projects in the fields of sustainable development, culture, welfare and social cohesion. Among others the fund finances microfinance institutions and institutions providing access to financial services for 'bottom of the pyramid' clients.
2 Hivos–Triodos Fund: provides directing savings accounts to microfinance activities worldwide.

3 Triodos Fair Share Fund: invests in established, regulated financial institutions from microfinance that have been financially profitable for two to three years. Investments are spread out over different continents, countries and regions.
4 Venture capital: Triodos offers venture capital investments in climate warming mitigation projects, organic fruit and vegetable trading, and socially responsible fashion production.
5 Triodos Values Equity Fund: through this fund you invest in shares of listed companies with a solid social and environmental performance.
6 Triodos Values Mix Fund: the portfolio of this fund contains shares and bonds of companies with strong sustainability characteristics.
7 Triodos Values Bond Fund: through this fund you invest in bonds of listed companies that are thoroughly assessed for the sustainability of their business processes.
8 Triodos Values Pioneer Fund: invests in innovative small and medium sized companies that are working on sustainable solutions for the future.

The first three funds invest in microfinance institutions globally, the fourth fund provides venture capital for sustainable companies and projects and the last four funds follow the socially responsible investment scheme investing in best-in-class firms and sustainable pioneers.

Other representatives of social banking oppose investments in companies that are listed on stock exchanges because the invested money does not support a firm directly. They prefer direct investments. However, these investments often bear higher financial risks than those in regulated markets.

Summary and conclusions on socially responsible investment

There are more and more socially responsible investment products on the market. Mostly SRI products and services use both positive and exclusion criteria. However, there are only very few products on the market that meet the needs of social banks completely. The majority of SRI funds invest in best-in-class equities and contain a number of assets that do not have a positive impact on the environment or the society or are even criticized for not being good corporate citizens. Therefore, some social banks prefer direct investments in firms and projects that match the needs and aspirations of the social bank and its clients. On the other side, direct investments in social pioneers are often connected with higher financial risks. Thus, there is the challenge for social banks to offer socially responsible investments with acceptable financial risks.

Carbon finance

At present it is widely accepted, and there is scientific consensus as well, that climate change occurs and that it is caused mainly by human activities. Therefore, different activities were started some years ago to mitigate climate change or to adapt to it. Activities are regulative actions and market driven actions. Because there is growing body of literature describing climate change and its implications we do not go into further details here and instead concentrate on carbon finance.

The connection between climate change and finance became even stronger in 2010, when the US Securities and Exchange Commission (SEC) provided guidance to companies about what they have to disclose in terms of climate risks and opportunities (Security and Exchange Commission (SEC) 2010). Thus, companies have to consider whether the impact of the existing and potential climate legislation and regulation is material for them and warrants disclosure. Companies should consider and disclose any material risks or impacts from international accords or treaties related to climate change as well as disclose material, indirect consequences of regulation or business trends such as decreased demand for goods that produce significant greenhouse gas (GHG) emissions (Security and Exchange Commission (SEC) 2010).

But how can we define carbon finance?

Carbon finance includes financial risks, opportunities and mechanisms resulting from a carbon-constrained world. Often, the basic assumption is that the emission of greenhouse gases is priced monetarily. Labatt and White (2007) define carbon finance as following:

> carbon finance:
>
> - Represents one specific dimension of environmental finance.
> - Explores the financial risks and opportunities associated with a carbon-constrained society.
> - Anticipates the availability and use of market-based instruments that are capable of transferring environmental risk and achieving environmental objectives.
>
> (Labatt and White 2007: 1)

The World Bank describes carbon finance in a different way: ‘Resources provided to projects generating (or expected to generate) greenhouse gas emission reductions in the form of the purchase of such emission reductions’ (The World Bank 2009). As the reduction of environmental harms, i.e. CO_2 emissions, is a field of social banking, we will give an overview about the topic in the following paragraphs. Before we present some products and services related to carbon finance we want to give a short overview about the risks of climate change for financial institutions. These are (Labatt and White 2007):

- Retail banking
  - Increased credit risks by clients directly affected by climate change or indirectly affected by climate change related regulations, policy or market changes.
  - Directly affected by physical risks (floods, storms, etc.).

- Corporate banking and project financing
  - Price changes in carbon markets.
  - Reputational risks due to investment in projects with high CO_2 emissions.
- Insurance
  - Losses for weather and other events caused by climate change.
  - Losses on business disruption policies.
- Investments
  - Loss of property assets.
  - Risk of investments in technologies, certificates or projects.
  - Additional costs because of climate adaption measures of projects or other investments.

One example of reputational risks due to an investment in projects with high CO_2 emissions is the Royal Bank of Canada's (RBC) public eye award (www.publiceye.ch, see Box 5.5).

Box 5.5 RBC and the public eye award (see www.publiceye.ch)

The world's filthiest ATM: like no other financial institution, the Royal Bank of Canada (RBC) facilitates the extraction of oil from tar sands in the province of Alberta. The dirtiest oil in the world is currently being squeezed out of soil from an area larger than Switzerland and Austria combined. Oil extraction from tar sands generates three times the CO_2 emissions as conventionally extracted oil. The amount of water pumped from the Athabasca River for extraction is enough to supply a city of one million residents. Afterwards, because of its toxicity, the water must be stored in a specially built storage reservoir – the world's largest. Toxic substances nonetheless show up in the environment: deformities appear in wild animals. Rarely seen forms of cancer occur more often in the indigenous peoples of the region. Furthermore, the oil firms fly in cheap labor from developing countries. These workers seldom leave the extraction area until they are shipped back home. RBC finances this violation against man and nature, in the last two years with investments totalling US $20 billion. And that is just the beginning of their plans.

RBC is highly ranked with respect to its sustainability performance. It is listed in the Dow Jones Sustainability World Index and engages in water protection projects. However, reputational risks connected to carbon finance may cover the sustainability performance of the bank.

Thus, what could be the role of social banks in carbon finance? Generally social banks could enter in all fields of the carbon finance market. Their role could be to guarantee effective and efficient carbon reductions in connection with positive social impacts. Therefore the German GLS Bank invests only in carbon finance projects if they are labelled with the Gold Standard. Furthermore, investing in CO_2 mitigation projects is only offered as compensation for so-called unavoidable emissions. In order to calculate these unavoidable emissions GLS offers a CO_2 emission calculator on their website (see Box 5.6).

Box 5.6 KlimAktivist CO_2 emissions calculator

The German social bank GLS offers a CO_2 emissions calculator on its website. After filling in the necessary data the user gets an estimation of his or her yearly CO_2 emissions. In addition to proposals how to reduce CO_2 emissions, GLS offers investments in renewable energy projects certified with the Gold Standard to offset the carbon footprint.

The projects the bank is investing in should provide climate, economic and social benefits. All financed projects have to pass the Gold Standard that incorporates the following five UNFCCC criteria for Clean Development Mechanism (CDM) carbon offset projects (www.cdm.goldstandard.org):

- additionality of emissions reductions compared to the 'business-as usual' situation;
- no adverse environmental impact;
- consistency with host country sustainable development strategy;
- emissions reduction benefits that are real and measurable; and
- no diversion of Official Development Assistance (ODA) to finance carbon offset projects.

Thus the following carbon finance activities are possible for social banks:

- supporting emissions trading;
- project finance for CO_2 mitigation projects;
- developing mechanisms to convert expected gains of CO_2 mitigation projects into monetary values usable as securities;
- loans and mortgages for CO_2 mitigating projects, housing, etc.
- investments, project finance and loans for renewable energy projects.

Summary and conclusions: carbon finance

Carbon finance has been a topic of interest especially for conventional banking and insurance, although social banks are at the forefront of financing projects and firms from the renewable energy sector. However, many of the social banks are reluctant to finance carbon-offset projects because they want to foster projects that reduce the carbon footprint at the source and not by offsetting. Thus many climate-change related products and services of social banks can be found in other sections of this book, i.e. in the sustainable credit management section (see, for example, the renewable energy loans of Alternative Bank.

Having said that, climate change and mitigation actions are one of the most important sustainability topics at present and the challenge for social banks will be to offer products and services with positive impacts on the reduction of CO_2 emissions.

Sustainability savings accounts and certificates of deposits

Sustainability accounts guarantee money flow between savings on the one side and loans and investments on the other side. Generally the balance in sustainability, environmental or social accounts is used for loans and investments in fields that are specified in these accounts (Labatt and White 2002). Often the acceptance of lower interest rates for the savings leads to lower interest rates for loans for clients meeting the sustainability criteria connected with the accounts.

However, the special savings accounts have never been more than a niche product in banks (Labatt and White 2002). The reasons for that could be the following:

- Social banks generally invest and lend all the savings using social or ethical criteria.
- The interest rates on savings accounts are relatively low at present. Thus ethical accounts connected with interest reductions are not attractive for many clients.
- Guaranteeing the connection between savings accounts and special loans or investments is not always possible because of an imbalance between savings and loans.
- Offering ethical savings accounts connected with interest reduction and conventional accounts in parallel can lead to a lack of credibility for the banks.

Thus, social or ethical banks often connect all the savings of their clients to ethical loans and investments. They do not finance clients who do not meet the ethical standards of the bank. Thus, for example, Triodos Bank is transparent and describes the clients that are financed by the bank on their website. On this basis savers can check which loans and investments their money is used for. There are similar models at other ethical or social banks, such as Alternative Bank Schweiz, GLS or Banca Etica in Italy. Thus Banca Etica writes on its website: 'The bank manages savings raised from private citizens, as singles or families, organisations, companies and institutions in general, and invests them in initiatives pursuing both social and economic objectives, operating in full respect of human dignity and the environment' (www.bancaetica.com).

At GLS bank clients have the opportunity to select the sectors in which the savings should be invested. Subsequently GLS publishes the distribution of the different sectors that were financed. The distribution of 2008 is presented in Table 5.2. In 2008 GLS disbursed loans with an amount of €613.3 million.

Table 5.2 Loans disbursed by GLS in 2008 divided by sectors

Sector	*Percentage*
Organic sector	7.7
Independent schools and kindergartens	16.6
Organizations serving people with disabilities	12.6
The elderly	9.2
Housing projects, environmentally friendly construction financing	22.9
Renewable energy	13.9
Organic agriculture	4.5
Cultural projects and facilities	7.1
Health sector	2.1
Others	3.4

Source: www.gls.de.

At the New Resource Bank (see www.newresourcebank.com) or the Alternative Bank Schweiz, customers can purchase certificates of deposit that are directed to solar energy projects or to different sectors, such as:

- renewable energies
- gender related projects
- education and culture
- alternative and social housing
- organic farming
- development cooperation
- social projects (see www.abs.ch).

Again, clients can select into what kind project they would like to channel their money and create impact.

Summary and conclusions: sustainable savings

As savings accounts are becoming less attractive with respect to the financial return in times of low interest, they offer an excellent opportunity to connect savings with loans for sustainable borrowers and investments in sustainable and social projects. Thus certificates of deposits are products that are offered by some social banks to guarantee a money flow that is transparent for the saver and creates a positive social or environmental impact. Thus social savings accounts and social certificates of deposit are products that are attractive for clients with low risk profiles and small amounts of money to save.

Microfinance

> The four billion people at the base of the economic pyramid (BOP) – all those with incomes below $3,000 in local purchasing power – live in relative poverty. Their incomes in current U.S. dollars are less than $3.35 a day in

> Brazil, $2.11 in China, $1.89 in Ghana, and $1.56 in India. Yet together they have substantial purchasing power: the BOP constitutes a $5 trillion global consumer market.
>
> (Hammond *et al.* 2007)

Furthermore, while in Europe and in the United States only 2–10 per cent do not have a bank account, in many developing countries between 65 per cent and 85 per cent do not (Solo 2005).

Since the microfinance pioneer Muhammad Yunus won the Nobel Prize for Peace in 2006, microfinance and especially microcredit became well known as a social-banking product that is able to fight poverty. The United Nations even declared the year 2005 as the International Year of Microcredit. Rhyne (2009) even calls microfinance a 'blue ocean' opportunity (Kim and Mauborgne 2004) given that a huge number of future clients of banks will live in emerging market countries. These clients, and thus microfinance, are a potential market for conventional banks as well. Newer developments even spread the concept of microfinance to micro-insurance and to microfinance in industrialized countries. An example of this new development is Grameen Bank from Bangladesh engaging in the US market. Another example is the German GLS bank that was assigned by the German government in 2009 to establish a microfinance network in Germany (see www.gls.de).

These services and networks should help people to set up their own businesses and to become independent from pure social-welfare or donations. However, according to Yunus, microfinance institutions should be social enterprises that should not concentrate on profit maximization, but on their social impact. Though interest rates for microcredit are relatively high compared to industrialized countries, they are lower than those offered by private lenders. Furthermore, inflation rates and currency risks have to be taken into account as well.

One characteristic of microcredit is the very high payback rate caused by mutually accepting guaranty and by providing the opportunity for subsequent loans. Therefore, borrowers and the representatives of the lender often meet in groups making the respective loans transparent. A second characteristic of microcredit is the absence of collateral. Frequently potential debtors do not have the possibility to offer securities or a verified credit history for a loan. That leads to a disqualification of people in need of loans at conventional banks.

The business case of BRAC illustrates the development and the activities of a microfinance institution in Bangladesh (see Box 5.7).

Box 5.7 BRAC's Microfinance Programme

BRAC's Microfinance (MF) Programme was launched in 1974 to encourage the increase of income for the poor through the setting up and expansion of income-generating activities and micro-enterprises. BRAC continues to play a pioneering role in providing diversified financial services to serve different segments of the population who lack access to saving and credits provided by financial institutions.

In 2008, BRAC's Microfinance Programme increased its member base to more than eight million, with a cumulative disbursement of nearly USD six billion.

BRAC Bank Limited, with institutional shareholdings by BRAC, International Finance Corporation (IFC) and Shorecap International, has been the fastest growing bank from 2004 to 2007. The bank operates under a 'double bottom line' agenda where profit and social responsibility go hand-in-hand as it strives towards a poverty-free, enlightened Bangladesh.

As a fully operational commercial bank, BRAC Bank focuses on pursuing unexplored market niches in the small and medium enterprise business, which hitherto has remained largely untapped within the country. Since inception in 2001, with 56 branches, 30 SME Sales and Service Centers, 430 SME Unit Offices, more than 150 ATMs, 30 Cash Deposit Machines and more than 1,800 Remittance Delivery Points BRAC Bank is one of the country's fastest growing banks. The bank has already proved to be the largest SME financier in just seven years of its operation and continues to broaden its horizon into SME, retail and corporate banking. Customer service and staff development towards delivering global standard service remains this year's priority.

See: http://gabv.org/Banks/BRAC.htm.

But what is the business field in microfinance for social banks and financial institutions in industrialized countries? One field is microfinance in industrialized countries for start-ups that are not financed by conventional banks. A second field is financing microfinance institutions abroad. A third field is the creation of microfinance mutual funds or other microfinance investment products. One example for institutions creating investment funds based on microfinance is the Canadian Sarona Asset Management (see www.sarona.com, Box 5.8).

Box 5.8 Sarona Asset Management investing in microfinance

The first investment of Sarona was in 1953, in the Sarona Dairy in Paraguay. Since then Sarona invests in, advises and creates many successful ventures throughout the world, many focused entirely in developing world markets. The investment firm managed CAD 50 million in 2009. Actually Sarona offers three funds for institutional investors, investing in debt and equity in micro, small and medium sized businesses and microfinance institutions in developing countries. The expected returns of those funds are between 5 per cent and 15 per cent per year though Sarona invests according to the triple bottom line targets: profit for the investors, economic benefit for developing countries and a focus on the environment.

See: www.sarona.com.

However, there are both criticism and benefits of microfinance. We present them in Table 5.3.

As one goal of microfinance is to help people out of poverty it often takes the role of national and international public organizations and governments. By

Table 5.3 Criticism and benefits of microfinance

Criticism	*Benefits*
Privatization of public safety-net programmes	Profits for the lenders
Dependency of borrowers on microfinance over long time	Long-term growth
Violent field officers	Learning for innovation
High interest rates	Reputation
No real improvement of basic development factors like health service, education, etc.	Life quality improvement for the borrowers (local economic development)
No integration of environmental aspects in microfinance products	Creation of financial service structures

financing basic human needs microfinance privatizes the fulfilment of these needs and thus creates a private safety net. As a consequence policy-makers and governments could neglect their responsibility for providing basic human needs.

Another area of criticism is the dependency of borrowers on the microfinance institutions. Often borrowers need other loans following the first to maintain their business. Thus it may happen that borrowers have to pay back loans for the duration of their lives and get more and more into debt. To prevent the vicious circle, micro lenders should combine financial services with technical advisory services, training for local partners and long-term project management.

The third criticism is connected to methods to guarantee the repayment of the loans. There are reports about field officers that use violent methods to put pressure on the borrowers – most of them are women – to repay the loan.

Connected to this, the high interest rates are criticized. From a Western, industrialized point of view with interest rates mostly below 10 per cent for commercial loans, interest rates up to 100 per cent per year are hardly understandable. However, there could be a number of reasons for the high interest rates. Obviously, high interest rates guaranteeing high returns for the providers of capital are not acceptable. If the interest rates are caused by high volatilities of the respective currency and high inflation rates they are justifiable if microfinance is accepted as a market-based solution for fighting poverty. Furthermore the interest rates are justifiable if the financial return for the borrower is higher than the interest rate.

A market-based solution will invest in projects that at least guarantee a certain amount of financial return. Basic development factors like health service or education are not frequently supported by microfinance. As a consequence, these basic factors that are needed to run even a small business are often not in place.

As a last point it is criticized that for a certain time the sustainability of a business with respect to the environment did not play an important role. Every business that generated income for the poor was supported, no matter what kind of product or service was offered by the borrowers.

On the other hand microfinance provides some benefits. At first it provides profits for the lenders as the default rate is very small. Second, it can support long-term growth by taking a long-term perspective into account. At present even conventional banks learn from microfinance principles like group lending and mutual guaranties and integrate these principles into their banking practice. Thus, it seems that microfinance is a driver for innovation in the financial sector as well. Furthermore, especially for conventional banks an engagement in microfinance activities has a positive effect on their reputation. One of the most important benefits of microfinance is the improvement in life quality for the borrowers. However, there is little evidence-based research that supports this assumption (Dichter 1996), even if the positive impact on life quality and development seems to be obvious. Last but not least microfinance creates financial service structures for those who did not have access to banking services so far.

But why is microfinance a field for specialized institutions and is, for the time being, not a business field for all banks? There are some challenges of microfinance that possibly prevented it from becoming a large-scale banking product. These are (Rhyne 2009):

- Understanding the clients: it has to be learned how to understand the needs of potential clients and how to meet their needs.
- Reducing costs: offering small loans for a high number of borrowers creates costs that often are higher than the returns of the microfinance products.
- Informality and risk management: frequently, a systematical risk management process is not possible, because there is neither a client history nor any securities to base the risk rating process on.
- Building the industry: dealing with millions of clients and small loans needs an efficient organization and structure that differs from the conventional, technology oriented banking.

Furthermore, Rhyne (2009) states that microfinance has to follow some principles to be a social and sustainable business. These principles are:

- quality of service
- transparent pricing
- fair pricing
- avoiding over-indebtness
- appropriate debt collection practices
- privacy of customer information
- ethical behaviour of staff
- feedback mechanisms
- integrating pro-consumer policies into operations (Rhyne 2009: 157)
- financing businesses that are both, environmentally and socially sustainable.

Summary and conclusions: microfinance

Microfinance is probably one of the most popular social banking products and enjoys a very good reputation. The Nobel award for one of the founders of microfinance, Mohammad Yunus, contributed to this positive reputation as well. The challenge for social banks based in industrialized countries is to select the appropriate microfinance partners guaranteeing business and practices that are in line with the social standards of the banks and their clients. Thus, it will be a challenge for social banks to establish microfinance principles – supporting small entrepreneurs without credit history and collateral – in industrialized and emerging countries as a means to support individuals to establish their livelihood. Especially in times of stricter banking regulations this task will not be easy to accomplish, but it could be a social and efficient opportunity to provide access to finance for small, medium and micro enterprises that still lack access to finance (Iddrisu 2010).

Project finance

Since the adoption of the Equator Principles (N.N. 2006) by ten leading banks in 2003 there is a global benchmark for determining, assessing and managing social and environmental risks in project financing.

But what is project finance? The Basel Committee on Banking Supervision defines project finance as

> a method of funding, in which the lender looks primarily to the revenues generated by a single project, both as the source of repayment and as security for the exposure. This type of financing is usually for large, complex and expensive installations that might include, for example, power plants, chemical processing plants, mines, transportation infrastructure, environment, and telecommunications infrastructure. Project finance may take the form of financing of the construction of a new capital installation, or refinancing of an existing installation, with or without improvements. In such transactions, the lender is usually paid solely or almost exclusively out of the money generated by the contracts for the facility's output, such as the electricity sold by a power plant.
>
> (N.N. 2005)

Generally, project finance is a service of big banks and financial institutions that often cooperate in financing one project. Because of the project size negative or positive environmental or social impacts of a project frequently become public and may negatively affect the reputation of the financing institution, like the Sakhalin II oil and gas project. We want to use this project to illustrate ethical issues in project finance. The information about the project and the involvement of banks and financial institutions was taken from www.banktrack.org.

A number of banks and export finance agencies are under public pressure because of financing or advising Sakhalin II. They are listed on www.banktrack.org. Seven out of the nine involved banks are signatories of the Equator Principles.

Sakhalin II is located in the Russian Far East. It is said by project sponsors to be the largest integrated oil and gas project in the world. The project involves three offshore oil and gas platforms and subsea pipelines to shore. The oil and gas will then be transported 800 km through onshore pipelines to natural gas liquefaction and export terminal and oil export facilities at Prigorodnoye, in the south of Sakhalin. A new oil platform was installed adjacent to the only known feeding ground of the approximately 120 critically endangered Western Gray Whales. After initially planning to build a subsea oil pipeline directly through the whales' feeding area, SEIC, the project developer, redirected the offshore pipeline just adjacent to the feeding area, continuing to threaten the whale population. Thus there is a conflict between business interests and the concerns of environmentalists.

Generally the role of the banks in this project is indirect. The banks provide the finance or even only financial consulting and are not directly responsible for analysing the environmental impact of the project. However, most of the involved banks are signatories of the Equator Principles and are criticized because involvement in the Sakhalin project violates the following principles and especially the principle on consultation and disclosure (for a detailed overview see the Equator Principles (N.N. 2006)):

- Principle 1: Review and Categorization
- Principle 2: Social and Environmental Assessment
- Principle 3: Applicable Social and Environmental Standards
- Principle 4: Action Plan and Management System
- Principle 5: Consultation and Disclosure
- Principle 6: Grievance Mechanism
- Principle 7: Independent Review
- Principle 8: Covenants
- Principle 9: Independent Monitoring and Reporting.

Even if the general responsibility of financing institutions for the environmental or social impacts of projects is unclear, the public discussion about the project involvement leads to high reputational risks for the respective banks.

After having presented the risks to reputation of project finance, we want to present and analyse social banking project finance and its impact. Many projects that are financed by social banks are from the renewable energy sector. The basis for calculating the return of these projects is the amount of electricity produced and the price per unit that will be paid for the electricity. Often a contract between the customer (sometimes a public entity) and the supplier defining the price per unit and the duration is used as collateral by the financing organization, because mostly the projects do not own other securities that could be used as collateral. Thus a number of renewable energy projects, such as wind-power, small water-power or solar-power projects are financed by social or ethical banks. Generally such projects require large up-front investment and under certain circumstances it can take more than ten years to reach a return on the investment.

Thus, in order to finance photovoltaics on leased roofs the German GLS or the Swiss Alternative Bank accepts the assignment of the feed-in remuneration, or for bigger projects the solar plant is accepted as security-assignment as well. The duration of the project finance is about ten to 20 years.

Summary and conclusions: project finance

Large-scale project finance is mainly a service of big universal banks and financial institutions. As social banks are smaller compared to their conventional counterparts, they concentrate more on lending. However, in the field of renewable energies, social or ethical banks are very active and were the pioneers in financing renewable energy projects. In order to engage in bigger environmental or social projects, social banks could cooperate and co-finance projects that are too risky for only one financing institution.

Summary and conclusion: products and services

Social and environmental banking products and services have become more and more popular. Thus the balance sheets of social and ethical banks and the portfolios that are managed using SRI criteria are growing. However, most of the social banking products and services are based on conventional products and services and add social, environmental or ethical criteria to them. Even the financial return of many of these products and services does not differ significantly from the returns of their conventional counterparts or is even better (Weber *et al.* 2008b; Galema *et al.* 2008; Weber *et al.* 2010).

Additional to financial criteria, often positive or exclusion criteria are used to rate borrowers, company shares or projects. This guarantees transparent financial products and services for those who are willing to invest their money in a social or sustainable way. As, in the meantime, conventional banks also offer products and services labelled as sustainable or socially responsible, the unique position of social banks is to offer a product portfolio that consists only of sustainable or socially responsible products and services. This unique position of social banks, that often includes the commitment to offer only products and services with a benefit for the real economy, gains higher momentum again after years of disconnection of the financial sector from other parts of the economy. In addition to that, real economy finance like loans or venture capital for start-ups is influencing social, environmental or sustainability performance much more directly than financial products like investments through the public stock market (Scholtens 2006).

Looking on basic differences between conventional and socially responsible products and services, microfinance differs mostly from conventional products. Microcredit is not based on conventional risk rating mechanisms like collateral and credit histories. They use concepts like group lending that have not been used in conventional banking to date. This leads to the question whether social banks should offer more products that differ from the conventional product design, such as loans, mortgages, mutual funds or project finance.

References

Alternative Bank Schweiz AG (2009) 'Die ABS Hypothek mit ABS-Immobilien-Rating', Olten: Alternative Bank Schweiz AG.

Annandale, D., Bailey, J., Ouano, E., Evans, W. and King, P. (2001) 'The potential role of strategic environmental assessment in the activities of multi-lateral development banks', *Environmental Impact Assessment Review*, 21: 407–29.

Bacow, L.S. (1998) 'Risk sharing mechanisms for brownfields redevelopment', in Benson, C.H., Meegoda, J.N., Gilbert, R.B. and Clemence, S.P. (eds) *Risk-Based Corrective Action and Brownfields Restoration*, Reston: American Society of Civil Engineers, 178–95.

Bizer, K., Führ, M., Barginda, K., Cichorowski, G., Weber, O. and Wiek, A. (2003) 'Evaluation des 3-Städte-Klimaschutzprojekts Viernheim, Lampertheim und Lorsch', Darmstadt and Zurich: Technische Hochschule Darmstadt und Eidgenössische Technische Hochschule Zürich.

Case, P. (1996) 'Land, lending and liability', *Chartered Banker*, 2: 44–9.

Coulson, A. and Dixon, R. (1995) 'Environmental risk and management strategy: the implications for financial institutions', *International Journal of Bank Marketing*, 13: 22–9.

Dichter, T. (1996) 'Questioning the future of NGOs in microfinance', *Journal of International Development*, 8: 259–69.

Eurosif (2007) *SRI Funds Service*. Online, available at: www.eurosif.org.

Galema, R., Plantinga, A. and Scholtens, B. (2008) 'The stocks at stake: return and risk in socially responsible investment', *Journal of Banking & Finance*, 32: 2646–54.

Hammond, A.L., Kramer, W.J., Katz, R.S., Tran, J.T. and Walker, C. (2007) *The Next 4 Billion*, Washington, DC: World Resources Institute and International Finance Corporation.

Iddrisu, T.Y. (2010) *Small, Medium, and Micro Enterprises (SMME) and Access to Finance: the Case of Ghana*, Waterloo: Master of Applied Environmental Studies in Local Economic Development Research Paper, University of Waterloo.

International Finance Corporation (IFC) (1998) *Environmental Assessment*, Washington, DC: International Finance Corporation (IFC).

Jayne, M.R. and Skerratt, G. (2003) 'Socially responsible investment in the UK – criteria that are used to evaluate suitability', *Corporate Social Responsibility and Environmental Management*, 10(1): 1–11.

Johnston, D., Lowe, R. and Bell, M. (2005) 'An exploration of the technical feasibility of achieving CO2 emission reductions in excess of 60% within the UK housing stock by the year 2050', *Energy Policy*, 33: 1643–59.

Kasemir, B., Süess, A. and Zehnder, A.J.B. (2001) 'The next unseen revolution. Pension fund investment and sustainability', *Environment*, 43: 8–19.

Kim, W.C. and Mauborgne, R. (2004) 'Blue ocean strategy', *Harvard Business Review*, 82: 76–84.

Köllner, T., Sangwon Suh, S., Weber, O., Moser, C. and Scholz, R.W. (2007) 'Environmental impacts of conventional and sustainable investment funds compared using input-output life-cycle assessment', *Journal of Industrial Ecology*, 11: 41–60.

Labatt, S. and White, R.R. (2002) *Environmental Finance*, Hoboken: Wiley.

Labatt, S. and White, R.R. (2007) *Carbon Finance*, Hoboken: Wiley.

N.N. (2005) *International Convergence of Capital Measurement and Capital Standards ('Basel II')*, Basel: Basel Committee on Banking Supervision.

N.N. (2006) *The Equator Principles*, London: Equator Principles Association.

Noor, R. and Syumanda, R. (2006) *Social Conflict and Environmental Disaster: a Report on Asia Pulp and Paper's Operations in Sumatra, Indonesia*, Montevideo: World Rainforest Movement.

Rhyne, E. (2009) *Microfinance for Bankers and Investors*, New York: McGraw-Hill.

Scheire, C. and de Maertelaere, S. (2009) 'Banking to make a difference', Preliminary Research Report, Artevelde: Artevelde University College.

Schmidheiny, S. and Zorraquin, F. (1996) *Financing Change: the Financial Community, Eco-efficiency, and Sustainable Development*, Cambridge, MA: MIT Press.

Scholtens, B. (2006) 'Finance as a driver of corporate social responsibility', *Journal of Business Ethics*, 68: 19–33.

Scholz, R.W., Weber, O., Stünzi, J., Ohlenroth, W. and Reuter, A. (1995) 'Umweltrisiken systematisch erfassen. Kreditausfälle aufgrund ökologischer Risiken – Fazit erster empirischer Untersuchungen', *Schweizer Bank*, 4: 45–7.

Security and Exchange Comission (SEC) (2010) *Commission Guidance Regarding Disclosure Related to Climate Change*, Security and Exchange Comission (SEC).

Solo, T. (2005) 'The high cost of being unbanked', *Newsletter*, Washington, DC: The World Bank Group.

The World Bank (2009) *Carbon Finance for Sustainable Development 2008*, Washington, DC: The World Bank Group.

Thompson, P. and Cowton, C.J. (2004) 'Bringing the environment into bank lending: implications for environmental reporting', *The British Accounting Review*, 36: 197–218.

Wanless, D. (1995) *The Gilbert Lecture 1995: Banking and the Environment*, London: The Chartered Institute of Bankers.

Weber, O. (2005) 'Sustainability benchmarking of European banks and financial service organizations', *Corporate Social Responsibility and Environmental Management*, 12: 73–87.

Weber, O., Fenchel, M. and Scholz, R.W. (2008a) 'Empirical analysis of the integration of environmental risks into the credit risk management process of European banks', *Business Strategy and the Environment*, 17: 149–59.

Weber, O., Scholz, R.W. and Michalik, G. (2010) 'Incorporating sustainability criteria into credit risk management', *Business Strategy and the Environment*, 19: 39–50.

Weber, O., Koellner, T., Habegger, D., Steffensen, H. and Ohnemus, P. (2008b) 'The relation between sustainability performance and financial performance of firms', *Progress in Industrial Ecology*, 5: 236–54.

6 Financing change through giving and donations

An integral part of social banking

Antje Toennis

Introduction

In our society, gifts are often understood as personal gestures of no importance to society at large. However, when we take a closer look, we find that there are important connections between gifts, the economy, society and the way people feel.

Banking reflects the way we think about economy and society, the values we apply to it, and how we act in our everyday economic lives. As Olaf Weber points out in Chapter 5, products and services that strive to reach a positive social, environmental or ethical impact are offered primarily by specialized social or ethical banks. Here capital is directed into areas with positive impact in these fields. Social banking works with a set of values that is different from traditional banking. Social banking draws a picture of a new economy, the kind of society we want to live in, where people and the environment are more important than profit. Profit can be a result of social banking but never the goal. Giving is a central aspect of this new picture, and social banks should provide consultation and services both for the people who want to give money and those charitable initiatives which are in need of funds. Gifts of money are important because there are areas in every society that are not profitable in an economic sense. Nevertheless, these areas, such as education, social services and culture, are at the centre of every society and thus in need of funding.

In this chapter, I argue that giving is not only part of the economy, but works to improve societies. I draw on two studies and a theoretical model to explain the social, economic and qualitative changes gifts can bring. The first study, concerning donated and sold blood, points out that trade is not the right form of exchange for every product and that giving can be a better way. The study proves that donated blood is of higher quality than sold blood and that donating also improves the social relations between donors and recipients. The second study takes for its subject a matriarchal gift economy, outlining other advantages that follow from gifting: a gift economy significantly evens out economic differences, thereby making a society more economically just. Also, because women hold valued positions in the economy, there is a higher level of gender equality. Third, from the perspective of a particular theoretical model, we see that without giving the economic process would come to a standstill, because innovation needs gift money.

Finally, turning to GLS Treuhand as an example of a financial organization that works with donors and charitable organizations, I discuss how social banks can support giving by incorporating donation consultation into their banking services. Tools for donors, such as certain types of endowments, funds or foundations are described.

Giving and gift economies

Following the latest economic crisis, an increasing number of people have begun to link economic problems with the destruction of nature, global warming, loss of community living, and gender and social injustice. It seems that at the core of all our problems lies the Western, profit-maximizing economic model: ‘The biggest problem of our lives is warlike economics’, said V. Bennholdt-Thomsen in 2005. Indeed, James Gustave Speth points out that it is no longer possible to act on environmental issues without discussing how our economy works to destroy the natural resources from which we live:

> Mainstream American environmentalism to date has been too limited. In the current frame of action, too little attention is paid to the corporate dominance of economic and political life, to transcending our growth fetish, to promoting major lifestyle changes and challenging the materialistic and anthropocentric values that dominate our society.
>
> (Speth 2010)

But what might an alternative economy look like? And what role might giving play?

There is not a lot of research on the economic meaning of giving in Western societies. For example, a conference entitled ‘The Economics of Charitable Giving’, held in Mannheim in 2009 (Arbeitskreis Europäische Integration e.V. 2009), included a wide range of topics concerning donations and charitable giving in relation to taxes, corporate social responsibility and corporate philanthropy, and investigations into who donates and what drives the size of donations. But none of the topics tackled the question of what giving means for a national economy, or for society, and which areas of society need to be funded because they are unable to generate income for themselves. This seems quite typical of research in economics. Thus, we need to look to other sciences – anthropology, ethnography, religious studies or sociology – to find research on the role gift giving can play in societies.[1]

For example, there is a British study on blood donations that shows how gift giving can improve the quality of a product and the relationship between those who give and those who receive (Titmuss 1970); there is an inquiry into how gift economies[2] can work towards a better and more just distribution of wealth within a society (Bennholdt-Thomsen 1994); and there are ideas on how financial gifts can be seen as a way to finance parts of society that are unable to support themselves (Steiner 1996).

These three approaches to giving share the belief that giving improves societies. Each approach points out specific benefits that are discussed in greater detail in the following subsections.

Giving blood

British social researcher Richard Titmuss' 1970 study on giving blood shows how the non-commercialization of blood collection both improves the quality of the blood collected and makes people feel that they are part of a community rather than anonymous producers, sellers and consumers of a commodity. Titmuss' area of expertise was welfare, and he used his research to argue that a hierarchical, materialistic society 'ignores at its peril the life-giving impulse towards altruism, which is needed for welfare' (The Titmuss–Meinhardt Memorial Fund, online).

Titmuss compared the commercial blood collection system in the United States with the non-commercial blood donation system in the UK, thereby distinguishing between the UK blood gift economy and the US commercial trade in blood. In the gift economy setting, a felt relationship between the donor and recipient develops: recipients feel close and grateful to the donors. In the commercial system, however, the relationship is that of producer and consumer. In addition, the very quality of the blood itself turned out to be different. US blood was less safe: it was, for example, infected with the hepatitis virus more often than donated blood in the UK. On top of that, US blood tended to be wasted more often in US hospitals and was much scarcer than in the UK (Erwand and Loibl 2007: 2). The overall finding of the study was that a donor system simply works better from both social and health perspectives, and politicians acted to regulate the system in the US (The Titmuss–Meinhardt Memorial Fund).

But the Titmuss study doesn't only shine light on the social and health benefits of a blood donor system, it also shows what happens in societies when they become 'economized' – when everything has a price. The study has been received in this way, and has been used to argue for the social and qualitative benefits of gift societies (Schwartz 1999).

Matriarchal gift economy

German sociologist and ethnologist, Veronika Bennholdt-Thomsen, points out that there is more to an economy than capital and work for wages or pay. Together with Maria Mies and Claudia von Werlhof, Bennholdt-Thomsen has developed a new perspective on the economy, which they have called 'subsistence economy' (Bennholdt-Thomsen 2008: 23). This expression is used to describe a form of economy that isn't bound to the necessity of growth and competition. Instead, we can live the good life within the means of our planet. According to these authors, the patriarchal fear of scarcity is the foundation of the predominant Western economic system. This fear leads to the mistaken conclusion that economies work best when they are centralized, concentrated, long on technology and profit-centred. In contrast, a subsistence economy is based on a matriarchal worldview: a picture of abundance, of 'the good life', of exchange between humans and between humans and nature (Bennholdt-Thomsen 2008: 24). Economic activity undertaken in this spirit enables both the economy and money to remain embedded in social relationships (Bennholdt-Thomsen 2005).

In their study of Juchitán – city of women, Bennholdt-Thomsen *et al.* show how an economy based on these principles can work. 'The aim is a good life and the life of the community rather than the fiction of "The more the better" or striving to become "Number One" at the expense of everybody else' (Bennholdt-Thomsen 2005). This economy is in women's hands: they do all the trading, which is at its centre. The division of labour follows rigid gender lines. This keeps women in the positions of trader and market-woman, and works to protect women from a take-over by men.[3] A lot of value-added production happens in the region. Juchitán's economy is organized like a big household, with a high degree of labour division. For example, one woman might specialize in a certain kind of pie production, another in a particular embroidery design. Rather than an abstract profit motive, the driving force behind the economy is the desire to provide for the community. Compared with other Central American Indian Regions, the whole Juchitán area is prosperous. The nutrition of pre-school children is even better than in the United States (Bennholdt-Thomsen 2005).[4]

Juchitán has a huge number of festivals, which are at the centre of the gift economy. The gift economy works as a so-called 'prestige economy', where prestige is gained not from owning the most, but from giving the most. A festival can be a large family celebration or it can involve an entire street. Each trading woman's ambition is to host a festival because this is how she can gain great prestige for herself and her family. The host carries the main responsibility and pays most of the costs, but others join in, contributing money and other gifts. There is a strict reciprocity code involved, and whoever has more, gives more (Bennholdt-Thomsen 2005).

The study shows, in the spirit of this gift economy, economic differences are to some extent evened out. Principles like 'who has more, gives more' lead to more economic justice, to a better distribution of wealth. Also, the money remains embedded in social relationships and is grounded in a real economy. Yet again, this study shows the social and economic benefits of giving.

Rudolf Steiner: giving as a crucial part of the economy

Austrian philosopher, social thinker and founder of anthroposophy,[5] Rudolph Steiner provides another perspective on the economy, one in which gifts are a crucial factor. In his course on economics, taught in 1922, Steiner articulated the idea that in a society there can be no innovation without giving. At the core of Steiner's concept is his notion of the three different qualities of money: 'payment', 'loan' and 'gift' (Steiner 1996: 89). 'Payment' money is used in buying and selling. This form of money is linked to the continuing reproduction of goods for consumption. Then there is 'loan' money. Lending plays another economic part, helping people to apply their intelligence and knowledge to what they want to do. Through loans they are enabled to invest in the means of production, thereby becoming producers, producing things they can then sell and receive 'payment' money for (Steiner 1996: 88). The third quality of money is 'gift' money.

Acknowledging that it is fairly uncommon to see giving as a crucial part of the economy, Steiner points out that without giving the economic process would come to a standstill, because there would be no possibility of innovation. The place for innovation in a society is what Steiner describes as the region of freed activity (*freies Geistesleben*). This includes all forms of education, especially a holistic kind of education that promotes the growth of every aspect of the personality, rather than education as the teaching of only certain skills and knowledge. For Steiner, there needs to be some scope for development or a society will keep reproducing the same skills and patterns. He explains this idea using the example of children: we give children everything they need and offer them the space and support to develop their full potential – at least that's the ideal.

People who work in the region of freed activity do not produce goods they can sell. They also should not have to sell anything because that would take away their freedom to try out new paths and see what develops. Gift money is needed to finance this sector. The gift money comes in different forms: it can be forced through taxes; it can be an inheritance/legacy that is given not to the next of kin but to the person who can use it in the best possible way for the common good of the society; it can be a free offering from wealthy people or companies. This gift money is provided to people or non-profit institutions working in the region of freed activity – people like teachers, artists or researchers. In this way, gift capital is the most productive of all capital because it doesn't only reproduce things the way they are but possibly brings out new ideas, skills and capacities.

If we apply Steiner's concept to today's economy, several transfers of funds can be seen as gift money. For example, the financing of a company's research department is done through the use of profits generated by the other departments. However, although the funds enable research in the first place, the freedom of the research may be compromised by the expectations of the company.

Thus Steiner would probably argue that in order for research (or education) to be in the region of *freies Geistesleben*, funds might be better administered by an independent institution. Steiner's gift money is freely given, meaning both sides of the transaction feel free. The donor chooses where to give money, gives happily and leaves it up to the recipients to decide how best to use it. The recipients know that they are permitted to take the money and use it for the common good. This is the ideal way. There are of course a number of problems that can develop within a donor–recipient relationship. These can include problems with hierarchy and abuse of power, the right to decide who gets the money, and the question of democratic process.

However, Steiner's ideas do highlight the role of giving in relation to both society and the economy. Innovation might indeed work best when gift money is donated to researchers, educational institutions and the arts to allow for freedom in these fields. As a consequence, more attention should be paid to different ways in which donations can be made, both individually and by the state.[6]

Conclusion

These examples point to the important role gift giving can play towards thinking and acting outside a profit-maximizing economy. We do not live in a world centred on gift giving, or in which industry, trade or individuals freely give their money as a matter of course to those areas of society in need of it. That is why we need to focus on consulting people who want to give, and on education to spread the idea of giving. We thus need to work for political and social change in our society, to develop a culture that supports giving. How could the tax system be changed in a way to support giving? How could giving be democratized? Who checks where private or corporate donors give their money? How can we create a society in which people don't feel the need to horde their money? It is probably a lot easier for people to give if they feel safe and provided for. One of the biggest things people save for is retirement. A great deal of money is stuck in huge pension plans because people fear poverty in old age. As long as there is no real alternative, such as a pension that works through a social security system (*Umlagesystem*), hording is unavoidable. There are structures in society that need changing in order to make giving easier.

While these kinds of social and economic changes will likely take a while, social banks can already offer services related to giving. Social banks and financial institutions can provide an arena for exploring, trying out and experimenting with the practice of giving. The next section shows how GLS Treuhand has been doing this for almost 50 years.

A new attitude towards money: the case of GLS Treuhand – giving as part of holistic banking

In 1961 a few anthroposophists gathered together to explore how it might be possible to finance 'free' education (i.e. non-state education) institutions, such as Steiner schools, art projects or the purchase of land for bio-dynamic agriculture. In order to develop a structure for this, they founded a charitable association called Gemeinnützige Treuhandstelle (Charitable Trust). Projects in need of financing could become members of this association, which would collect money from affluent people or industrial companies to be distributed amongst its members. Based on Steiner's ideas about the different qualities of money, the Gemeinnützige Treuhandstelle[7] decided to work towards a sensible distribution of gift money, and to support a totally different way of dealing with money.

When it came to investing some of the acquired funds, it became clear that a trusted bank was needed. Since it was impossible to find an institution that provided bank services in the same spirit of an ethical, social, sustainable and ecological way of dealing with money, the members of the GLS Treuhand then founded a new, social bank in 1974. Today this bank is called GLS Gemeinschaftsbank eG. The abbreviation 'GLS' stands for 'Gemeinschaft für Leihen und Schenken' (community for loans), showing that both giving and lending are still seen as two aspects of social banking.

Since 1961, GLS Treuhand has grown into an organization with over 290 members, all of which are charitable organizations. In 2009, a total of 6.5 million euro was spent funding projects, grants and individuals in the areas of development cooperation, organic agriculture, ecology and the environment, (complementary) health, orthopedagogy and social therapy, arts and culture, schools and nursery schools, democracy, human rights and social issues, religion, and spirituality.

As a charitable association, GLS Treuhand offers advice and consultation to benefactors and donors. Customers are supported in making use of their assets according to their personal ideas and goals with the aim of making future-oriented societal changes possible. Money is passed on to specific committed initiatives and individuals in the charitable sector, facilitating the transformation of ideas into projects. GLS Treuhand also funds existing projects, particularly in the areas of education and culture, which operate within a non-profit model, and are thus unable to generate their own financing. Over the years, GLS Treuhand has created a huge network of non-profit and charitable organizations. These contacts are offered to donors, enabling them to make informed decisions.

Consultancy for donors

The donors' particular areas of concern and interest are always at the heart of the consultations. GLS Treuhand has worked with a range of instruments, among them donations, endowments, foundations and last wills, developing them specifically for gifting. Sometimes, depending on how much time a donor needs for her or his decision-making process, a consultation can take months or even years. This process clearly differs greatly from opening a bank account or deciding where to invest a certain amount of money for a specific time period. Usually, giving is a process involving not only economic reasoning but also selection of the right instrument, or form, for the gift. The consultation process is typically concerned with ethical, social and psychological questions.

The consultation process is free of charge and funded through GLS Treuhand's own endowments. However, some customers elect to support the work of GLS Treuhand by donating money directly to its endowments. In this way, GLS Treuhand does not 'use up' its own assets in the provision of consultation services.

Finding the right legal instrument – tools for giving

In order to ensure that donors are able to find the appropriate instrument for their gift giving, GLS Treuhand offers a range of instruments for gifting, endowment and legacy, as well as legal advice. All necessary legal information and support is provided through cooperation with an independent lawyer or notary.

Consultants work with potential givers towards finding the right expression of their desire to give – the right form for their gift. The following paragraphs set out some of the instruments.

Donation is one way to give money. Donations can be made in the form of free money, given to GLS Treuhand itself without any conditions. An Allocation Committee then decides which projects the money would best be given to. Donations can also be made to GLS Treuhand's own Future Foundations. These work in the areas of 'free' education (i.e. non-state education), development aid, complementary health, (organic) agriculture, social life and renewable energies. Donors who give funds to any of these foundations can decide whether their money goes to a particular project, or they can leave the decision up to the foundation.

Donations are also possible through direct cooperation with GLS Gemeinschaftsbank. Customers can put their money into special savings accounts. Interest earned is automatically directed to the Future Foundations for Development Aid and Agriculture.

Donors can also give to the base capital of any foundation administered by GLS Treuhand. This way the money remains within the principal of the foundation for at least ten years, and only the earned interest is used to fund projects. For the donors, it makes a difference in terms of tax deductions whether the money is a donation or given to a foundation's base capital.

Sometimes donors are not able to be sure about the amount of money they are able to give. Funding needs in their own families might be fluctuating or their companies might unexpectedly require investment. In such cases, GLS Treuhand offers giving under obligations or conditions. This provides that a certain amount of money can be donated under the condition that the donor might need to have it back. In the meantime, interest earned with the money can be used to fund projects. Also, the money can support charitable projects in the form of interest-free loans. When the donor's situation changes and the donor can be sure about the gift, the condition can be lifted and the gift turned into a permanent donation or payment into the base capital of a foundation. If the donors need the money back, it can be easily returned to them.

A special tool is the Umbrella Foundation for Individual Giving (Dachstiftung für individuelles Schenken). This single foundation houses over 60 (2009) individual endowment funds, each one of which works like a 'little foundation'. Compared with affiliated or unaffiliated foundations, there are some advantages to this legal form. One of the Umbrella Foundation's particular strengths is flexibility when it comes to funding. While charters often offer only limited possibilities, the charter of the Umbrella Foundation allows for a multitude of opportunities across the charitable sector. This means donors are able to switch funding sectors depending on their interests and the changing needs of society. At the same time, it is possible for every endowment fund to have its individually stated purpose, its own name and its own Awarding Committee. Administration is made simple by the investment of the combined capital of the Umbrella Foundation. This way benefactors do not have to bother with decisions about investments. Also, better interest rates can be earned through investing greater sums of money. Another administrative benefit is the single auditing report done for the entire Umbrella Foundation by an independent consulting firm. This saves money, which can then be spent on each fund's specific funding goals. Furthermore, assets (base capital) can be entirely used up, enabling endowment fund initiatives to liquidate their assets and make good use of their accumulated funds – which makes sense if an endowment fund wants to pay for major renovations to an institution that it regularly supports, such as a hospital.[8]

One example of an endowment fund within the Umbrella Foundation for Individual Giving is the fund 'Gottessegen' (God's blessings). This endowment, created by a community of heirs, funds workshops that support people with disabilities through therapeutic treatment and other forms of support.

If the amount of money a donor wants to give is of a significant size, consultants at GLS Treuhand might suggest the creation of a new foundation. These foundations can be affiliated, with GLS Treuhand acting as legal trustee. This is recommended if the donation is between €300,000 and €3,000,000. Over €3,000,000 an independent Foundation can be set up. Either way, donors can decide on investment of their assets. There are legal differences between affiliated and unaffiliated foundations, resulting, for example, in your being audited either by the tax authority or by the state's foundations oversight committee.

Consultants at GLS Treuhand suggest setting up foundations for a fixed time frame of about 30 years, the equivalent of one generation. Since the problems faced today might change and new problems arise for the next generations, foundations need to be flexible. This means the mission, or charter, of the foundation should also be flexible. Additionally, it should be possible for a foundation to come to an end and use up its assets within one generation. That way, money is kept flowing within the economic cycle.

Administration services

Once the most suitable legal instrument for giving is found, GLS Treuhand offers administrative services. Depending on the needs of the donors, either the entire administration or only parts of it can be undertaken. This includes all the formalities dealing with the establishment of the foundation. For the regular work of the foundations or funds, committees can be organized, even specialists on certain issues can be found to support decision-making within the committees. Also, bookkeeping, donation receipts, balance sheets or financial statements can be provided. Fees are charged for administrative services. Contributions lie between 0.4 per cent and 0.75 per cent of the administered assets, depending on the sum of the assets.

Investment of assets

Looking at the agenda of a major Association of Foundations meeting, or at their publications, one can surmise that the relationship between banks and foundations is focused on the investment of assets (Kottke 2009). Especially following the most recent financial crisis, foundations seem to be seeking more conservative investment in order to minimize loss. This might be the correct strategy. For GLS Treuhand too, the classic investment criteria of profitability, security and liquidity are valid. However, there are other investment criteria, such as the idea that investment should be ethical and sustainable. This means money is invested sensibly and in a socially effective way: such as the financing of regenerative or sustainable energy research projects or concerns, beneficial social facilities (hospitals, kindergartens, etc.), and ethical-sustainable enterprises (GLS Gemeinschaftsbank, Weleda, electricity company Schönau (renewables), etc.).

GLS Treuhand also pursues the classic aims of investment: attention is paid to sensible dispersion for risk minimization; an adequate yield is aimed for, to enable promotion of charitable purposes with lasting effect; provisions for unforeseen liquidity needs are put in place through investing part of the capital in instruments, which can be easily sold at any time. Different investment classes with defined criteria have been developed to serve the goal of meaningful investment. All investments should serve the causes the foundations themselves support:

- Properties and buildings are only received through donations by customers. GLS Treuhand does not acquire or hold properties and buildings for speculation purposes and also does not take part in real estate funds.
- In relation to shares, investment goes exclusively to enterprises, which support ecological sustainability and social change.
- Loans are given only to organizations, which share our goals of a better society.
- In the area of securities, we invest only in ethical and sustainable funds and directly in fixed-interest bonds, predominantly state loans, and to a lesser extent, bank loans and enterprise loans. There is no speculation in shares or share funds.
- Savings bonds and fixed term deposits are bought exclusively from GLS Gemeinschaftsbank, where all the giro accounts are also kept. Over 90 per cent of all investment and banking is done with GLS Gemeinschaftsbank as close cooperative partner.
- Parts of the assets are given as interest-free or interest-preferred loans to support charitable organizations.[9]

GLS Treuhand as a creative pool for thinking about giving and foundations

Besides consultation and administrative and funding management services, GLS Treuhand aims to be a think tank on giving and related issues. Time is reserved for discussion of basic principles and ideas, such as seeing money as a means of communication, or how to use money in a sustainable way to support a just, ecologically sound and ethical world.

Keeping money in flow is one topic discussed. Being aware of potential problems that can ensue from the investment of money leads to a new understanding of giving. For example, problems arise when there is simply too much money around. People who invest money tend to look for the highest return, thus creating speculation in certain areas of investment, like real estate, commodity or gold markets. If this money were given away to charitable causes, fewer 'bubbles' would be created. Besides, money donated is put to much better use than when it is lost in failed investment.

Another topic discussed is time limits for foundations. While generally and legally foundations are created for eternity, people at GLS Treuhand question this practice and try to help set up foundations with limited time frames. Within one generation funding needs can change because society changes. Problems that are essential today, like funding for the development and implementation of renewable energies, might be overcome in 30 or 50 years. Using up the base capital and spending it on a specific cause or project might be a sensible thing to do when it can give a beneficial push to the cause or project.

Aspects of giving, as understood within the context of the twenty-first century, are also discussed. GLS Treuhand employees debate the relevance of certain models of giving, such as those discussed at the beginning of this chapter. Also, the role of foundations in our society is discussed, as well as questions around how to make giving a more democratic process. Where the money for donations comes from, who has generated it and who decides where to spend it – all have to do with that question.

The spiritual quality of money and giving is another area of interest. When money is given away, it dies a little death and is somehow resurrected in a new form. There seems to be a quality about giving that is outside rational understanding.[10] Questions in relation to this have to do with how we are all linked to our money and the expectations we have of it; how we are responsible for what we create through how we use our money; how we can let go of it if we have more than we need; how giving breaks down the separation between an individual person and the community as a whole.

Discussion of these and other questions is an ongoing process, and is understood within the context of a learning organization that constantly aims to broaden and deepen its understanding of the relationship between its own work and giving.

A note on communicating with customers about giving

Communication on giving needs approaches that differ from marketing models. For a customer, opening a bank account is very different from giving away money. Hence, the relationship between the person who wants to give and the person who facilitates the giving is personal and unique. This should be reflected in all communications about the services offered. However attractive and informative, leaflets and brochures are only a first glimpse and should be followed up by consistent personal communication that honours the act of giving.

Summary and conclusion

Social banking works to improve society in areas such as economics, ecology and social justice. Social banking has a holistic approach involving trade and consumption, production and investment, education, research and culture. The financing of these different areas needs a differentiated and sophisticated range of banking services that necessarily includes giving for those areas that cannot fund themselves. Furthermore, studies show the social benefits of giving. Not every human and economic need is best dealt with through trade. Sometimes donation, as in the case of blood donation, improves both the quality of a product or service and the social relationships between the people involved.

Nevertheless, it continues to be relatively rare for consultation on giving to be integrated into social banking. GLS Treuhand has a great deal of experience with donor counselling, and competence in the establishment and maintenance of endowments, foundations and legacies. This experience is there for social banks to draw on.

References

Arbeitskreis Europäische Integration e.V. (2009) *Programm: The Economics of Charitable Giving*, conference held at Zentrum für Europäische Wirtschaftsforschung, Mannheim, 8 and 9 October 2009. Online, available at: www.aei-ecsa.de/dokumente/tagung_charitable-giving_programm.pdf (accessed 2 April 2010).

Bennholdt-Thomsen, V. (ed.) (1994) *Juchitán – Stadt der Frauen*, Reinbek bei Hamburg: Rowohlt.

Bennholdt-Thomsen, V. (2005) *A Matriarchal Society in the Age of Globalisation*, paper presented at the '2nd World Congress on Matriarchal Studies'. 29–30 September and 1–2 October 2005 in San Marcos and Austin. Online, available at: www.second-congress-matriarchal-studies.com/bennholdtthomsen.html (accessed 24 March 2010).

Bennholdt-Thomsen, V. (2008) 'Die Subsistenzperspektive', *Kurskontakte*, 150: 22–4. Online, available at: www.kurskontakte.de/article/ausgabe/150.html (accessed 24 March 2009).

Derrida, J. (1992) *Given Time 1: Counterfeit Money*, Chicago and London: University of Chicago Press.

Erwand, A. and Loibl, D. (2007) *Catherine Waldby: Stem Cells, Tissue Cultures and the Production of Biovalue*. Online, available at: www.univie.ac.at/virusss/documents/270756063.pdf (accessed 24 March 2010).

Kottke, N. (2009) 'Von der Psychologie lernen. Behavioral Finance – Impulse für die Stiftungsvermögensverwaltung', *Stiftung und Sponsoring*, 6: 32–3.

Schwartz, J. (1999) 'Blood and altruism – Richard M. Titmuss' criticism on the commercialization of blood', *Public Interest*, 136, Boca Raton. Online, available at: http://findarticles.com/p/articles/mi_m0377/is_136/ai_55174702/?tag=content;col1 (accessed 3 April 2010).

Speth, J.G. (2010) 'A new American environmentalism and the new economy', lecture held at the 10th Annual John H. Chafee Memorial Lecture National Council for Science and the Environment. Washington, DC, 21 January 2010 Online, available at: www.smallisbeautiful.org/publications/speth10.html (accessed 2 April 2010).

Steiner, R. (1996) *Economics. The World as one Economy*, Bristol: New Economy Publications.

The Titmuss-Meinhardt Memorial Fund: Richard Titmuss (1907–1973). Online, available at: www.ntpu.edu.tw/sw/titmuss2.htm (accessed 5 March 2010).

Titmuss, R.M. (originally published 1970; new edn 1997 edited by A. Oakley and J. Ashton) *The Gift Relationship: From Blood to Social Policy*, London.

Volz, F.R. (2008) 'Freiwillige Armut – Zum Zuammenhang von Askese und Besitzlosigkeit', in Boeckh, J. (ed.) *Handbuch Armut und soziale Ausgrenzung*, Wiesbaden: VS Verlag, 180–94.

Waldorf Answers (2010) 'What is anthroposophy?' Online, available at: www.waldorfanswers.org/Anthroposophy.htm (accessed 3 April 2010).

7 Social banking at the crossroads

Sven Remer

Introduction

In this chapter we undertake an analysis of the general prospects of social banking and of the specific possibilities for social banks, including some factors with a likely influence in this context.[1]

But, to start with, some explanations and qualifications of our approach to this topic are necessary. First and foremost, because of the very nature of our topic and because of a general lack of literature on social banking, in this chapter we take a rather *conceptual approach.* This is, we base our arguments primarily on our own observations, supplemented by some insights gained from conversations with practitioners working in the sector. Furthermore, when using the term 'social banking', we refer to the overall sector of social banks as described in Chapter 1 of this book, namely, licensed banks with the mission to have a positive impact on people and planet. We use the term social bank/ing also in contrast to conventional bank/ing, whereby we refer by the latter to those banks that have been set up with the prime objective of increasing/maximizing their shareholders'/owners' financial profit. In addition, we focus mainly on social banks in Europe, not because we consider them more important than those in the South but because this is where our experience lies. Finally, it is clear, there is no *the* social bank. Whilst often driven by similar, non-monetary values and operating principles, social banks differ, at least in terms of their maturity and size. They span a wide range from Ekobanken in Sweden with less than 20 employees and a balance sheet of some €34 million to Triodos Bank in the Netherlands with about 600 employees and a balance sheet of almost €3 billion. This obviously impacts their individual resources and capabilities, which, in turn, (co-)determine their future prospects. As such, any generalization about them unavoidably will do injustice to some. However, we feel the similarities between social banks, particularly with respect to their missions but also with respect to their comparatively small size, allow contrasting them as a group to the group of conventional banks. We therefore base our analysis on the sector of social banking overall, but we qualify our discussion by explicitly excluding or referring to certain organizations when we feel this is necessary.

With the above in mind, in this chapter we argue that 'social banking is at the crossroads'. To us, social banking, as we have come to know it over the past four decades, is at the most decisive point of its development thus far. By this we *do not* suggest social banking is at the 'brink', possibly turning irrelevant soon. Quite the opposite, as we will describe in the following, social banking today and in the foreseeable future is needed more than ever before. Social banks have arguably already achieved a lot more than their limited size would suggest. And social banks now have an enormous – and arguably unique – chance to increase their outreach and impact. The question is, however, whether and how well they make use of this chance, and to what extent social banks will (be able to) change to do so.

Before we look into the prospects of social banking more deeply, in the following, we first recap what social banks have set out and what they have managed to achieve to date. We consider this reflection on the past essential to 'ground' any speculation on the possible future of social banking.

Objectives and achievements of social banks to date

Banks are at the heart of the society and economy. Their core function is that of an intermediary who transforms and channels money streams from those that have spare funds to those that need funds (Saunders 2000). Because of this intermediation role and because of their role in the money creation process through handing out loans, banks can significantly influence important developments, including those that concern social, economic and environmental problems.

This comes with a responsibility that most conventional banks arguably have failed to accept and to put into practice. Admittedly, ever more conventional banks begin to enter the sustainability arena set up by social banks – for various reasons, e.g. to avoid risks, to feed PR/marketing, or to exploit new business opportunities (Weber 2005).[2] This tendency further seems to have picked up speed since the latest financial crisis resulted in an erosion of public trust in banks. But, overall, conventional banks still do not even remotely make use of their full potential in this context. They were and are still primarily interested in profit maximization. Over the past two to three decades, this increasingly led them away from the core banking function of taking deposits and handing out loans in the real economy and towards speculative activities in the ever more virtual financial world. But at the same time conventional banks cause ever more 'collateral damage' in the real world, for instance by funding environmentally and socially hazardous large projects, by contributing to the over-indebtedness of large parts of the population, or by contributing to speculative bubbles that ultimately harm all. As such, we would caution to compare the socially- and/or environmentally oriented activities of conventional and social banks just in terms of the absolute figures stated in their CSR or Sustainability Reports.

Social banks, by contrast, focus primarily on the core banking activities of taking deposits and handing out loans. As Scheire and de Maertelaere (2009: 20) note, '(T)he group of northern ethical banks in the Global Alliance for Banking on Values (GABV), for instance, are financed for 75.3 to 91.2 per cent by their clients deposits'. Moreover, they all have been set up with the mission to have a positive societal impact. This is evident from Box 7.1, which shows excerpts from the mission statements of those social banks that are members of the Institute for Social Banking and/or the Global Alliance for Banking on Values and that have already been introduced in the first chapter of this book.

Box 7.1 Excerpts of the mission statements of various European social banks (mostly own translations)

Alternative Bank (ABS), Switzerland. Grants loans … to support ecological and social projects.

Banca Popolare Etica, Italy. Is a place where savers … meet socio-economic initiatives, inspired by the values of a sustainable, social and human development.

Charity Bank, UK. Tackles marginalization, social injustice and exclusion, and facilitates social change through investment.

Cultura Sparebank, Norway. Promotes projects with a social and ethical quality. Profitability is secondary, but, of course, economic viability of the projects is a prerequisite for financing.

Ekobanken, Sweden. Is also interested in sustainable business that takes the environment and human being into account.

GLS Gemeinschaftsbank, Germany. (Strives for) sustainable development and it aims for a responsible exposure to money in favour of human beings and nature.

Merkur Bank, Denmark. Is founded on the idea of conscious handling of money, and on criteria that include environmental, social and ethical aspects.

Société financiere de la NEF, France. Builds a direct link between savers and borrowers who carry out sustainable projects meeting social and ecological criteria.

Triodos Bank, The Netherlands. (Has the mission) to enable individuals, institutions, and businesses to use money more consciously in ways that benefit people and the environment, and promote sustainable development.

As is evident from Box 7.1, all social banks aim to address economic, social and environmental problems presenting obstacles to a more sustainable development of humankind.[3] In sharp contrast to their conventional peers, their often-explicit objective is *not* to maximize shareholder profit (Scheire and de Maertelaere 2009). However, it also has to be stated clearly, despite their 'social mission', social banks are not charities but banks. As such, social banks, as all other businesses, social or not, *must* have the objective to sustain themselves economically in order to achieve their (social) missions.

Based on the above outlined objectives of social banks, to examine their achievements, one has to look at two broad areas – their ability to contribute to a more sustainable development, and their ability to prosper or at least sustain themselves as businesses. This we will briefly do in the following, starting with the contribution of social banks to a more sustainable development overall.

Social banks' contribution to sustainable development overall

As regards their contribution to a more sustainable development overall social banks undoubtedly have demonstrated, in thousands of inspiring and successful projects, that a different type of banking is possible, one that not only makes economic but also social and ecological sense. By funding people and projects geared towards sustainability, they certainly did positively influence the development at least in certain areas.

However, it is fair to say, the actual extent of their impact has been small and impossible to pinpoint in detail. This is because social banks are tiny compared to their conventional peers, because there were many other forces (including conventional banks) working in an opposite direction than the social banks, and because there are hardly any comprehensive data available on the 'sustainability performance' of social banks. But to get at least some idea where we (and the social banks) stand in this context, in the following, we take a broader perspective on the developments with view to the economic, social and environmental problems social banks set out to address.

With view to the *economic problems*, a key impulse for the founding of most social banks has been to provide financial services and products to those people and projects that have been un(der)served by conventional banks because they were considered to be too risky and not sufficiently profitable in an environment solely driven by the idea of economic efficiency and profit maximization. Moreover, many social banks also set out to change our economic thinking and acting by showing that a different approach towards money and banking is possible.

Just by taking a brief look at the long lists of their loan receivers published by many social banks, there is little doubt that they indeed have served many people and projects that would have been unlikely to obtain funding from conventional banks. However, also due to the rapid growth of the world's population, many more people are still excluded from financial services. Whilst this problem is particularly pronounced in the South, it also exists in the North – to a much larger extent than most would believe. For instance, a recent report produced by Réseau Financement Alternatif for the European Commission finds that (parentheses added):

> [A]t the end of 2003, ten per cent of adults aged 18 and over in the EU 15 countries and 47 per cent of adults in the new member states had no bank account at all [the 'unbanked']. ... A further eight per cent in the EU 15 and six per cent in the new member states had only a deposit account with no payment card or cheque book [the 'marginally banked'].
>
> (European Commission 2008: 17–18)

At the same time, even many of those that have been 'served' by (conventional) banks have lost all they had during the latest financial crisis. In this context, some point out that 'exploiting poverty caused the financial crisis' (Kohn 2008). Whilst this happened in the North, it had disastrous consequences in the South. Thus the World Bank states:

> [T]he spreading global economic crisis is set to trap up to 53 million more people in poverty in developing countries this year on top of the 130–155 million driven into poverty in 2008 by soaring food and fuel prices, bringing the total of those living on less than $2 a day to over 1.5 billion.
>
> (World Bank 2009)

This also is solid proof that not much has changed for the better in terms of our economic thinking in general or our attitude towards money in particular (World Economic Forum 2009). Particularly the past two to three decades were characterized by a globalization of both the real and the financial economy. During this period, almost all conventional banks – including many cooperative and saving banks – developed more and more away from their core purpose, which essentially is taking deposits and handing out loans. But, as it turned out, it was much easier to 'earn more money with money' than it was to earn some money with real projects. In a general trend of 'financialization', most (conventional) banks have focused on developing ever more profitable products and services and have 'herded' into lucrative activities that increasingly were unrelated to the real economy (World Economic Forum 2009). As Lars Pehrson, CEO of Merkur Bank in Denmark, points out:

> As shareholder value and market fundamentalism became dominant in the mindset, statements such as 'a bank is a business like any other business' and 'banks are in this world to make a profit' became more and more frequent. ... That the banks have a *mission* in society became subordinate.
>
> (Pehrson 2010: 53)

Whilst major investors and leading banks were heading this trend, many consumers were contributing their part too. Anyone who could afford to deposit or invest spare funds seemed – and still seems – to be guided by one principle only: profit maximization for investments and savings, and interest minimization for loans. How the money was earned and what use it was put to, mostly did not and does not matter to the banks or their customers. As a consequence, the financial system increasingly has been failing to deliver to many, namely to the majority of those that did not enjoy 'spare funds' and that were not working on profit-maximizing projects. Conventional banks would avoid these people and projects not necessarily because they would lose money on them, but because they could make a lot more elsewhere, and seemingly much more easily. Clearly, against those forces, social banks had little chance to have a noteworthy impact.

Turning now to the *social problems* social banks set out to address, the situation does not look much better. A key impulse underlying the founding of many social banks has been to improve the conditions of the less fortunate group of people who are socially deprived, not only, but also, because they were cut off from basic banking services such as savings accounts or small loans, which many today consider basic human rights. This group comprised of a wide range of poor and socially deprived subgroups, amongst them ethnic minorities, (single-parent) women, the challenged, the elderly, or those simply unlucky enough to live in areas that were 'redlined' and therefore not served by conventional banks. As described in the previous section, conventional banks excluded such groups because of the alleged risks and because serving them was considered to be economically inefficient and 'better' clients were at hand.

This notwithstanding, it must be acknowledged, over the past two decades or so, one could see some improvements, many of which also have been initiated by social banks. The biggest breakthrough in this context arguably originated in the South with the founding of the Grameen Bank in Bangladesh in 1983 by Professor Muhammad Yunus, the 2006 Nobel Peace Prize laureate. He fathered what is now generally known as microfinance – the provision of small loans usually to groups of women in socially deprived areas to start small businesses. Many estimates put this group globally into billions (Solo 2005). The success of Grameen Bank, that proved it is possible to successfully serve this group with default rates usually way below those of the conventional banks, inspired many imitators, also in the North. Still, microfinance has only just started to show its potential – and problems (cf. Bateman 2010). Conventional banks are beginning to get engaged in microfinance – mainly by arranging for the refinancing of microfinance organizations and/or by providing the relevant infrastructure (Chapple *et al.* 2007). But, so far, microfinance only represents a tiny part of their business activities. Thus, there are still billions of people cut off from vital funding needed to realize their business ideas and to make a decent and dignified living. Add to this the millions of people who have lost their jobs and homes because of the recent financial crisis, it is obvious that the social problems continue (to grow), also in the North. An ever-larger group of people is finding it increasingly difficult to get a foothold on the social ladder, or is simply slipping off it.

Besides microfinance, another socially oriented financial product that has experienced some sort of a 'boom' over the past decade are socially responsible investment (SRI) funds investing for their clients in shares of companies that have been previously screened to meet certain social and environmental criteria (Social Investment Forum 2009). However, whilst experiencing a significant growth in size and number, as of now, these funds are dwarfed by the majority of conventional funds that exclusively pursue a profit-maximization strategy.

Furthermore, as outlined in the previous section, there is a general funding gap for small and locally oriented projects that do not aim to maximize profit but to improve social conditions, for example by setting up multi-generation housing facilities. These are considered too risky and unprofitable by conventional banks.

This issue is now additionally exacerbated by the fact that, thanks to the financial crisis, public support for these people and projects has further dried up.

Again, despite all their efforts, social banks were simply to small to halt or even reverse the overall negative developments in the social field.

Looking finally at the *environmental problems* social banks aimed to address a similarly bleak picture exists. An important founding motive for several social banks – particularly after the Chernobyl disaster in 1986 – was to support projects and initiatives that aimed at addressing environmental problems, e.g. supporting organic farming, emission reduction, renewable energy and/or local production/consumption, etc.

Social banks certainly had a substantial impact in this context. For instance, they were responsible for initiating the wind farming industry by setting up the first investment funds for this purpose, long before the conventional banks discovered this as a lucrative business. But it is also true that the reluctance of conventional banks to get active in the environmental field is beginning to change with changes in public attitudes and increasing pressure from NGOs. Most conventional banks now have environmental management systems to control and reduce the environmental impact of their own operations (The Global Reporting Initiative 2008). A recent example in this context is the Deutsche Bank that promotes its environmental consciousness by 'greening' the two towers of its headquarters in Frankfurt and setting up a webpage highlighting its CSR (corporate social responsibility) activities, amongst them also those that deal with environmental aspects (see www.banking-on-green.com). Many big banks have also subscribed to voluntary standards, such as the ISO 14001, the Carbon Disclosure Project, the UN Principles for Responsible Investment (UNPRI), the UN Global Compact/Global Reporting Initiative (GRI), the Equator Principles, and the Wolfsberg Principles, etc., which all have been developed over the past decade to contain the banks' appetite for exclusively profit-maximizing investments. As mentioned before, more and more banks have begun to offer some sort of green products such as SRI funds, which also consider the environmental impact of investee companies. A limited number of conventional banks have even begun to include sustainability (including environmental) criteria in their loan application processes, which also makes sense for them financially (Weber *et al.* 2008). This is mainly in the form of negative screening that makes obtaining funding for environmentally damaging projects more difficult – but hardly yet in the form of positive screening that would ease funding for environment friendly projects. Finally, there are some early signs for new markets to develop in the area of environmental finance, with emission trading schemes being the most advanced (Labatt and White 2007).

However, overall, these activities of the conventional financial institutions still form only a miniscule part of their overall business. Consequently they have had little or no impact on the persistent lack of funding for environmentally oriented projects, particularly if they are very innovative and 'untested'. And too many banks are still consciously supporting environmentally hazardous projects (for a good overview see: www.banktrack.org). At the same time we experience a rapid and increasingly dramatic advance of man-made environmental problems on all fronts: climate change, deforestation, soil erosion and desertification, decline in fresh water supply, and loss of biodiversity are just a few examples of these problems that increasingly challenge our very survival (Pachauri and Reisinger 2009). To state the obvious again, social banks have not yet been able to curtail the environmental deterioration they set out to address.

With view to the above portrayal of the deteriorating situation in economic, social and environmental terms, it would be unfair to conclude that social banks have failed to have at least some positive impact towards a more (or at least not less) sustainable development. They have enabled many thousand people and projects to work for a more sustainable development, and they have proven that it is possible to do so in an economically viable way. Thus, particularly given their small size, they have arguably achieved a lot, even if their impact was overcompensated by stronger forces working into the opposite direction. At the same time though, as we will discuss further below, their actual achievements in terms of realizing their sustainability mission are also difficult to assess because social banks overall didn't make much effort in measuring their own impact.

We now turn to the other core objective of social banks besides their sustainability mission, their *own economic sustainability*. Here, their achievements are somehow easier to measure and depict, although they are not unambiguous.

Social banks' own economic sustainability

The examples of the social banks in Chapter 1 show they have been doing well for quite some time, particularly with respect to the growth of their balance sheets. And some have been doing exceptionally well during the recent financial crisis when most conventional banks 'underperformed'. This is illustrated in Figure 7.1. Overall, the balance sheets of social banks presented in Figure 7.1 have shown noteworthy growth rates during the observation period, ranging from 8 to 25 per cent on average per bank.

The fact that social banks have done well during the recent financial crisis is no coincidence. Over the past 40 years or so, social banks have developed substantial expertise in and innovative funding methods for selected sectors of the real economy. This helped them to serve what conventional banks considered inefficient, risky and unprofitable people and projects, in a way that not only makes economic but also social and ecological sense. Furthermore, based on their values and operating principles, social banks did not indulge in shortsighted speculation like most of the 'herd'. This made them increasingly attractive to new customers searching for a safe haven for their deposits.

However, the recent fast growth of social banks in terms of their balance sheets is not necessarily matched by an increase in their profitability. On the contrary, most social banks show a relatively low level of profitability. This is evident from Figure 7.2 that illustrates the profit as a percentage of the balance sheet sum of several social banks over the past years.[4] All European social banks apart from Charity Bank (not shown in Figure 7.2) published a net profit for the

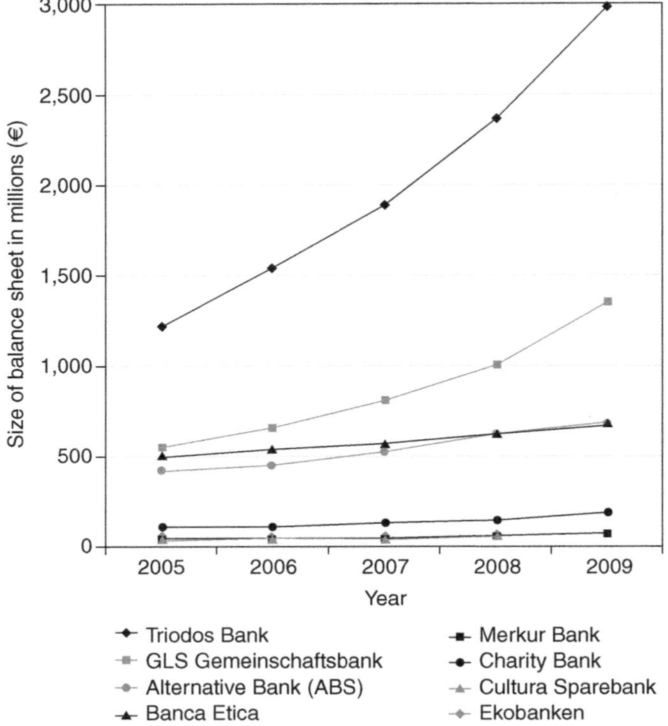

Figure 7.1 Developments in the size of balance sheets of selected social banks.

years for which data were available. However, this profit was overall small – ranging from 0.1 to 0.85 per cent of the balance sheet (averaged over the observation period for each bank), and it showed considerable volatility.

From Figures 7.1 and 7.2, it is obvious that social banks have been performing well in terms of some economic measures but not others. Whilst growing their balance sheets and funds under management, most social banks did not increase their profits at the same rate. The specific reasons for the relatively low profitability of these banks might vary from case to case. But the falling interest rates as a result of the recent financial crisis undoubtedly have played a major role. The lending business, which is at the core of social banks' activities, is highly dependent on general interest rates and very competitive, especially for good debtors.

Furthermore, their focus on lending comes with another challenge for social banks. Transforming deposits into loans for sustainability-oriented companies and projects to the desired extent is not always possible for a variety of reasons, some of which we will discuss further below (see pp. 156–157). As Figure 7.3 shows, social banks, in 2008, on average had less than two-thirds of their balance

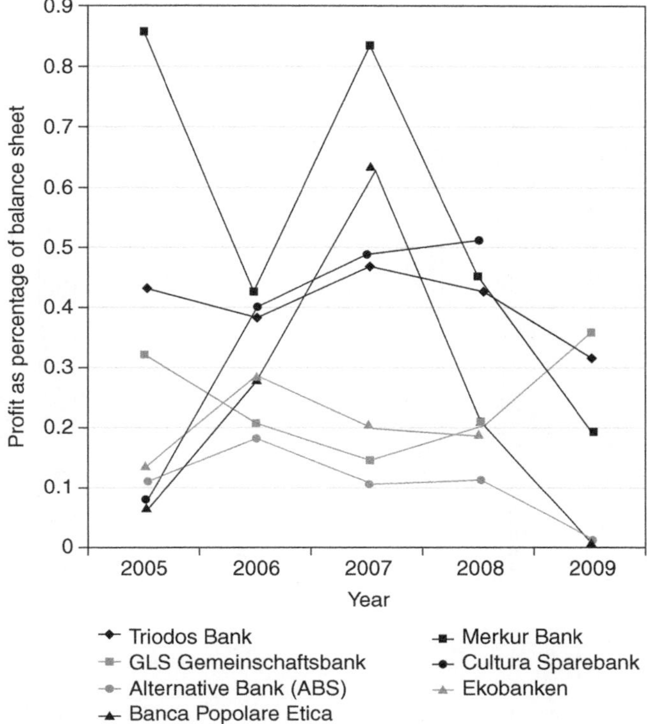

Figure 7.2 Development of profit as percentage of balance sheet for selected social banks.

sheets outstanding as loans, and the overall trend for 2009 also is said to be similar by several industry experts.[5] Thus, one might argue, at least in recent years, social banks have not managed to fulfil their core function.

Finally, it must be kept in mind that the sector is still tiny compared to the overall banking sector. For instance, the ten 'large' social banks (each with a balance sheet of over $100 million) that form the Global Alliance of Banking on Values (GABV) together have assets that exceed $10 billion, and they serve more than seven million customers in 20 countries (GABV 2010). But compare this with a single large conventional bank such as the Deutsche Bank with total assets of €1.5 trillion (2009), with about 2,000 branches (of which about 1,000 are located in Germany), 80,000 employees, around 14 million customers, and with a profit of almost €5 billion (2009) (www.deutsche-bank.com), and the relative limits to the impact of social banks are obvious. None of the European social banks is comparable to the main players in banking in terms of the size of their balance sheets. Only two have balance sheets greater than €1 billion, and only four greater than €500 million. Banca Etica, for instance, the fifth largest Euro-

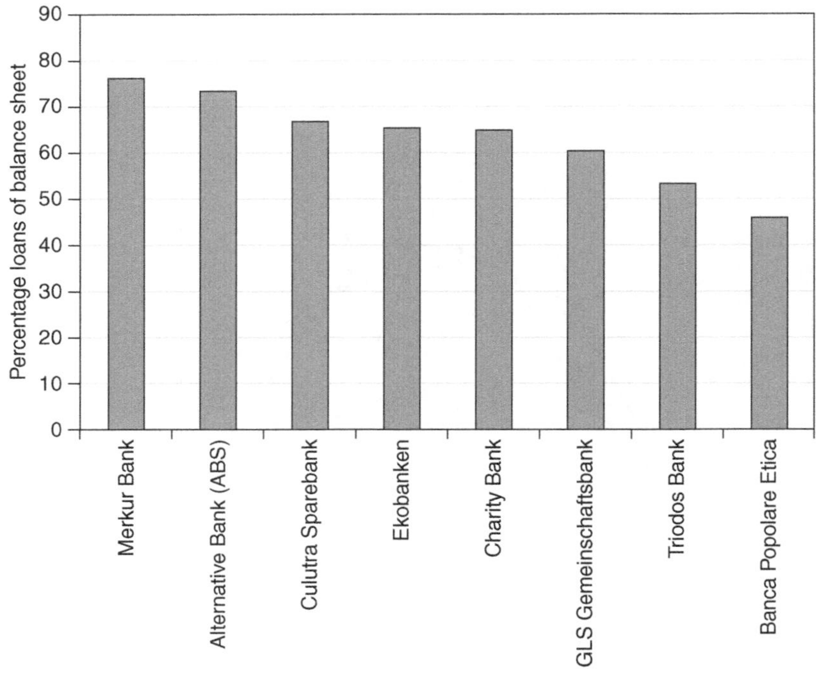

Figure 7.3 Conversion rates of total loans to balance sheet for selected social banks (based on data for 2008).

pean social bank, had a balance sheet of slightly over €600 million in 2008. Similarly, also in terms of their staff numbers social banks rank low on the banking landscape, with the biggest one (Triodos) having just about 600 co-workers. Most of them also have only one or a few branches in their home country. In most Northern countries, social banks serve far less than 1 per cent of the population. Thus, undoubtedly having performed well in terms of their balance sheets, social banks overall still remain a niche phenomenon, steadily growing but dwarfed by conventional banking (Scheire and de Maertelaere 2009).

General prospects for social banking

With respect to the general prospects for social banking, the fact that the economic, social and environmental problems seem to intensify rather than ease arguably calls for a different approach towards banking. And more and more people begin to realize this. As Scheire and de Maertelaere (2009) note:

> The challenges of [the] financial crisis, and the role of banks, in particular, have risen high on the agenda. There is a strong call for responsible,

> transparent and socially responsible banks. Society, including politicians, businessmen, academics and bankers understand banking should return to its basic intermediate function, reinvesting collected deposits in the real economy. Combined with a growing ecological, social and ethical consciousness fuelled by the food crisis, the climate crisis and the limited success of the fight against poverty, more and more voices in society are calling for a substantial shift of investments towards an ecological and more human economy.
>
> (Scheire and de Maertelaere 2009: 3)

This essentially is why social banks have been set up. They strive to serve the un(der)-served and to 'have an impact' on people and planet by addressing the various problems related to economic, social and/or environmental issues that have been neglected – and to some extent even been caused – by conventional banks. Thus, they are clearly called upon to increase their outreach and impact. But, until recently, social banking remained a niche without much recognition and impact in the wider world. Typical for niche species, without drastic changes in its outside environment, social banking was on a development path best characterized by incremental change, building upon and further refining its specialist expertise to serve the other co-habitants of this niche in a symbiotic microcosmos in the shadows of conventional banking.

However, the ongoing 'sustainability crisis' combined with the recent developments in the financial markets present a 'shock' to the outside world that could now provide social banking – or at least some of the organizations in this sector – with an unique opportunity to leave the niche (or at least to grow it substantially) and enter a totally new avenue for further development. Grabbing this opportunity, the few early adopters could fundamentally change the way we all *think* and *do* banking in the future, namely, with a focus not only on economic but also on social and environmental criteria. Thus, social banking now could have a direct and indirect impact that reaches far beyond its prior horizon.

This assertion finds the support of Scheire and de Maertelaere (2009), who note, with a particular focus on the social banks that are members in the Global Alliance (GA) for Banking on Values:

> With the current financial system crisis and the failure of the business model of mainstream banks, the momentum is there for GA banks to break out and openly inspire mainstream banks. The business models executed by GA banks are out of the experimental phase and have proven to be successful in markets that were considered to be risky and difficult. Some aspects of the banks' business models are concrete answers to fundamental critiques that have been raised to mainstream bank behaviour. GA banks have shown that banking can be done differently. Inspiring the banking sector might create a strong leverage effect that could never be reached by these banks' human and financial capital.
>
> (Scheire and de Maertelaere 2009: 42–3)

Into the same direction also points a recent analysis of the ethical-ecological banking sector in Germany by zeb (2009), the largest German management consulting firm specialized in the banking and finance sector. It notes that banks dedicated towards social banking – based on business models that are based on trust, transparency and sustainable business conduct – in the previous years have been experiencing two-digit (sometimes over 30 per cent) growth rates. And zeb expects the significant growth of such social banks to continue. Key to their success, according to zeb, is their orientation towards the changing values in parts of the society. Based on an analysis of various market and future studies, zeb expects that values and operating principles such as social quality of life, environmental consciousness, democratic decision-making, transparency, honesty, mutuality and social security will be of growing societal relevance. According to zeb, this fits well with the four essential features of the social banking concept:

1 the consequential investment in ethical-ecologically sustainable projects;
2 the transparent publication of the loan book to validate the claimed usage of funds;
3 the possibility for depositors to decide themselves, in which sectors their deposits should be channelled; and
4 the risk-minimizing focus on the real economy, i.e. a no-speculation policy.

With their particular positioning, zeb (2009) further notes, social banks target the 'post-materialistic' customer group. But, as zeb also notes, with less than 200,000 customers, the German social banks, so far, have only managed to reach a small proportion of this core customer segment that is currently estimated to comprise more than six million people. Moreover, this core segment, according to zeb, is bound to rise because of the loss of customer trust during the course of the banking crisis and the forecasted changes in the value systems. As such, zeb expects the potential customer segment of German social banks to rise to a noteworthy ten to 12 million (or around 10 to 15 per cent of the German population) over the next years to 2020.

Based on this, Dr Katrin Lumma, partner at zeb, concludes (own translation):

> Social banks show impressively how one can, with contemporary customer-target approaches, gain new customers and market share. As our study suggests, these are no one-off effects. We sincerely believe that success and significance of social banking will keep on growing.
>
> (zeb 2009)

Therefore, zeb (2009) recommends conventional 'banks to take serious the growing demand for "Social Banking"'. Superficial modifications of the conventional banking business models, according to zeb, will not suffice in the long term to regain and stabilize the trust that was lost by customers over the financial crisis. Instead, zeb argues, banks should anticipate and make use of the fundamental changes in the attitudes of the public. In this context, criteria such as sustainability and social consciousness will be of increasing importance. They provide an opportunity to conventional banks to reposition themselves in the highly competitive private clients sector.

However, another very recent study on social banking by the reputable German economic think tank ZEW (2010), based on a survey of 236 finance experts, paints a slightly more differentiated picture. It suggests that there is no guarantee for social banking to succeed in the long term. Instead, the recent growth of the sector could be a temporary and possibly short-lived trend as a consequence of the financial crisis. If this is the case, the sector overall might not grow much beyond what we see now.

The ZEW (2010) study also identifies a growing trend towards social banking. And 43 per cent of the experts surveyed by ZEW expect the growth of today's social banks to be sustainable and to continue over the next years. In this context, the finance experts see the most important reasons for the growing importance of social banking in the banking clients' 'mistrust towards conventional banks' (96 per cent of the experts consider this important), followed by the clients' 'growing interest social and ecological topics' (94 per cent of the experts consider this important) and the clients' 'trust in social banks' (92 per cent of the experts consider this important), whereby the latter can be seen as a result of social banks' good reputation, less risky investment strategies and transparent business practices.

However, the ZEW (2010) survey also reveals an element of uncertainty regarding the future of social banking. Around one-third of those surveyed by ZEW believe that social banking is 'just a temporary phenomenon'; and almost a quarter of those surveyed did not want to voice an opinion in this context. Furthermore, despite the visible success of today's social banks, 'only' 57 per cent of the experts believe that other banks will follow the example of social banks – whilst 43 per cent of the experts remain sceptical as to whether other banks will orient themselves more towards ethical-ecological or social objectives because they believe ethically and ecologically motivated products often have a lower return and are therefore not attractive to price-sensitive customers.

In a more pointed version, this latter assessment is also reflected in a very recent article in *Die Bank*, a well-established German journal for banking policy and practice. There, it reads: 'Much of the traditional Social Banking was more claim than reality, and ultimately reduced the yields for well-meaning customers' (Bendig *et al.* 2010: 70).

The scepticism that partly speaks out of the above not withstanding, to us, the question is not *whether* social banking will stay, but *how much* it can increase its outreach and impact – in absolute terms and relative to the conventional banks that increasingly engage in socially-oriented products and services whilst simultaneously maintaining their conventional activities that often cause 'collateral damage'.

As de Clerck (2009) puts it (using the term 'ethical banking' rather than 'social banking', but essentially referring to the same banks):

> Some questions require continuous attention: Will this emerging financial business sector be able to achieve the relative scale and the professionalism to challenge the dominance of mainstream finance? Will the exceptions of the financial industry become the exceptional and a factor in modern society? Will a profound way of dealing with ethical choices be overruled by the superficiality of business development – also in ethical banking? Can ethical banking as a process with an instrumental character avoid becoming institutionalized? Can ethical banking be a portal for trust forces, morality and responsibility to feed money processes and the financial system with basic values and practices that can be a counter power to uncontrollable morbid growth?
>
> (de Clerck 2009)

In this context, we are confident that at least some social banks have the potential to grow into the league of conventional banks, and thus increase their outreach and impact. Others, however, might – willingly or not – stay small and focus on serving a limited group of local clients.

We are aware that the different parties on the social banking 'scene' have different objectives and different visions about the future of this sector. Yet, to us, a desirable 'vision' of the sector would comprise of a significant growth of social banks, not only in terms of their *number* but also in terms of their *size*.

More social banks are needed to cover wider parts of the population with products and services that are specifically tailored towards the regional and local sustainability challenges. *Bigger* social banks are needed to spread the word of social banking on a broader scale and, equally important, to fund bigger projects efficiently. Moreover, bigger social banks might also find it easier to branch out and thus create 'more' social banks. For this purpose (some of) today's social banks are obvious candidates. They have already reached a size and maturity that would allow them to grow even bigger in the currents of the recent financial crisis. For them, we feel, it would be nonsensical not to grow, if they have the opportunity and the will to do so.

It should be mentioned here that we explicitly acknowledge the value of the decision by some of today's social banks to only grow 'organically', not making use of the current growth opportunities but making sure that they stay close to their local customers and to their original values. They show that growth is not a 'necessity' but can be consciously chosen, or rejected. Clearly, this is a valuable lesson to be learnt, particularly at a time when it has become evident that some organizations can be 'too big to fail'. Moreover, if all of today's social banks grow, they are likely to leave a gap that needs to be filled by new social banks – or other socially oriented financial institutions – willing and able to serve small, 'inefficient' clients. What we ultimately need is a diverse and resilient 'Ecology of Finance', where a variety of different types and sizes of socially oriented banks and financial institutions, based on their individual strengths, compete and cooperate for the common good (nef 2009).

However, in this chapter, we exclusively focus on the future possibilities of those social banks that perceive an opportunity to grow, and a desire to make use of it.

Analysis of specific possibilities for social banks

In the following, we analyse some specific possibilities – in terms of opportunities and threats – for social banks that result from the situation sketched out in the previous section.

But we begin with an outline of our general analytical approach that orients itself towards the well-established tool of SWOT analysis, a technique credited to Albert Humphrey, who worked at Stanford University during the 1960s and 1970s. This technique refers to:

- strengths as internal attributes (e.g. resources/capabilities) of a company that are helpful;
- weaknesses as internal attributes (e.g. resources/capabilities) of a company that are harmful;
- opportunities as external conditions (e.g. developments and/or demands) in the environment that are helpful; and to
- threats as the external conditions (e.g. developments and/or demands) in the environment that are harmful to achieving a company's objectives.[6]

To translate the above generic definitions for our purpose, in the following, we refer to opportunities and threats, respectively, as those external developments or demands in the environment of social banks that could have a positive or negative impact on realizing their mission to increase their outreach and impact with respect to a more sustainable development whilst simultaneously safeguarding their own economic sustainability. Strengths and weaknesses, respectively, are then those internal attributes of social banks that help or hinder social banks to deal appropriately with the respective opportunity or threat.

This being said, each external opportunity and threat is met by both internal strengths *and* weaknesses. For instance, a social bank might have certain internal strengths that help to make use of an external opportunity, but it might also have certain internal weaknesses in this context. In the same vein, a social bank might have a certain internal strength that should help it overcome external threat, but it might also have certain weaknesses in this context.[7]

In the following, we structure our text according to opportunities and threats, whereby we describe for every opportunity and threat, the (combination of) strengths and weaknesses we consider particularly relevant. For a first overview of the subsequent structure of the text, in Table 7.1, we summarize those opportunities and threats, which we will deal with in more detail subsequently. At this point one might also refer to the summary section at the end of this chapter where we provide an overview of our analytical approach and, in Table 7.2, of our main results.

Opportunities

Whilst we believe there are plenty of opportunities for social banks to achieve their objectives in the future four areas are particularly noteworthy: new public

Table 7.1 Summary of selected opportunities and threats, and strengths and weaknesses of social banks

Opportunities	*Threats*
New public consciousness Social banks can use the new public consciousness to increase their outreach and *indirect* impact way beyond what their limited size would suggest.	*New value systems* With new stakeholders, social banks face new value systems, some of which might run counter to their original values, at least in the eyes of some early stakeholders.
New funds under management Social banks, based on the new funds deposited with them, can increase their *direct* impact by funding more and larger projects and initiatives that aim to foster sustainability.	*New structures and procedures* Growth in terms of funds managed, customers and employees, along with new regulation necessitates social banks to implement new structures and procedures.
New products and services Social banks can develop innovative financial products and services in response to the growing customer demand for products and services promoting sustainability.	*New competition* Social banks increasingly compete with conventional incumbents and new entrants, at least some of which want to 'green-wash' their predominantly conventional activities.
New technologies and media Social banks can use technologies, such as the Internet and social media, to realize their missions and play an active role in fundamentally changing the nature of banking, in a socially-oriented direction.	*New recruitment and training* Rapid growth necessitates social banks to hire and train new staff that often has been trained and socialized in conventional banks, with different values and without the relevant experience in the focus sectors.

consciousness, new funds under management, new products and services, and new technologies and media.

New public consciousness

Over the past three decades there was to be observed a general change in consumer attitude towards more sustainable lifestyles. This trend found its most recent manifestation in the identification of the so-called LOHAS (*l*ifestyle *o*f *h*ealth *a*nd *s*ustainability) consumer group by marketing experts (Cortese 2003). This overall trend towards more sustainability mainly concerned consumptive goods, however – from food or clothes to cars. Financial products and services, by contrast, were hardly on the radar of critical consumers. This, however, changed radically with the financial crisis in 2007. Since then the banking sector – that previously had enjoyed a comfortable and discrete life 'in the shadows' – is in the limelight. People began to think, and publicly talk about banking differently (Clark 2009). Many bank clients started to realize that there was a serious conflict of interest between them and their banks (and their customer advisers).

For social banks, the crisis has had diagonally opposite effects: the public attitude towards them changed for the better. Not long ago, these banks had either been completely unknown to the public or even been ridiculed for being 'unprofessional' and 'too idealistic' in their niche. But when it surfaced that the social banks had made it through the crisis almost unscathed, their executives suddenly became much demanded guests on many popular TV talk shows and interviews, being asked to reveal the secrets of their success (Scheire and de Maertelaere 2009). And, in 2009, Triodos Bank was awarded, in an international competition with more than 100 entries, the prestigious 'Sustainable Bank of the Year' Award by the *Financial Times* and the International Finance Cooperation.

Obviously, all this new public consciousness and attention offers several great opportunities to social banks. One very important one is the opportunity to boost their *indirect* impact and 'outreach'. Since the beginning of the current crisis, social banks' ability to actively influence the public and political debate on money and banking has increased manifold. This must not be underestimated, as it always has been very high on the agenda of social banks. Peter Blom, Chairman of the Executive Board of Triodos Bank, for instance, when asked about the impact of his bank, pointed out:

> The impact of our work is channeling people's money – now five billion euro from almost 250,000 people – to sustainable projects that serve the common good. That is direct impact. Our indirect impact is to show clearly that banking can go in another direction to the mainstream. We're contributing to the discussion around banking, and we are doing it on the basis of a solid business model. So we're not promoting the idea that banks are bad and should behave better, we're actually showing that banking itself can be done better.
>
> (Niven 2010: 112)

However, until very recently, most social banks found it difficult for their (warning) voices to be heard in public. Now being at the centre of public interest, social banks have a possible outreach way beyond what their limited size would suggest. They can show that an alternative way of dealing with money is possible, and they can draw attention towards the issues they were set up to address – in the economic, social and/or environmental area, thus further raising awareness for their cause.

As regards the *strengths* of social banks with respect to the opportunity of the 'new public consciousness', one of the core strengths of social banks certainly is the (current) weakness of conventional banks. Conventional banking has suffered a big blow to its key asset, the ('blind') trust of its customers.

Social banks, by contrast, are perceived as neither having contributed nor having suffered from the recent financial crisis. As the apparent 'winners' of this crisis, social banks are now being taken increasingly seriously as professional and trustworthy banks. This presents a major reputational boost for them – who previously were seen (if at all) as organizations that tried 'to do good', but did not manage 'to do well'. Undoubtedly, this made many (including business-minded) people open up towards them for the first time. Furthermore, once (potential) new customers begin to engage more with the social banks, they become aware of their deeper values and operating principles driven not by profit maximization but by striving to make sense of and with money. Their transparency, no-speculation policy, focus on the real economy and local community etc. make social banks ever more attractive alternatives to those already interested in more sustainable consumption and those disappointed by the ruthlessness of the conventional banks.

Yet, the above notwithstanding, social banks also suffer from some *weaknesses* that might prevent them from making full use of the change in public consciousness. Arguably the core weakness of social banks with respect to the opportunity offered by the new public consciousness is that they, despite their rapid growth over the past few years, still remain tiny as compared to almost all other (conventional) banks. So, it is fair to assume that even if social banks' visibility on the public screen has increased dramatically, only few people will have ever heard of them. Another weakness of social banks in this context arguably is that they, for better or worse, are more conservative than many conventional banks in terms of marketing, PR and lobbying.[8] At least some of them feel (or felt until recently) that engaging in these activities would run counter to their core values and principles. A really good business should rely on word of mouth. However, for a long time, most social banks mainly served a select clientele that generally shared the banks' values. As a consequence, they developed their own jargon not necessarily understood by the outside world. Overall, social banks have a reputation for being too ideological or academic and therefore might find it difficult to reach the wider parts of the population. Yet, in this context, it must also be acknowledged that, because they were and still are working on relatively low profit margins and are cash-constrained, most social banks do not have sufficient resources to spend heavily on activities that made their conventional peers so strong in lobbying for their cause. This certainly is a major limitation of social banks trying to increase their visibility and indirect impact.

Another arguable weakness of social banks with respect to the opportunity offered in form of the new public consciousness can be seen in their lack of research and insufficient communication with respect to their non-monetary impacts. All social banks – explicitly or implicitly – claim to follow a triple bottom line approach, with a focus on the social and environmental impacts of their activities. This is also why they enjoy a steady influx of funds from customers who want to make a difference. But, for a long time, neither the social banks nor their customers seem to have been interested in analysing or even questioning the actual impact any further. There was no move for systematic impact maximization (analogous to 'profit maximization' in the conventional banking world). Steps taken by some social banks in the direction of impact assessment and reporting – such as the publication of lists with projects funded, of CO_2 reductions associated with parts of the business activities and product portfolio (see Alternative Bank Switzerland), or of 'Social Impact Reports', are arguably limited in their comparability across project alternatives and across banks. Even if the public attitude today is very much in favour of social banks, it can be expected that future customers will sooner or later demand more comprehensive and comparable indicators of the social and environmental impacts of their funds deposited at social banks. If social banks could show 'proof' of their total impact, this would likely increase public willingness to listen to and engage with them even further, and it would put pressure on their conventional peers to do similar. This assertion also finds some support from Scheire and de Maertelaere (2009), who argue with respect to the Global Alliance for Banking on Values:

> [T]o gain more massive public attention and support, the Alliance could take a big step forward by measuring their member banks' impact. The Alliance gathered economic figures from all of its members in its first year. What's lacking is a collection and measurement of the impact the banks have had on society. How many people have been helped to get out of poverty? How much CO_2 has been avoided? How many jobs have been created? … Measuring these impacts will not only show that banking can be done differently, but also that banking can make a difference.
>
> (Scheire and de Maertelaere 2009: 44)

New funds under management

As outlined above, changes in public awareness towards social banks lead ever more people to open up to this apparent alternative on the banking landscape. And once aware of these niche banks, people often realize that they are not only safer and more sensible than conventional banks but that many of them also offer at least average interest rates and good quality/accessibility of service. As a result, ever more begin to vote with their wallet, carrying their funds from conventional banks towards social banks, which are currently experiencing an unprecedented growth in the number of new customers and deposits. Importantly, the new customers don't seem to regret their decision, as became recently evident when the comparatively small GLS Bank was awarded the 'Best German Bank of 2010' – an award based on a survey of 34,000 people by a popular TV news channel and an online business paper (see www.gls.de).

The *opportunities* offered herein for the social banks' missions are obvious. Beyond the general awareness and possibility to promote their cause (as described above), many social banks are now flush with deposits. This could enable them to substantially increase their *direct* impact, by providing (new) products and services to more people and more (and larger) projects that aim to foster sustainability more than ever before – individually or as a group. The Global Alliance for Banking on Values, for instance, is now publicly talking about 'touching the lives of one billion people by 2020' (see www.gabv.org).

However, it is fair to say that the large and rapid influx of new funds also comes as a challenge to many social banks. As mentioned before, most social banks define themselves as savings and loan banks. Their core activity consists of transforming deposits into loans for sustainability oriented companies and projects. But, as Figure 7.3 shows, this is not always possible. At least in recent years most social banks' conversion rates (deposits to loans) were sub-optimal. This was for a number of reasons, some of which were hardly under the control of the social banks such as the fact that, with the recent economic downturn, many (potential) borrowers postponed their planned investments, did not apply for a loan, or did not draw the loans granted to them. Other reasons that were more under the control of social banks we will discuss further below.

At this stage it should just be noted that most social banks currently sit on a substantial amount of excess liquidity (from new deposits), which needs to be transformed into loans and investments for sustainable projects and initiatives, unless social banks want to turn this great opportunity of new funds under management into a threat. This threat could arise because social banks have to park these excess funds and have to pay interest on them as well. They usually do so, also because of liquidity reasons, by depositing them at their central banks and/or by buying government bonds. Yet, this comes at a price, literally and metaphorically. Parking excess funds in more or less liquid form pays only little interest, further adding to the low profitability of social banks sketched out in the previous section. Moreover, such parking probably is not what depositors had in mind when depositing their funds at a *social bank*. So, if this situation continues for too long, it could come at a price for the reputational capital of social banks, i.e. their reputation for finding and funding only social/sustainable projects.

As Scheire and de Maertelaere (2009), in their analysis of the deposit-loan reconversion rates of the GABV banks, state:

> [S]ome European ethical banks like Banca Etica … and Triodos Bank … and, to a lesser extent, GLS Bank … seem to be struggling with their popularity. The perception of these banks as being savings and loans banks that use deposit money to finance ethical, ecological, and social projects and companies is in danger when they are no longer able to find enough borrowers to grant loans.
>
> (Scheire and de Maertelaere 2009: 23)

Therefore, as of now, the new funds present a somehow ambiguous opportunity to the social banks, not just a blessing but also a threat. Nevertheless, if social banks really felt that they could not manage the incoming funds anymore, they have ways to reduce them. The most obvious one would be to lower interest rates on deposits to levels that would reduce further inflows. This can already be observed in some cases. Moreover, some social banks also actively encourage (potential) depositors to consider other, much needed, forms of using their funds, e.g. for investments or even donations to sustainable projects. In this context, the aforementioned growing group of LOHAS could play an increasingly important role for social banks. This is because LOHAS has now begun to extend their ethical consumption into financial matters. And thanks to their relative economic strength, they are likely to be interested not only in opening deposit accounts but also in products and services beyond core banking – such as wealth management and direct equity investments in sustainable ventures. It could help social banks to reduce their dependency on the low-profit lending business and the corresponding requirements with a view to equity capital if they managed to channel some of the deposits in equity that is even more needed in times of strong banking regulations.

As regards the *strengths* of social banks with respect to their 'new funds under management', their value-driven operating principles and criteria (e.g. focus on the real economy, rejection of speculation, and sustainability oriented screening of loan applications and investments) certainly play a major role. Related to this, a strength of social banks in this context is their expertise and networks in their focus sectors that strive to contribute to sustainable development through organic farming, independent schooling or alternative healthcare, etc. This provides them with a good overview and a good chance to be the first to learn about promising opportunities, thereby reducing transaction costs. Their expertise and 'insider information' also helps them to realistically assess and appropriately deal with the potential risks of projects faced by them in these sectors. Together, the above should help social banks to channel the new funds into areas where they can have a real impact, not only from an economic, but also from a social and environmental perspective.

An additional plus of social banks is their willingness to network and cooperate with their peers. They arguably have a much higher propensity to cooperate than do their conventional peers. This allows them to finance projects too large or too risky for an individual bank, and it could also help them to – temporarily – solve the above-described problem of 'excess funds'. For instance, as Scheire and de Maertelaere (2009) highlight, one of the projects of the new Alliance for Banking on Values could be the establishment of an own interbank market within the Alliance whereby excess funds in the North could be used to support microfinance institutions in the South. This could help improving the poor reconversion rates of the ethical banks in the North and to reduce the high vulnerability of poverty alleviation banks in the South that results from their dependency on the regular interbank market.

Dwelling on the *weaknesses* of social banks that might present possible obstacles for them to make sensible use of the new funds available to them, it is fair to say that social banks were taken by surprise by the speed and the extent of the latest financial crisis – and by the rapid influx of large amounts of new deposits. The immediate result was described above. As mentioned, this has numerous reasons, some of which are largely beyond the control of social banks. But some also can be seen as their weaknesses.

Obvious in this context is the small size of social banks, particularly with respect to human resources. More deposits simply mean more work. Even with substantial expertise and experience, a thorough assessment of a loan project or an investment opportunity that is not just based on profit, but also on a multitude of other – sustainability related – criteria often takes time. The time problem is inflated by the fact that the sudden growth necessitates social banks to swiftly hire new staff, including experienced loan managers. But the kind of loan managers social banks need – those with experience in banking *and* in the social banks focus sectors – are not easy to find. Usually, social banks have to train their new staff either with respect to sector knowledge or with respect to banking (also see the section below on 'new recruitment and training', pp. 175–180). Both take considerable time. Therefore, it might just take a while before social banks can transform all their new funds into sensible and sense-making projects.

But another noteworthy issue in this context is the small equity capital base of several (not all) social banks. This is already an existing problem that has now become exacerbated by the new funds resulting from the crisis.[9] Regulators prescribe certain equity–loan ratios for banks to remain liquid and to be able to guarantee provisions for potential loan defaults. Thus, a low equity capital base restricts at least some social banks' lending activities, even if they have suitable projects to lend to. This might become even more of an issue in the near future, when new regulations (e.g. Basel III) are likely to introduce even more restrictive requirements regarding the equity capital of banks. Related to this, yet another obstacle for some social banks with respect to the sudden influx of funds could be the flipside of one of their key strengths, i.e. their limited sector and customer focus. As Scheire and de Maertelaere (2009) put it:

> [I]t is pretty clear we are talking about niche banks. These banks offer loans to a well-defined category of clients or for well-defined uses of the proceeds of the loan. Loans are offered to individuals, organizations and companies in certain sectors.
>
> (Scheire and de Maertelaere 2009: 12)

This also affects their pipelines of suitable loan applications and investment opportunities. The sectors social banks focus on present only a tiny part of the total economy. Whilst there is no scarcity of people and projects searching for funding, even with substantial expertise in sustainability oriented sectors, it is not necessarily easy to find sufficiently large numbers of suitable people and projects that make sense from an economic perspective *and* comply with the value-based criteria of social banks. Hence, social banks will find it much more difficult to transform large new deposits into loans and investments than would their profit-only-oriented peers.

New products and services

Notwithstanding the fact that social banks, as described above, currently might find it difficult to swiftly transform the massive influx of new deposits into projects they consider worthwhile funding, we believe that this is going to change, at least in the mid-term. Given the overall deteriorating economic, social and environmental developments and trends outlined earlier, there is bound to be a rising demand – by a larger and more diverse group of clients – for more and more innovative financial products to support a more sustainable development.

Again the new group of LOHAS might play an important role in this context. Economically strong but conscious about their lifestyle and consumption, they are likely to be increasingly interested also in new, sustainable financial products. One of the already more well-known examples of such new products – currently marketed primarily by conventional rather than social banks – are socially responsible investment (SRI) funds, which experienced a strong growth over the last decade (Social Investment Forum 2009). While the SRI activities by conventional banks might represent only a fraction part of their overall business, it is fair to assume that they still dwarf the total sum of all activities by social banks in absolute numbers.[10]

However, it is likely that conventional banks will keep on avoiding funding small-scale innovative projects, particularly if the latter focus more on sustainability rather than on profit maximization. And with conventional banks continuing to support unsustainable projects, it can be expected that the above-mentioned problems will grow, as will the scope (and need) for social banks to provide innovative funding for (people and projects aiming at) new solutions, in innovative ways and with innovative business models. Again, the opportunities offered to social banks in this context are obvious. They will face increasing demand for more and cheaper funding (because, as the sustainability movement matures and grows, so do its projects) to foster sustainable development. And this also comes with an increasing demand for innovative products and services.

As regards the *strengths* of social banks with respect to the opportunity of 'new products and services', one important aspect certainly is the fact that they have been in the business of providing core banking products and services long enough to be at least at par with most other banks in this field. They know the existing bank products, including their strengths and weaknesses. But equally important, another key strength of the social banks in this context is their long experience and network within their focus sectors such as organic farming, independent schooling, alternative healthcare, etc. Having specialized in this clientele allows social banks to identify the real needs and to appropriately deal with the risks associated with funding such ventures much better than conventional banks could do. In this context, it is also important that social banks, based on their long experience with a variety of ventures from the same sector, have proprietary information, and can often provide extra advice to their clients in order to reduce their risk and increase their chances of success (whilst conventional banks might simply hike the interest rates or the required ROI to 'manage' the associated risk).

Both their experience in core banking activities and their expertise in select sectors are further complemented by a long tradition of financial innovation to provide funding for those projects and initiatives that have been left unserved by conventional banks. There are many examples of such innovations, arguably the most famous being microfinance in the South (i.e. providing funding without security to groups of people/women that individually would be difficult to fund) (Bhole and Ogden 2009). This now is also being introduced as an innovation by (social) banks in the North (Counts 2008). In Germany, for instance, GLS Bank recently started managing a €100 million microcredit fund.

But there are also many examples of genuine innovations by social banks to be found in the North. Amongst them, for instance, are new forms of savings accounts, or savings accounts for new customer segments (e.g. students), direct loans from depositors to borrowers, green credit cards, special sustainable housing mortgages, and even supporting regional/alternative currencies with the necessary banking infrastructure, etc. To pick just one organization out of the group of social banks as an example, Descours *et al.* (2010) describe some of the innovations introduced by La Nef in France:

> Ever since its creation, la Nef has tried to innovate, to create products and services, which had not existed before … recently la Nef gave birth to several initiatives by joining forces with other structures willing to do the same … through Terre de liens [literally Soil of links] the civil society can buy and be in charge of farms in order to let organic farmers work. For the last two years, over 5000 consumers have been gathering to obtain 15M€ of capital shares to collectively own farm properties. … SOLIRA was created by la Nef and specialists of photovoltaic energy to offer citizens the possibility of directly investing their savings in roofs covered with photovoltaic panels.
>
> (Descours *et al.* 2010: 99–100)

Some of the innovations initiated by social banks have subsequently been picked up by conventional banks. Arguably the most famous example in this context stems from Triodos Bank:

> [It] has pioneered the Netherlands' first wind funds, a financial product that has become standard in most banks now. The result of the fund was not only to provide a shot in the arm to the renewable industry, but also to prompt discussions that led to the creation of the Dutch Tax Credit Scheme. The scheme allows individual investors in a renewal energy fund to claim a tax credit on their investment. Over time this has led the majority of Dutch Banks to launch renewable energy funds themselves.
>
> (Niven 2010: 109)

In addition, social banks – partly based on conviction and partly based on sheer necessity – also have had a long tradition of cooperation with their peers, both to develop economies of scale for certain product types and to realize projects too big for an individual bank. Merkur Bank, for instance, sells Triodos' investment funds and finances larger projects in Denmark together with GLS Bank from Germany (Pehrson 2010).

Notwithstanding their above outlined strengths, social banks also show some noteworthy *weaknesses* when it comes to serving the increasing demand for new, innovative and affordable products and services. To begin with, as already described above, social banks mostly operate on comparatively low overall profit margins. They mainly serve low-profit clients (e.g. from the third sector or from agriculture), and they do not enjoy the same economies of scale as their conventional peers. Thus, they have a disadvantage in terms of their cost structure. Furthermore, they do not engage in speculation or other financial market activities that have the potential to generate high profits that could be used to subsidize other, more social, activities.

In this context it is also worth mentioning that social banks so far were more focused on serving their active side clients – with funds provided by dedicated passive side clients who shared the values of the bank and therefore were willing to forsake better returns than they could have obtained by depositing their funds with conventional banks. Yet, as mentioned in the introduction to this section, there is scope to develop more – and more profitable – products and services for passive side customers too. Asset management and SRI funds for the new LOHAS groups might be one direction to explore in this context, possibly also in cooperation with peers, to reduce the risk for individual banks.

At the same time, notwithstanding the general propensity of social banks to cooperate in order to realize projects an individual social bank could not realize on its own, there are natural limits to the innovative capacity of small organizations. Innovation requires 'slack resources', of which social banks usually do not have too many. Even if they were to join forces in order to innovate, there are obviously limits to cooperation for such small organizations, particularly if they are – as is the case with social banks – geographically dispersed with usually only one social bank per country. So, the limited size and sparse resources will present an ongoing hindrance in terms of their ability to satisfy the demand efficiently and effectively with innovative *and* affordable products and services.

Another issue for social banks with respect to the development of new products and services could be that they, so far, only served a small group of sectors, deemed particularly important for sustainable development. However, over time, new sectors came up that also have great potential to provide promising solutions to our sustainability problems. Often they are to be found in the high-tech sector. Yet, so far, most social banks have stayed away from the high-tech sector, partially because they do not have the relevant expertise and partly because the ventures in this sector usually need larger funds than social banks are able to provide (at least until recently).

In this context, it is also worth pointing out that social banks do not do much, if any, fundamental research – an aspect that had already been dealt with before in the section on new public consciousness (see pp. 152–155). Whilst big banks all have their own in-house departments to figure out 'how to make more money with their money', most social banks do not have (the resources to pay for) experts who can focus their energy exclusively on figuring out how to make more sense with their money. Instead, they mainly rely on their loan- and investment managers to learn (more) about the sectors they are (already) operating in. Notwithstanding the fact that this approach is useful in that it makes sure that the social banks stay in close contact with their clients and their clients' needs, it obviously narrows their horizon in terms of totally new developments that might happen outside their core sectors. Given that social banks are 'boutiques' that differentiate themselves based on their special expertise in certain sectors, in the longer term it could present a real problem for them to keep up their innovation capabilities. As other sectors (e.g. pharmaceuticals) show, despite being dominated by large corporations, there is a chance for small players (e.g. biotech ventures), but only if they are engaged in highly innovative research.

Closely related to the above, and in light of the social banks' rapid growth, it might also turn out to be of relevance that they are now forced to hire more staff, with less expertise in the social banks' core sectors. Particularly against this backdrop, a weakness of social banks certainly is that they, unlike their conventional peers, do not enjoy public services in terms of training institutions that churn out well-trained and highly skilled new recruits. As will be dealt with in more detail below (see pp. 175–180), social banks need a special kind of staff, with banking and focus sector expertise. This does not come in a package at the universities. Social banks have to train their new staff on the job to provide them with the relevant sector expertise (if they have a banking/business background) or send them to banking academies to arm them with the relevant technical skills (if they have experience in the banks' focus sectors). All of this takes time, and time is scarce.

Together, all of the above could suggest that social banks' innovative potential does not grow in tandem with the growth of their balance sheets. At least to some extent, they might have to accept that part of their outreach will comprise functioning as examples and trendsetters rather than serving the trends with their own products and services. Still, we are confident that social banks have the relevant experience and expertise, and now also the relevant funds coming in, to respond to the demand for new and innovative financial products and services, which is bound to rise in line with the problems we face.

New technologies and media

As a final *opportunity* for social banks these days, we would like to highlight the chances that lie for them in 'new technologies and media'. Information and communication technology (ICT) has long influenced all areas of business. Arguably, however, the impact of ICT has been particularly strong in the banking and finance sector. Finance and banking primarily deal with a virtual product, electronic money that can be easily transmitted around the globe in binary codes. Therefore, the sector has been particularly receptive to ICT. This has changed the face of banking considerably. The omnipresent ATMs are as much a sign of this as are telephone and Internet-based 'direct' banks. One of the results also has been that the banking sector has become increasingly impersonal. But the recent past has seen yet another very dramatic development in terms of ICT that promises to change the face of finance and banking even further and more fundamentally: the Internet-based 'web 2.0' technologies, also referred to as 'social' media, such as Facebook, YouTube, Twitter, and various blogging software tools.[11] These new technologies and media have the potential to change and to threaten the banking industry at its core. They are increasingly used to design new business models that challenge the role of banks as the exclusive intermediaries in the financial markets who transform the funds of depositors into loans for borrowers, without bringing together the two parties directly. It was this intermediation service, together with their risk-handling capabilities, that provided the foundation of banks' business model, and profits. But with the new social media, this foundation has begun to erode (Lochmaier 2010).

The new buzzwords are 'Social Banking 2.0' and 'P2P (peer to peer) banking', direct cash transfers between depositors and borrowers, without any additional transformation by a bank. In addition, there are more and more social media platforms that enable visitors to inform each other about good investment opportunities and the like. The main function of the 'financial' service provider in this context mostly is that of an IT platform service provider who doesn't need a banking licence and all the regulatory issues that come with it. Examples are Prosper (United States), Zopa (UK) or Smava (Germany), all online platforms that provide non-bureaucratic P2P lending in the North, or Kiva (United States) that provides similar services but focuses on direct microcredit from the North to the South. Though none of these organizations is older than five years, their loan portfolios are already several hundred million euro – with minimal spending on infrastructure and staff.[12]

Notwithstanding the fact that the new social media have the potential to challenge the traditional banking sector, they also offer great *opportunities*. Over the past few years ever more banks and financial service providers began to realize the potential of these technologies, particularly in terms of PR and marketing. Many conventional and social banks today actively use these technologies to inform – and sometimes also to communicate with – existing and possible new customers and stakeholders. They are present on Facebook and similar platforms and even 'tweet' to their customers. Indeed, almost all banks now make use of the new ICT and social media technologies, at least to some extent, and some newly set up banks are primarily based on them (e.g. Fidor Bank or Noa Bank in Germany).

But, whilst more or less all banks use them, we feel, the new technologies and media offer a particularly huge opportunity for social banks. On the one hand, this is because the technologies help reducing costs by automating many internal processes, thus creating substantial cost savings. On the other hand, this is because the new media allow for both large-scale marketing activities and personal dialogues with (prospective) clients and the wider community of stakeholders – at a much lower cost than would be possible when setting up a branch network or using other means such as print media or TV. So, even if social banks have to invest relatively more of their budgets into these technologies and media, once installed, they should help the small social banks to compete on a more even level with their larger conventional peers.

At the same time, the new media could also help social banks to get in touch with a younger generation of customers. For long a time, they mainly served a particular clientele, which normally comprised of a higher proportion of academically educated and wealthy people than would be seen in most other banks. However, their clients were also older than those of some other banks. With the new technologies and media, social banks now have an opportunity to attract a higher portion of young tech-savvy clients, an important asset for the future development of these banks.

Finally, as mentioned before, the new social media have the potential to challenge the business model of banks, by cutting out the costly intermediaries between depositors and borrowers. As Bendig *et al.* (2010: 73) note: 'the "net community" checks carefully whether and how (increases) in efficiency also result in social benefit'. This presents a real threat for many banks, particularly if they are not perceived to add much value to the transaction. At the same time, this could provide new opportunities for social banks. For instance, one might speculate that social banks might find themselves (partly) moving from handling money streams themselves towards providing knowledge and credibility to financial platforms based on new technologies and media. They might cooperate with and advise non-bank P2P platforms, whilst focusing their own money business more on those transactions that actually need transformation to gather bigger funds and reduce the associated risks.

Thinking of the *strengths* of social banks with respect to the 'new technologies and media', it is fair to say, social banks, out of sheer necessity (because they could not afford a branch network and had to keep costs for routine services to a minimum) have long been using various forms of ICT media to provide basic banking services. Most of them have technologically advanced online facilities, including customer service teams, to handle the basic banking services such as payments or opening accounts. As such, most have already gained substantial ICT experience and often build up a corresponding technology infrastructure. This should help them to also enter into the era of new social media.

However, it is obvious that social banks' ICT experience and infrastructure is at best at par with conventional banks, but does not provide the former with a competitive advantage. This is different with respect to a soft factor that is very important in this context: trust (Luo *et al.* 2010). People, quite naturally, are concerned when it comes to entrusting others with their money. For most of their history banks succeeded in cultivating a reputation of trustworthiness. This lasting trust also helped overcome fears when banking moved into the virtual realm a good decade ago. Even Internet-only banks benefited from the trust people had in their banks. However, during the recent financial crisis, conventional banks have lost much ground in this area. Yet, this situation was different for social banks who gained a wide reputation for integrity and trustworthiness. This is an invaluable asset, particularly in the virtual realm.

Equally important, social banks have had a long history of active stakeholder engagement. Most of them are engaged in an open and transparent dialogue with their customers and other stakeholders, not only to inform about their activities but also to jointly search for new approaches to old and new threats and to get vital input for developing relevant products and services. Moreover, several social banks also let depositors decide what projects or sectors they want to see their deposits being lent to; and they publish the actual loans and investments made. In addition, at least some social banks (e.g. GLS Bank) have had a long experience with arranging direct (P2P) transactions. All this now clearly also helps social banks to enter into an even broader dialogue with their stakeholders by using the new social media. As outlined before, the new media have the potential to challenge the business model of banks as financial intermediaries – particularly if these banks are not perceived to add much value to the financial transactions. But it seems fair to expect that customers at both ends of the banking business will appreciate that social banks are not only more trustworthy in their communication but – based on their expertise and networks in sustainable sectors – can add more value to many (basic) financial transactions than their conventional peers could.

Whilst we believe that social banks will benefit from the new technologies and media, several *weaknesses* mean that their success in this arena is by no means guaranteed. Once again, a core weakness of social banks in this context lies in their still limited size and visibility. Whilst social media help to communicate with stakeholders, they are of less use to attract these stakeholders in the first instance. Here, the conventional big players have a clear advantage in the form of much larger funds available for PR and marketing in both traditional and new social media. Worried about their reputation and the loss of trust of their clients, they now spend more than ever before on these activities, and they often cooperate with modern and trendsetting marketing, PR and web-design agencies.

In this context, much will therefore depend for social banks on modernizing their general communication. Whilst some of them have recently started to rebrand themselves and to redesign their websites in order to make them more attractive also to the younger and more tech-savvy generation, some web-appearances of social banks still appear outdated and unattractive. This could deter a good number of potentially interested people from entering into a virtual dialogue with them.

Another, related, problem for the social banks employing these new technologies and media might be that, for a large part, their success relies on the direct social interaction and personal knowledge of bank employees and customers. A virtual dialogue – and more generally a virtualization of social interactions – might not be what many of their dedicated old/long-time clients (and some of the banks' employees for that matter) are interested in, and it might go against their values. If social banks now become too modern and too virtual too quickly, they might lose touch with this dedicated core customer base.

We now turn towards what we consider threats for the future of social banks.

Threats

To begin with, it should be recalled that, in this chapter, we refer to threats as those external developments or demands in the environment of social banks that could have a negative impact on realizing their mission to increase their outreach and impact with respect to a more sustainable development whilst simultaneously safeguarding their own economic sustainability. Although, in the previous section, we highlighted the new funds under management as a key opportunity for social banks, we simultaneously see the current growth of many social banks as a key threat, particularly because it is not 'organic' but externally induced, and very, very fast growth. This makes it difficult for the social banks to adjust, and bears consequences on many aspects of their activities, of which we feel four are particularly worth highlighting here. These are, the *effects of new value systems*, *new structures and procedures*, *new competition*, and the need for *new recruitment and training*.

New value systems

All social banks are based on their values as *the* key differentiating factor compared to other banks. Their employees, customers and owners overall share (at least most of) these values as their own and are therefore willing to put up with some shortcomings of social banks (e.g. in terms of remuneration, interest rates and dividends). But rapid growth always presents a threat for the values and operating principles of value-driven organizations, including social banks. With growth, there come new necessities, some of which might be in contrast to the values of the early and incumbent employees, customers and owners.

So, given the current significant growth rates of most social banks, it is no wonder that the growth vs. values/principles debate presently is the most discussed topic on the social banking scene.[13] The fear of many is that with growth, there will be increasing pressure on (some might call it incentives for) social banks to morph more and more into mainstream organizations, leaving behind their core values and operating principles, with negative internal and external consequences. With respect to the *internal* consequences, for instance, personal conversations reveal that some longstanding co-workers of the social banks fear the loss of flat hierarchies, trust-based relations and open transparent discussions (also on values and principles) they have been used to. This, in turn, might impair not only the generally good working atmosphere but also the core of social banks, many of which perceive themselves not only as alternative banks, but also as alternative businesses, with transparent and democratic management and business practices. At Merkur Bank, for instance, there is a tradition of setting aside one hour a week for a common study of a subject, often a subject of the employees' own choosing (Arup 2010). This might not sound much, but it adds up to half a working day per month, and it is certainly more than one would find in most conventional banks. Another recent example from one of the rapidly growing social banks is the conversion of a meditation or relaxation room into new office space. Clearly, in particular the early employees who got used to such 'perks' would find it difficult to see them go.

With respect to the *external* aspects, it is feared that with their rapid growth social banks, for reasons of efficiency and profitability, might focus less on their social impact, at least at grassroots level. They might reduce their level and depth of service to smaller clients who could make a difference but might have little earning or growth potential. Instead, they might focus more on bigger and efficient clients who might demand products and services that, by their very nature, run counter to some of social banks' old values and principles (such as their focus on the local real economy or their no-speculation policy). A quote by Janniken Østervold (2010) from Cultura Bank in Norway also points in this direction:

> Our major challenge is to grow without compromising our ethical profile. We all agree that it would be a good thing to double or triple in size, because then we will be able to finance larger projects and we will be less vulnerable. But if we are to grow fast, where will we find all the really good projects? The deposits? The capital? We should not be tempted to take in all kinds of customers just to grow.
>
> (Østervold 2010: 130–1)

In a similar vein, Kirstin Arup (2010) from Merkur Bank argues:

> every client is a mini network whose contribution is important, and who may bring impulses from Merkur to other people that we are not in contact with. It is one thing to know … [this], but quite another to remember it in the busy daily work.
>
> (Arup 2010: 93)

However, it should also not remain unmentioned that there are differences in the perception of the threat to the core values of social banks that might come with growth. For instance, when asked about GLS Bank's accomplishments in an interview, Thomas Jorberg, spokesman of the Board of GLS Bank, summarizes it this way: 'The most important accomplishment in my view is that we have managed to grow without compromising on our values' (Lützel 2010: 86).

But independent of the question of how justified these fears are, it is clear that social banks' value-based business models are much more difficult to manage in a way that satisfies all, even in more normal times. A big challenge with respect to the values, for instance, is that most of them are so relative, difficult to define and to measure. Conventional banks usually have one core value, shareholder value, which is easy to measure and to base decisions on. But social banks have a host of different values to be taken care of. Some of them are concerned more about the external business activities (e.g. transparency) and some more about the internal relations (e.g. democracy). Some can be well documented in writing (e.g. positive or negative criteria) and some are shared more tacitly (e.g. human development or spirituality). Furthermore, values are hardly ever fully shared between people. Whilst everybody would claim to have certain values (that go by the same names), most would describe them differently. In the same vein, it is usually difficult to measure how well values are lived up to. And, in the real world, there will always be tradeoffs, between non-monetary values and economic necessities. All this obviously nurtures the possibility that particularly those values that cannot be easily quantified and documented but are tacit, and those values that are of less direct relevance for outside activities but more internally oriented fall victim to other values and necessities.

Therefore, the above fears are not only understandable but, at least to some extent, they are also necessary for the organization. If social banking is to succeed, it has to be based on strong values and also on the people who cherish and protect them. Social banks, as all value-driven organizations, have to thoroughly engage with and cherish their core values, at least as long as they help them to tackle the issues they want to address. This includes defining their values more clearly and measuring their actual social impact – as a reflection of how well they live up to their values. This also includes being open to constructively considering possible changes to their value system where changes in the environment so suggest.

Thinking about the *strengths* of social banks with respect to the 'new value systems', one core strength in this context remains the fact that, particularly when compared to most other organizations, their values are still deeply rooted – in their people, principles and practices. Social banks' values directly influence their operating principles, which in turn guide their practices. Obvious examples in this context are the value-based positive or negative criteria, which social banks employ for assessing loan applications and investment decisions.

Moreover, to change these documented criteria and related processes (e.g. to soften the exclusion criteria for funding) would involve a conscious decision by the management, which would have to find the agreement of the many dedicated stakeholders, amongst them, the employees and the owners of the bank. If they felt that the bank has moved too far away from its core values – documented or not – they would likely intervene. And they often have the means to do so. Most social banks still have comparatively flat hierarchies and substantial employee representation. Furthermore, social banks are usually organized as cooperatives, with their members (and often also employees) not only being dedicated followers but also critical friends and often even owners. They are not in it primarily for the money but for the values represented and realized by the bank. They often forsake possible dividend or interest for their investment in the banks' equity shares. This, in turn, is a crucial ingredient at least for some social banks being able to operate on a relatively low profit margin (although others also show that it is possible to pay dividends and have a social impact). Hence, there is also a formal governance structure in place that is much more values-focused than would usually be the case in conventional banks. The management might find it risky to change operating principles in a way that runs counter to the members' convictions and values.

In addition, one might argue that it is again the weakness of conventional banks when it comes to non-monetary values that personify the strength of social banks. As stated before, values are difficult to measure and their assessment often works on a relative basis. Yet, particularly when compared to conventional banks, social banks certainly score well in terms of how they live up to their values. So, in a way, the negative mirror image of conventional banks could serve social banks and their stakeholders as a continuous reference for reflection upon and assessment of their own values.

Thinking about the *weaknesses* of social banks in terms of new value systems, the limited size and the associated workload for employees comes to mind first. A continuous formal or informal reflection of and engagement with the underlying value system takes time and energy. However, as most social bankers will agree, in these fast-paced times, there is simply too little time and slack. Whilst social banks have a long tradition of engaging with their values internally (e.g. informally during joint breakfasts etc. or formally in joint seminars and reading seminars), it is fair to say that, in many cases, these discussions have become less frequent, particularly in the fast-growing banks. Either there is no time at all for them, or co-workers are too swamped with work to engage in such discussions during or after work. This problem has certainly intensified over the course of the latest financial crisis.

Another aspect that comes to mind is the 'conservatism' of social banks. The fact that many of the social banks' values are deeply rooted in the organization (i.e. early employees, owners and customers) also comes with a flipside. Social banks might be seen, at least in part, as inflexible when it comes to further developing the values and the corresponding principles. However, it is also clear that, with the environment changing, it is necessary to reassess one's old values to see whether they still address the problems and issues one faces. Changes in the environment of social banking might well lead to the development of new values and principles, as well as to a necessity to give up on some old ones. For example, in the early days of social banking, safeguarding cultural diversity has arguably been much less of an issue than it is today in the age of globalization. Similarly, new technologies (such as certain types of biotechnology) today might offer possibilities to deal with sustainability issues whilst at the same time run counter to the traditional core values of social banks.

At the same time, as mentioned before, there is an ever more pressing need for the fast-growing social banks to hire new staff – which often has been originally trained and socialized in conventional banks, and therefore is not accustomed to their new employers' value system and corresponding discussion. Particularly, but not only, for them a formalized thorough engagement with values-related issues, for instance in form of trainings or seminars, would seem recommended. However, again, there is too little time and slack. Furthermore, the growth comes with extra demands for the staff's formal qualifications and trainings, e.g. technical or legal aspects. And the corresponding specialist trainings – either in banking skills or in focus sector aspects – often dominate the training schedules of new (and old) staff, so that there is not much time left for seminars etc. on values.

Finally, related to the above, social banks have made little or no advance in terms of systematic research in this context, for instance on suitable parameters to proxy how well they live up to their own values. Only recently some banks have started to measure or assess, for instance, their CO_2 emissions of their loan products (e.g. Alternative Bank Switzerland) or their broader social impact (e.g. Charity Bank). But without further and more systematic analysis of their own values (and the corresponding impacts), social banks forsake the opportunity to engage with them more consciously. By this, they risk losing touch with their values and/or not realizing when it is time for a re-orientation of their value or their practices. Obviously, this sort of research could also feed into the corresponding training activities.

New competition

Social banks have enjoyed life in a niche market for a long time, mostly unchallenged by the world outside, possible customers and competitors included. This, however, is beginning to change. And so the competitive strategy of social banks might have to follow suit. Social banks attract ever more funds from customers that have formerly been banking with conventional banks. Moreover, those social banks that want to make use of the current opportunity to grow now put considerable effort and resources into marketing activities aimed at such customers from conventional banks. Even if the number of customers changing sides is still relatively small from the perspective of conventional banks, it will not be long before the latter begin to take notice and try to stop this trend. In this context, it should also be referred back to the recent study by zeb (2009) mentioned in the introduction to this chapter, which forecasted a customer potential of 15 to 20 per cent of the population (in Germany). Clearly, this spells increasing competition.

At the same time, more and more conventional banks now jump the bandwagon of sustainable banking mainly to regain public trust, but increasingly also because they realize the business opportunity of going green (Weber 2005; Social Investment Forum 2009). Often accompanied by extensive marketing efforts, conventional incumbents green parts of their businesses, including their headquarters (e.g. Deutsche Bank) and offer at least some green or socially oriented products, such as SRI funds. If required, they can buy in at least some of the expertise to facilitate the swift development of products and services they had previously no experience in.

Hardly any true social banker would mind involving others in the same cause. After all, the main purpose of social banking is to make the world a better place, and not to hinder others from trying to do so. However, the devil lies in the detail. The motivations of these old and new banks certainly vary. Some of them are likely to have a genuine interest in fostering sustainable development. (Many) others, however, are more likely to be driven by the desire to green-wash their image and win back customers by look-alike green or socially oriented products and services – whilst continuing with their conventional practices and thus further contributing to the problems social banks try to address. Then, competition increasingly becomes an issue, even for the most un-competitive social bankers.

Therefore, overall, with the social banks arriving on the radar screens of customers and conventional banks, a heating up of the competitive situation can be expected. The small social banks will therefore need to get their competitive strategy right, if they want to increase their outreach and impact. This strategy might or might not have to differ for the passive side (deposits and equity) and the active side (loans and investments) of the banks' balance sheet.

Common business school knowledge (e.g. Porter 2004) suggests there are two generic sources of competitive advantage, *differentiation* or *cost-leadership* (Porter 2004). Social banks, so far, have mainly followed a differentiation strategy both on the passive and the active side. Partly out of necessity and partly because they chose to, they served a limited clientele with a limited range of (more or less) differentiated products and services. On the passive side social banks differentiated themselves as being value-driven with operating principles strictly focused on using deposits to foster sustainable development. For this purpose they offered, for instance, deposit accounts with a selection of sustainably oriented areas to choose from. On the active side social banks differentiated themselves with their specialized expertise and experience in selected focus sectors. This enabled them to get engaged in (i.e. to provide loans to or invest in) people and projects that otherwise would have been cut off from funding and to support them beyond the funds provided. The value-added of this differentiation is well captured by Scheire and de Maertelaere (2009; parentheses and emphasis added):

> Many people will argue that the added value of the loans of this group of banks [members of the Global Alliance for Banking on Values], compared to the loans offered by their mainstream contemporaries, is not directly to be found in the nature of the loan itself. They will not deny the intrinsic value of a loan to its recipient, but given the same conditions they will probably argue that a loan of US$100 from, for example, ING Bank will not be less valuable to the borrower than a loan of US$100 from Triodos Bank. However, the prerequisite here was that the conditions for both loans were the same and that is exactly where the difference is to be found. *Due to the lending criteria of the mainstream banks – consisting strictly of economic and financial criteria – many sectors will not get served.* Too often this means sectors that add considerable social and ecological value. These are sectors that are highly needed given today's context. However *they will often not get served, or be unsatisfactorily served, through the mainstream market.* It treats of innovative ecological projects that bear a high risk or social-enterprises that are undercapitalized and therefore considered of maximum risk too. As [ethical banks] are inspired by the values of sustainable and human development they adopt very different lending criteria compared to mainstream banks. In addition to traditional economic evaluation procedures, the companies undergo an evaluation aimed at analyzing and assessing the consequences of their activity on common welfare and the natural environment. To be able to do this, these ... banks have developed their own models, which are applied to both the loan book and the ethical investment funds they are managing. ... As such, they raise the access to credit for underserved sustainable sectors considerably. Therefore, we

> believe that one of the main added values of these [ethical] banks' lending and investment is to be found in their financial inclusion of sectors that are underserved in the market.
>
> (Scheire and de Maertelaere 2009: 31–2)

From a pure financial perspective, these products and services were often less attractive to the average bank customer than those available (if in fact available!) from conventional banks. But their value-added enabled social banks to compete based their differentiation strategy. Conventional banks, by contrast, are not focused on particular sectors (and therefore lack special expertise in those sectors) but are able to offer a wider spectrum of products and services, and can use economies of scale to offer comparatively attractive conditions. As such, they mainly compete based on a cost-leadership strategy.

Broadly speaking, we would expect social banks to keep on competing based on a differentiation strategy and conventional banks to keep on competing based on a cost-leadership strategy. However, we also see both sides adopting parts of their respective opponents' strategies.

The different options for both parties cannot be discussed in detail here, but we shall briefly describe one plausible scenario for social banks. Particularly those social banks that opted to grow by attracting and serving new customers that previously have been with conventional banks now find themselves in a new competitive territory. Those mainstream customers might indeed be increasingly interested in value-driven banking products and services. But, in the foreseeable future (and with the memory of the crisis fading), they are likely to remain more cost and price sensitive than were the old dedicated customers of social banks, whilst at the same time demanding the full range of banking products and services they were used to from their former conventional banks. Thus, social banks might find it increasingly necessary, if not to compete on costs and price, at least to offer a broader range of products and services at conditions similarly attractive to those offered by conventional banks. This not only holds for the passive side where (potential) new depositors certainly will find it easier to change sides if this change does not coincide with significantly lower interest rates or higher fees. It also holds for the active side. Here, we would expect social banks to remain the lender of first choice for first-time borrowers. These customers typically were (and will remain) relatively unattractive to conventional banks because identifying the most promising amongst them, and serving them efficiently, requires significant sector expertise, which most conventional or new banks do not have. However, once they have built up a positive credit history with a social bank, existing customers (e.g. potential second-time borrowers) might not find it beyond them to obtain (possibly cheaper) funds from a conventional bank. This would leave social banks with relatively more labour-intensive low-profit first-time borrowers.

Clearly, if social banks do not communicate their value added convincingly enough, and if they cannot increase their efficiency and do not offer a broader range of (more profitable) products and services to a broader range of (of more profitable) clients, this will translate into a further pressure on their profit margins, and by this on their chances to increase their outreach and impact.

As regards the *strengths* of social banks with respect to the 'new competition', an important factor again can be seen in the weakness of conventional banks. Whilst the latter are losing, the former are further gaining the vital trust of their stakeholders. Social banks now more than ever can benefit from their reputation as value-driven and transparent organizations, primarily aiming for the greater good and not so much for their own profit maximization. But equally important certainly is the fact that social banks, particularly when compared to their conventional peers, have special expertise and networks in their focus sectors such as organic farming, independent schooling or alternative healthcare. This provides them with a better overview of the developments in those sectors, and with a better feeling for what customers in these sectors need. As one consequence, new customers from within these sectors regularly get referred to them by word of mouth. In addition, social banks are often the first to learn about promising funding opportunities within these sectors. Their expertise then also helps them to more realistically assess and appropriately deal with the potential risks of the projects in these sectors. All this contributes to social banks not only being able to compete based on differentiation strategy, but it also helps them to reduce transaction costs within their focus sectors.

Related to this, we would argue, the ability of social banks to innovate also can be seen as a strength in this context. In many instances social banks were set up to make possible the funding for certain projects and initiatives that were deemed impossible by their conventional peers. But the intimate insider knowledge of social banks with respect to select sectors together with the explicit willingness to support projects that foster sustainable development, allowed social banks to venture new routes in banking, as has already been discussed (see pp. 158–162).

Another relevant strength of social banks in terms of competition arguably lies in their – often innovative – ownership structures (see pp. 168–169). Many of them are set up as cooperatives with their dedicated members often willing to forsake some return on their investments to support their bank.[14] Thus without the pressure of maximizing the profit for their shareholders, social banks can serve their customers (at least in some parts) on lower profit margins than their competitors could. This, in turn, is important to realize their mission to provide *affordable* products and services with a social impact.

Finally, it is also worth mentioning that social banks try to keep their expenses for salaries and infrastructure etc. low. They do not splash out on lavish bonuses, perks or fancy buildings, corporate jets, etc. The money saved on this might be partly used to offer more attractive conditions to the passive side customers and shareholders. Indeed, at least some of the larger social banks (e.g. GLS Bank) are proud to offer what they call 'average market rates' to depositors.

The above strengths notwithstanding, social banks suffer from substantial competitive disadvantages, or *weaknesses* in terms of both costs and differentiation.

What comes to mind first in this context again is their limited size and visibility compared to their conventional peers. As such, and even despite the new public consciousness also with respect to the social banks, many potential customers simply might never know about them. Partly related to this, another competitive weakness of social banks is their disadvantageous cost structure. Whilst conventional banks usually operate very efficiently, enjoy economies of scale and do not serve what might be considered unprofitable clients, social banks are still specialist boutiques. They have special values, serve a special clientele in special sectors, and they also provide (some) special products to clients. For instance, social banks often overcome the apparent risks involved with serving seemingly risky borrowers by taking the time to learn to know their clients and providing advice to them. Clearly, this is resource-intensive, and has an impact on the cost structures and efficiency (at least if measured in traditional, economic ways) of social banks. As such, it also sets limits on their pricing flexibility (e.g. on the passive side), particularly at the moment when social banks have to 'park' their excess funds for little interest.

Possibly not quite as obvious are social banks' competitive weaknesses in terms of their differentiation. Here, we feel, an important weakness lies in the way they market (or not) their being different from their conventional peers. Again, costs are likely to play a role in this context, as tiny social banks obviously do not have the same PR or marketing funds available as the big conventional banks do. However, we feel the problem runs deeper than shallow pockets. It also has to do with the social banks' communication, at least until recently. Social banks, with their publicly declared non-monetary values and transparent operating principles, are generally believed to do good. This particularly holds for their dedicated early (depositor) customers, who were willing to forsake higher interests rates or a more complete range of products and services possibly to be obtained from other banks. And this, one might further argue, has contributed to social banks being somehow self-content. There simply was no need to prove that their values and operating principles actually translate into the betterment of the world. As a consequence, social banks' marketing communication mainly focused on just publicizing the projects funded – leaving it to those interested to identify the overall value added of such projects as compared to those funded by conventional banks. But, with some delay, non-financial reporting now also has become an increasingly important issue in the banking industry. More and more conventional banks begin to publish externally audited environmental, sustainability or CSR reports on their non-monetary impacts. For instance, Deutsche Bank dedicates a good part of its homepage to issues of corporate social responsibility (see www.db.com) and it has even set up a webpage to highlight all its sustainability related activities (www.banking-on-green.com). Most social banks, in contrast, were and still are reluctant to do so, also based on the argument that their sustainability report simply was their annual report, or their published list of funded projects. However, whilst there is some logic to this argument, it might not be so obvious to the growing group of (potential) new customers, who might not differentiate between the actual sustainability of a bank that reports on it in a neat brochure and one that actually strives for sustainability in all of its activities – but is not so good at reporting it. Apart from this, today, many – primarily business journalists and analysts – simply see it as good practice for companies to publish such reports. Thus, social banks, if they do not want to raise any suspicions, will feel more and more pressured to publish such reports. They have to demonstrate their social impact to all stakeholders and not only to their longstanding core clients who often already know their bank intimately.

However, such reporting could also present an issue for the social banks not only because it is comparatively expensive for small organizations but also because it, in the eye of the superficial observer, could make organizations appear comparable that are inherently not comparable, because one group exclusively engages in sustainable activities whilst the other group is much more indiscriminate.[15]

Finally, and related to the previous aspect, even if social banks might now be willing to report more systematically about their activities and how they are different from those of conventional banks, they might not have sufficient data on their hands. As already discussed above (see pp. 152–155) social banks, for too long, hardly tried to systematically capture and analyse their (positive and negative) impacts. This was partly for the above-mentioned reasons, i.e. the fact that social banks were self-content and did not feel the need to elucidate even their positive impacts to anyone. But this was likely also because of the difficulties involved in capturing the non-monetary – e.g. social or environmental – impacts of their activities. Social banks' success criteria are multidimensional, including economic, social and environmental aspects. These aspects are much more difficult to determine than are profits or losses and they are also much more difficult to communicate. Thus, there is a need to develop indicators that measure the social impact of social banks in a valid, reliable, objective, comparable and transparent way.

New recruitment and training

Another threat we see for social banks these days concerns the need for new recruitment and training as a result of the rapid, externally induced growth (in this context one should also refer to Chapter 4 in this volume).

To begin with, the employees are certainly key assets of social banks. If they existed only on paper, mission statements, values, operating principles and any alleged expertise and networks, could easily be copied by competitors. However, the fact that they are embedded in the organizational culture and ultimately in the employees of social banks is what makes them so difficult to replicate, and what provides the competitive edge of social banks.

As outlined before, social banks are essentially boutiques that – not only but also – serve a select clientele with select products, based on particular values and operating principles not found in other banks. This requires a rather special breed of employees with a unique blend of capabilities. They need not only a thorough grounding in the underlying motives and values of their own organization but also an in-depth understanding of their clients' sectors, problems and requirements. This also calls for an aptitude on the part of the social bankers to base decisions (e.g. on loans or investments) on a much larger and broader set of criteria than would be requested from their conventional peers. Moreover, they should be able to critically reflect upon and constructively and creatively develop further their own and their clients' practices in light of new insights to find new solutions to the ever-changing demands for sustainable development.

As such it is not too surprising that employees, on all levels of social banks, have a diversity of backgrounds. Some of their founders were not bankers but lawyers or even musicians. Many employees have the experience of two or more different studies or professions. Add to this the fact that many employees also have hands-on experience in the sectors social banks specialize in, and it becomes clear why they are neither easy to find nor easy to replace. Clearly all this helps social banks to stay in tune with new developments and to avoid herding and group-think that is so characteristic for many conventional banks. However, it should go without saying that the kind of growth most social banks have experienced over the past few years has stretched their human resources to the limit. As most of us, also none of the social banks were really prepared in terms of human resources and infrastructure for the pace and ferocity of the latest crisis on the financial markets. Social banks have been small for most of their history and now suddenly found themselves facing an unexpected stream of new customers and funds. These developments could not be planned for and adjusting to them takes time, during which the existing employees have to work hard. This not only leads to physical exhaustion, but increasingly also to discontentment and stress on an individual level. Too much work can destroy the best atmosphere amongst the most motivated employees. And this arguably presents an even greater problem in case of organizations that attract new staff because they seem to be different from the conventional organizations, more social and more humane. As a result, some social banks now suffer from staff turnover rates that are not so different from those of similarly sized conventional banks. This brain drain could put a strain on the (tacit) knowledge resources of social banks, and ultimately on their competitiveness.

Thus, to adjust to the new opportunities and stay competitive, a key task for the fast-growing social banks is recruitment of new staff. Triodos, for instance, reported a remarkable 20 per cent increase in the number of employees from 2007 to 2008. This comprises of three main groups – lower level employees that help to deal with the core banking services such as dealing with customer requests and opening accounts, more specialized employees such as asset or loan managers, and top level executives who help to build or create the missing infrastructure and departments. Given the above-mentioned peculiar requirements for social bankers, finding, attracting and integrating large numbers of suitable new staff is not an easy task. Social banks need boutique employees, not only but particularly from the mid ranks upwards: value-driven people with up-to-date banking knowledge, with solid social skills and competences and with profound knowledge of the sectors of interest to the bank. Those employees are not as easy to find as are employees of conventional banks.

A quote by Kristoffer Lüthi from Ekobanken provides support for this assertion:

> [The] challenge is to find co-workers with the relevant combination of financial skills and a deep understanding of the underlying values of creating a more ecological, social and cultural society, that lies behind our business. Every person working for Ekobanken needs, in some way or another, to be an ambassador for our ideas.
>
> (Lüthi 2010: 126)

The most obvious source for such specialists would be other social banks. But with normally only one or very few social banks per country, even if it wanted to, a social bank searching for new employees could not simply snatch them from a peer, as would a conventional bank.

At the same time, it must also be kept in mind that the recent events in the financial markets were so extreme that, even if the future of social banks might be promising in the mid to long run, it is quite difficult to predict what the developments will bring in the short run. (How long) will the stream of new deposits last? (When) will the conventional banks get back on track, and (to what extent) will they try to enter social banking? The answers to these questions have an impact on many aspects of social banks' activities, but certainly also on their recruitment policies, which – different from many conventional banks – are not based on a 'hire and fire' mentality. Once they recruit people, they strive to make them an integral and lasting part of the organization. All this makes the recruitment an intricate business for social banks.

Hand-in-hand with the recruitment of the new employees goes the need for training of new and old employees. The rapid growth does not allow for much training on the job but necessitates social banks to mostly hire new outside staff that often have been trained and socialized in conventional banks, with different values and without the relevant experience in the focus sectors of social banks. As such, they usually need extra training to engage with the respective aspects. Yet, with the growth of the organization, also the existing employees need to further their technical and sector related skills. And all employees need to engage with the core of social banking, i.e. the organizational values and how they relate to both the individual values and the (possibly changing values in the) organizational environment. Unfortunately, however, social banking is not taught yet in universities and banking academies.

Therefore, summarizing the above, a key threat for social banks is to recruit new staff and to train new and old staff in order to keep their competitive edge over conventional peers.

Looking at social banks' likely *strengths* with respect to the 'new recruitment and training', it is fair to say that most social banks certainly do not suffer from a scarcity of applications from those enthusiastic to work for them. Most social bankers (to be) do not target this sector by chance but because they specifically want to work for an organization with values and missions with which they can identify. This general trend is spurred by the changing attitudes and consciousness in the public towards sustainable lifestyles.

But clearly, also in this context, a key strength of social banks these days is the weakness of the conventional banking sector. Some conventional bankers switched sides to a social bank because they wanted to practice their private values also professionally. The general changes in the public attitude towards sustainability have been accelerated by the financial crisis, and particularly amongst bankers, who now increasingly open up to the idea of working for a social bank and ultimately are ready to leave their relatively secure and well-paid jobs.

Furthermore, because of their strong relationships with their stakeholders, and particularly with their core-sector customers, social banks have a good chance to identify and attract new recruits from this source. Whilst small, this recruitment market is not irrelevant for social banks as they rely heavily on expertise on the sectors they focus on. The specialists in social banks are primarily loan assessment officers with a long experience in the sectors the social banks do business with. But, in addition, social banks obviously also need many other experts, e.g. in the areas of asset management, controlling, etc., as do all banks. Add to it that social banks are now paying at least average rates, often aided by attractive features such as flexible working times, sabbaticals and extra pay for new parents, it is clear why it now is attractive for some to be(come) a social banker.

Turning now briefly to the second challenge in this context, training, one could argue that social banks have a strength in as far as they are aware of the need for and experienced in the provision of tailor made in-house seminars. Having never enjoyed the availability of suitable courses in universities or banking academies, social banks have a tradition of organizing their own training, with the joint founding of the Institute for Social Banking being the most visible outcome so far.

With respect to *weaknesses* of social banks in the context of recruitment and training it should not be left unmentioned that, because social banks are operating on low profit margins, an often-heard issue in the context of recruitment concerns the allegedly low remuneration of social bankers that would keep qualified people from applying to them. It is true that social banks don't pay lavishly and usually also don't offer bonus schemes. Many social banks have fixed ratios for the payment of the lowest to the highest ranked employees (the Alternative Bank Switzerland, for instance, has a fixed maximum ratio of 1:5 for the payments of the lowest to the highest ranks). But, at least for the lower and mid ranks, social banks usually pay similar to or even better than conventional cooperative and savings banks. So, if the salary issue comes into play at all, it does so mainly at the management level. This is because social banks need new conventional (banking) expertise in functional areas such as marketing or controlling to support and manage their growth.

Still financial aspects undoubtedly play a role as a weakness of social banks in terms of recruitment and training. Staff has to be hired and trained now to transform the new deposits into loans and investments that generate profits in the future. Given their relatively low profitability, social banks are certainly restricted in terms of hiring and, equally important (see pp. 145–146), training new staff to the extent they might wish to. Training means time and money, and both are in short supply in social banks, today at least as much as before the crisis.

Another weakness of social banks in this context arguably is their limited size and visibility. It is fair to assume that they still do not appear on the radar screens of many possible job-shifters, and some of those that come across them might consider them too risky an organization to work for just because of their limited size. In the same vein, also their limited physical size could be seen as a weakness. Hiring new staff necessitates additional, usually expensive, office space. GLS Bank, for instance, is currently contemplating its second major extension in just six years. This consumes valuable resources and puts further pressure on their profitability and possibly also on their equity capital, with consequences for their ability to lend out the excess funds they are currently sitting on.

Turning now to the other issue that comes with new recruitment, training, this currently can be seen as an important weakness of social banks. Social banks today usually hire either qualified bankers from conventional banks, who have been socialized in a very different environment and usually do not have the relevant sector knowledge (or, but more rarely these days, sector specialists who might not have a solid banking expertise). Clearly, to become an integrated part of the social bank and to help realize their mission, this new group of recruits needs training in various aspects of social banking, including its ideals, products, services and stakeholders.

Yet, whilst traditional banking can be learned at academies or universities, social banking is only just beginning to appear as a subject at universities and academies, and it will be a while before the first graduates come to the market. Sector-specific knowledge, furthermore, has to be acquired mostly on the job. As long as social banks grew slowly, this was not too much of a problem. The banks could recruit new staff from their networks of people with relevant sector experience and shared values, and, if necessary, send them to get the missing banking know-how at a conventional banking academy. Moreover, there was also sufficient time for new staff to be trained in-house by older colleagues who could pass on their often tacit knowledge over time. But all this changed dramatically with the recent developments. There now is much less time to train these people informally in-house. Furthermore, it seems fair to say, exclusive in-house training, particularly when the 'house' is small, is of less value for broadening the staff's horizon, and for making it aware of what is happening 'outside'. Not least because social banks consider themselves part of a larger movement of activists for sustainable development, it would seem there is scope to learn from and with each other through regular exchanges not only on the level of the top executives (as already happens in the context of associations such as INAISE, FEBEA or

GABV) but also on the level of the ordinary staff, which faces the chores of the day-to-day operational business.

In this context, it could be referred to a tradition by European social banks to organize joint international seminars, which ultimately resulted in the founding of the Institute for Social Banking, ISB (www.social-banking.org), which is co-sponsored by the leading European social banks. The ISB has made considerable progress with a view to further developing training offers for its founding members. However, the ISB is still small and, as of now, resource constraints prevent it from realizing its full potential in this context. Hence, what is missing is a thorough and systematic formal training for social bankers, in-house and externally.[16]

Related to this is the issue of research, again. Training without research (defined, for instance, as a systematic analysis of what is happening in practice) feeding into it, is likely to be unfocused at least to some extent. With social banking not having yet entered the realm of academia in general – and of research in particular – what is there to be taught, and who decides? What makes a good social banker and, equally important, what makes a good social bank – and what are its actual impacts? So far, no textbooks exist on social banking, and no bespoke or unified theory of social banking. Part of the reason certainly lies in the different origins of social banks. Several are based on the philosophy of Rudolf Steiner, but others have their roots in the environmental or civic society movement. Each of these origins brings with it its own perspectives, ideas and norms. And even if one is to accept that social banks have the joint objective of fostering sustainable development at their core, it is no secret that there is no theory of sustainability or sustainable development, and, right or wrong, ever more consider sustainable development just an empty phrase without a coherent theoretical base. In the same vein, one could argue social banking is normative but atheoretical. But a theory of social banking could be beneficial not just for the sake of it, but for providing a basis for strategic orientation and for identifying a common ground and reference for measuring and communicating social banks' impact and thus differentiating them more clearly from the look-alikes that just jump the bandwagon, which might lead them out of the crisis, in which theories such as shareholder profit maximization and market fundamentalism had led them.

New structures and procedures

As a final threat for social banks, in the following we would like to briefly highlight the internal and external demand for 'new structures and procedures'.

For most of their history social banks were small. Their hierarchies were mostly flat. Their employees knew each other – and many of their customers – personally and often even privately. Not all employees had fixed job profiles and moving positions within the organization was no rare event. As a positive consequence, at least until recently, most employees had a good overview of what was going on in the organization, and there was little need for formal structures and procedures. But when organizations grow, their structures and processes have to be adjusted. This is also true for social banks. Thus, given the growth many social banks are currently going through, particularly after the recent financial crisis, the challenges lying ahead of them are plenty.

With the growth, and with banking regulations tightening, there comes an increasing need for formalization, specialization, departmentalization and separation of certain functions. Employees in different departments hardly know each other anymore, and with the administration and back office growing, proportionally less staff has direct contact with the bank's clients. With many new employees arriving each month, it is increasingly difficult to train them all on the job, not to mention in different departments (see also Chapter 4 in this volume). There also has to be a clear allocation of responsibilities and accountability. This comprises of documented job descriptions and operating procedures. More generally, to remain manageable and controllable, bigger organizations need controlling and risk management systems. Because banks deal with other peoples' money, their systems have to be particularly well refined and documented. They have to install various measures and systems to guarantee confidentiality, amongst others, of their clients' data and banking activities. This particularly affects their IT and payment systems. Adding to this, the social banks' new customers demand a broader range of products and services, such as brokerage, safekeeping of securities and asset management. Each of these products comes with special legal and organizational requirements (see for instance the Basel II requirements) (N.N. 2005). This assertion also finds support by Lüthi (2010) from Swedish Ekobanken:

> We have many challenges, however. For instance, getting access to banking infrastructure is very difficult for a small bank in Sweden. All the major systems are practically owned by the largest banks. It is costly for a small bank to pay the required fee for accessing this infrastructure. To solve this we started a co-operation with one of the larger players, which allows our corporate clients access to the major systems and services. But our current size prevents us from offering e-banking and credit card to our private clients. For them, we remain a bank for savings and loans rather than for transactions and a current account. But our goal is to grow and create the necessary resources and infrastructure to provide all our clients with more services.
>
> (Lüthi 2010: 125)

Finally, it must be kept in mind that whilst the recent financial crisis is likely to bring about stricter regulation, the new requirements are still hazy. As of now, it remains unclear whether the new regulation will be of the one-size-fits-all type (which is not unlikely) or whether it will differentiate between banks with differing business risk models (which would make more sense). All this makes it quite challenging for social banks to design the most appropriate structures and procedures. Again, Kristoffer Lüthi (2010) provides support for this assertion: 'The costs of carrying through the regulations together with the increasing demands on infrastructure is the biggest threat to Social Banks.'

Let us come to the *strengths* of social banks with respect to 'new structures and procedures'. To state the obvious, social banks are banks, with at least the same experience in (core) banking activities and the respective requirements as all other banks (of their size). Furthermore, whilst some of the above-mentioned formal structures and procedures might be new to the social banks (e.g. with a view to brokerage or asset management), they are not to the banking industry as such. Therefore, social banks can and do buy into the relevant expertise with the many new employees they recruit from conventional banks.

In addition, it seems fair to argue, social banks with their strong value-orientation and value-driven operating principles that guide much of their internal and external activities, have a strong in-built (self-) regulatory corrective element. What might be seen as a trivial offence (if not legally sanctioned) in most ordinary companies, might be seen very differently in a value-based organization such as a social bank. Related to this, one of the key strengths of social banks certainly lies with their enthusiastic and engaged employees, many, if not most, of which identify themselves strongly with the (mission of) their banks. This could translate in social banks finding it less restrictive to establish formal structures and procedures, and also in them having to rely less on formal structures and procedures where not legally required.

Turning now to the weaknesses of social banks with respect to the "new structures and procedures" an important factor certainly was that their growth was so rapid that they had little time – and even less spare resources to prepare and adjust to the new requirements. Whilst many of their conventional peers had decades, many experts and substantial funds at their hands to develop into full fledged banks offering the complete range of banking services, social banks had neither. Moreover, the new structures and procedures are only one of the many new demands and challenges social banks face in these fast-paced times, when they have to re-design so many of their practices.

Another weakness of social banks in this context could result from the non-conformist attitude of some of their employees, who might be described as 'conservative alternatives'. To them, formal structures and procedures in some way will run counter to the corporate culture in small value-driven organizations, which consider it one of their core strengths to be unconventional and different from the conventional organization. Thus, the challenge is to develop necessary structures in such a way that both the management and the employees of social banks accept them.

Finally, as outlined above, social banks mostly do not offer the full range of possible banking products and services, such as brokerage or asset management, which are now being increasingly demanded by and offered to new customers. Whilst this was not a weakness initially – because there simply was not the necessity to develop the corresponding structures and procedures that are now legally required – social banks have to catch up.

Below, we first summarize our above 'analysis' to conclude with what it does tell us for the current situation and possible outlook for social banking.

Summary, conclusion and outlook

To begin with, based on what we have outlined earlier in this chapter, to us there is no doubt that the need for social banking today is bigger than ever before. As our brief overview of the economic, social and environmental developments and trends at the beginning of this chapter suggests, we do need banks that are working not just for the maximization of their shareholders' wealth but for 'people, planet and prosperity of all their stakeholders'. Social banks have been set up to do just this. And they have shown that a different approach towards banking and money can be realized in an economically viable way.

At the same time, it is also clear, social banks are still too small and too few. Social banking still takes place in a 'niche'. It doesn't matter how good and sensible the activities of social banks are, only a few people will have ever heard about them. And all their inspiring achievements are dwarfed by the much less inspiring activities of many other parties, including conventional banks.

But there is hope. The niche for social banks is growing bigger, and also experts from the conventional banking sector feel that social banks could reasonably expect to increase their outreach from currently less than 1 per cent to 10 or 15 per cent in the near future (and this only refers to the North; chances are that in the South the outreach of social banks is going to be much higher). Given the long-running trends towards more sustainable lifestyles and given the disastrous impacts of the most recent financial crisis not only on public wellbeing but also on public trust in conventional banks, this appears indeed to be not overly optimistic.

Social banks today are at the crossroads where a new avenue for the realization of their missions on a large scale is opening up rather unexpectedly. Yet, in this way, there are not only opportunities waiting for social banks, but also some noteworthy threats, or challenges.

Opportunities and threats

There are a number of good *opportunities* on the horizon for social banks; amongst them are the 'new public consciousness', 'new funds under management', demand for 'new banking products and services' and 'new technologies and media'.

Whilst we feel that all of these opportunities are important, to us, the first one, '*new public consciousness*', is by far the most important. Social banks are small, and despite their substantial growth are likely to remain relatively small in the foreseeable future. However, thanks to the new public consciousness, they now have an extraordinary opportunity to increase their outreach and indirect impact way beyond what their actual size would suggest. Arguably for the first (and possibly also for the last) time they now find themselves being listened to by a wide audience. They can demonstrate that a different way of banking and finance is possible, one that makes not only economic sense but also social and environmental sense. This surely will convince ever more customers to vote with their wallets (and accounts), which ultimately might also result in other, conventional, banks changing their direction, towards a more responsible and sustainable behaviour. True enough, the memories of the recent financial crisis might fade. But even then we wouldn't expect the public consciousness to reverse completely. Instead we see the current developments similarly to what could be observed over the past three decades in the market for organic food that was also spurred by some (environmental and food) scandals but now is firmly established and steadily growing. So, it might have taken a long time, but once rolling this stone will be difficult to halt. If a sufficiently large part of the public shows interest in those alternative but sensible ideas, ever more organizations will want to participate and thus co-create this new market. Thus, if social banks now manage to grab this opportunity, they can make a huge step forward in realizing the core of their missions, i.e. contributing to more sustainable development in banking and finance.

From this perspective, the new '*funds under management*' of social banks are clearly important, too. They provide social banks with an opportunity to increase their direct impact by funding more and bigger projects they deem worthy. But those new funds of social banks are still negligible compared to the funds managed by today's conventional banks. Without wanting to sound derogative here, one could see those funds almost as 'play money' – i.e. money social banks can use to 'experiment' with (obviously in a way that is economically viable) in order to find and realize – exemplary – solutions to the many problems we face. Where appropriate, this might and should also include a stronger focus on gift money.

In this context, to us, the demand for '*new products and services*' by small and large projects and initiatives is at least equally important. Social banks have a long history – and corresponding experience – in innovating financial products and services to foster sustainable development in an economically viable way. This will also help them to reach out to new and more profitable customers – such as the LOHAS – that have a need for banking products more advanced than the core products currently offered by social banks. The examples provided by social banks, as 'innovation hubs', then might be picked up by other banks and brought to scale. This is a model tested already for a long time in other industries such as the pharmaceuticals where small but innovative biotech 'boutiques' essentially are responsible for the innovations that are then taken up by the big pharmaceutical companies that enjoy economies of scale and have all the relevant experience in marketing and distribution.

The '*new technologies and media*', finally, should also help to 'spread the word' of social banking to an extent that would have been unthinkable until recently because of the limited size of social banks. At the same time, these new technologies and media also support those activists that check and report upon the mis-/deeds of conventional banks, making it increasingly difficult for the latter to simply 'green-wash' their public images. Add to this the fact that the new technologies and media also begin to challenge the intermediation function of banks, and particularly of those that don't add much value to transactions, it is clear that they offer a non-negligible opportunity for social banks to realize their own missions on a broader scale.

This not withstanding, there is also a set of *threats*, or challenges, waiting for social banks. In this context, we feel, 'new value systems', 'new competition', the demand for 'new recruitment and training', and the need for 'new structures and procedures' are important ones.

Again, we would suggest that the first of these challenges, which results from the '*new value systems*', is the most critical one. Together with the expertise and networks in focus sectors of their co-workers, the values and value-based operating principles of social banks are their main differentiating factors. Most value-driven organizations face the challenge to stay true to their values in light of organizational development and in light of changes in the organizational environment. This is not different for social banks, but their recent growth that followed the dramatic events in the financial markets was more extreme than what most other value-driven organizations ever experience. In this situation, thoroughly engaging with their values also seems important for social banks because they are, as of now, based on a normative worldview rather than a grounded theory and fundamental research, which could help explain and examine how these values are best being translated into an actual social and environmental impact.

As far as the threat through '*new competition*' is concerned, we feel that there cannot be enough banks and financial institutions working in a socially and environmentally responsible manner. The problem, however, is that many of those old and new conventional banks that now jump on the bandwagon of sustainable banking are likely to do so mainly for motives other than the greater common good. Instead, they strive to regain some of the public goodwill and trust lost during the crisis and to profit from the increasing segment of conscious customers. But at the same time they continue with much of the conventional and unsustainable business they were engaged in before the crisis, causing substantial 'collateral damage'. As such it seems fair to talk about 'green-washing' rather than 'going green' in many cases. Yet, this could obviously have negative consequences for social banks, which might find it increasingly difficult to differentiate themselves from their conventional peers that benefit from deeper pockets for PR and marketing.

Another issue we have identified as a threat (better: 'challenge') for social banks comes with the demand for new '*recruitment and training*' as a result of the sudden and rapid growth. This is an important issue because, besides their values, their employees are the other key assets of social banks as they are where the values and expertise of social banks are embedded. However, social bankers are a 'special breed' that does not graduate from universities or banking academies. Instead, most social bankers today had to learn their trade informally on the job – either as sector specialists that moved into banking or as bankers that acquired the relevant sector expertise over time. Yet, today, social banks have to hire a lot of new staff that has been trained and socialized in conventional banks, unaccustomed with either the values or the focus sectors of social banks. Hence the new recruits have to be (re-)trained to fit into their new organizations. But, because of the workload and the time constraints these days, this hardly can occur on the job anymore. What is needed instead are new formal training courses that have yet to be developed alongside with the training materials since there is no textbook available yet on social banking (although with the foundation of the Institute for Social Banking in 2006, a first promising step has been taken in this direction).

Finally, another threat or challenge for social banks lies in the need for '*new structures and procedures*'. This results from both the rapid growth of social banks that necessitates having more formalization and departmentalization and the regulatory requirements that are already strict for banks and are likely to become even stricter in the aftermath of the financial crisis. Implementing new formal and functioning structures and procedures is a challenge for most organizations, but particularly so for social banks that are comparatively restricted in terms of time, people and cash. Furthermore, the formalization of internal and external relationships might run counter to the attitude and style of what is usually a non-conformist organization.

In the following we briefly summarize our discussion on the strength and weaknesses of social banks dealt in the main section of this chapter.

Strengths and weaknesses

Social banks, over the past four decades, have developed a number of key strengths that should help them to make good use of the above-mentioned opportunities and that could also help them to appropriately deal with the simultaneous challenges. However, to fulfil their potential and to increase their outreach and impact, they also will have to work on some indisputable weaknesses of theirs.

In this context, one of our objectives in the analysis above was to find out about the key strengths and weaknesses of social banks *in light of* the external opportunities and challenges, as a first step to make some more grounded predictions about the possible future of social banks.

For this purpose, in our discussions above, we tried to identify and describe what we felt were important strengths and weaknesses for each individual opportunity and threat respectively.

But obviously, different bank(er)s might (perceive to) have different strengths and weaknesses. Thus, even if we believe we have identified some important strengths and weaknesses in our analysis above, there are too many of them – and in too many shades – to be dealt with in detail here, and we do not claim to have covered the full spectrum of possibly relevant strengths and weaknesses even remotely.

At the same time, it is clear that the same (or a similar) strength or weakness obviously can be of relevance in light of several opportunities or threats respectively. This is also evident in the fact that, in the above main section of our analysis, the same or similar weaknesses and strengths of social banks were identified in the context of different opportunities and threats.

To allow for at least some more general conclusions, Table 7.2 therefore provides an overview of the above discussions, allocating the identified strengths and weaknesses to the respective opportunities and threats.

As can be seen in Table 7.2, we condense the strengths and weaknesses discussed in our analysis above into six – very broad – groups each, which are made up of several (sub-) aspects that we have described in our analysis above.

As (groups of) '*strengths*' of social banks we have identified their 'reputation', their 'competitors' weaknesses', their 'expertise in selected sectors' alongside their 'expertise in basic banking' and their 'dedicated set of stakeholders'.

As (groups of) '*weaknesses*' of social banks we have identified their 'limited size', their 'conservatism' with view to their communication, their 'limited theory and basic research', their 'limited in-/formal training', their 'limited financial means' and their 'limited range of activities'.

Clearly, forming such groups means some loss of detail. Therefore, for a better understanding of the respective strengths and weaknesses, the interested reader might want to refer back to the above sections on the individual opportunities and threats.

At the same time, we also want to identify whether there are any '*key*' *strengths* and *weaknesses*, respectively, that can be worked on by the social banks to help realize their mission and potential. For this purpose, in Table 7.2, we use *stars* ('*') to indicate what we feel are the *three most important strengths* and *weaknesses*, respectively, of social banks identified in our discussion above in light of a particular opportunity or threat. For reasons of simplicity and accessibility, in our subsequent discussion, we will primarily focus on these. However, in the text above, we have also discussed some additional strengths and weaknesses, as indicated by a plus sign in brackets ('+') in Table 7.2.

Finally, to give our subsequent discussion some direction, in Table 7.2, we sort the respective strengths and weaknesses not in order of appearance in the text but in descending order according to the overall number of stars ('indicative score') we have allocated to them. This thus presents *our subjective evaluation* of the relative importance of the discussed key strengths and weaknesses of social banks.

But, to state it very clearly, this is *not meant to be an objective or even scientific analysis* (if anything it is a reflection of our own text analysis from hindsight). We feel that Table 7.2 represents a good enough summary of *our* perspective on the current situation of social banks. But we are well aware that there will be many more perspectives, which might or might not come to similar conclusions. It goes without mentioning that individual banker/s will perceive themselves to have differing strengths and weaknesses, and possibly also face differing opportunities and threats. However, they might still find Table 7.2 (or a similar table for that matter) useful to identify their very own strengths and weaknesses in light of their particular opportunities and threats.

Our main objective here is to offer some basis and structure for future discussion amongst practitioners and academics. We hope this will serve to make the sector more self-aware and thus even more successful.

Table 7.2 Overview of internal key strengths and weaknesses in light of the external opportunities and threats of social banks

Internal	*External*								*Indicative 'score'*
	Opportunities				*Threats*				
	New …				*New …*				
	Public consciousness	*Funds under management*	*Products and services*	*Technologies and media*	*Value systems*	*Competition*	*Recruitment and training*	*Structures and procedures*	
Strengths									
(Reputation for) deeply rooted values and corresponding operating principles	*	*		*	*	*	*	*	7
Competitors' weaknesses (e.g. in terms of reputation and actual business practices)	*			(+)	*	*	*		4
Expertise and networks in selected sectors fostering sustainable development		*	*			*	*		4
Dedicated and engaged stakeholders (e.g. employees, clients, owners and peers)		*		*	*	(+)		*	4
Expertise in core banking products and services (e.g. deposits and loans)	*		*	*				*	4
Ability to innovate products and services to foster sustainable development			*			(+)			1

Weaknesses									
Limited size in terms of human resources, time and visibility	*	*	*	*	*	*	*	*	8
Limited financial means (e.g. low equity and profitability, relatively high costs)	(+)	*	*			*	*		4
'Conservatism' (i.e. 'normative rigidity' with view to values and communication)	*			*	*	(+)		*	4
Limited theory and basic research (e.g. on 'value-added'/'impact')	*		*	*	(+)	*	(+)		4
Limited range of activities (in terms of products, services and sectors)		*	(+)					*	2
Limited in-/formal 'training' on the fundamentals of social banking			(+)		*		*		2

In the following, we briefly summarize key observations from Table 7.2, highlighting only some strengths and weaknesses, which we feel are particularly important at least in the context of the opportunities and threats identified in our analysis.

Starting with the key *strengths*, as one would expect for value-driven organizations, we find '*reputation* for deeply rooted values and corresponding operating principles' to be a particular important asset of social banks that not only should help them to make use of identified opportunities but also to overcome the identified threats.

This key strength of social banks is followed by a number of further strengths of arguably lesser but still noteworthy 'importance' in light of the opportunities and threats identified by us. These are '*competitors' weaknesses*', '*expertise and networks in selected sectors*', '*dedicated and engaged stakeholders*' and '*expertise in core banking products and services*'.

Of those, we would like to highlight the first, '*competitors' weaknesses*'. This is also the factor in favour of social banking that scored highest in the ZEW (2010) study mentioned further above (see pp. 149–150). We feel this is a rather critical issue because it lies vastly outside the influence of social banks.[17]

At the same time, it should also be mentioned that slightly surprising to us was the result of our 'hindsight-analysis' that the various '*dedicated stakeholder*' appeared as an important strength across several opportunities and threats. We did not have this item on our radar when starting with our above discussion. Then again, this is not a real surprise in the context of organizations that consider themselves stake- rather than shareholder driven.

Of somewhat less relevance in our analysis appears the social banks' '*ability to innovate*'. Yet this should not be taken as a sign that this is an irrelevant strength. It can well be argued that, were it not for their continuous attempts to innovate banking and finance products and services, social banks would not exist. As such, the relatively low indicative scoring of this aspect might reflect the fact that other strengths of social banks are currently indeed more significant and/or point towards a weakness in our deliberations and analytical approach.

Turning now to the *weaknesses* of social banks, as was to be expected for small organizations, the overall '*small size*' of social banks in our analysis turned up as a key weakness across all identified opportunities and threats. It is important to emphasize here that, in our categorization, this 'small size' does rather refer to the 'physical size' and visibility of social banks rather than to the size of their balance sheet – which is part of what we categorized under '*limited financial means*'. The latter obviously is an important weakness of social banks in its own right, and as such plays a role at least in half of the opportunities and threats analysed by us. If one were to combine these two groups of weaknesses (and this would have been justified given that the limited financial means of social banks obviously are one key reason for their limited size and non-financial resources), this would result in a group of key weaknesses arguably far more important than the other groups. Clearly this underlines the importance of growing not only their balance sheet but also their profitability for those social banks that want to grow their outreach and impact.

With respect to the weaknesses of social banks we would also like to highlight what we called their '*conservatism*'. This obviously is a double-edged sword since their 'conservative values' (one might also call them 'sustainable' values) is exactly what differentiates social banks from their conventional peers. As such, we want to emphasize here that we don't see the social banks' value-oriented conservatism as a weakness; quite the opposite. However, we feel how these values are communicated and are engaged with – externally and internally – shows scope for improvement.

In a similar vein, we are aware that the '*limited range of activities*' by social banks in terms of their products, services and sectors by itself cannot be seen as a weakness, because this focus and self-restriction provides the basis for many of their strengths, i.e. expertise and networks. Nevertheless, in light of some of the opportunities and threats, we felt it is fair to consider this particular feature a weakness that calls for a broadening of both the range of products and services and the range of sectors served by social banks.

Finally, it is worth emphasizing that, in our analysis, the lack of '*theory and basic research*' also shines through as a fairly important weakness of social banks on its own, and even more so with view to the simultaneous lack of formal and informal training. Clearly, if social banks, as they do, compete mainly based on differentiation, sooner or later they will have to prove (and report on) their actual impact more systematically than they used to. Their new stakeholders are likely to be more demanding in this respect than were their old dedicated stakeholders. Moreover, a more thorough engagement with their actual impact will also help them to refine their strategy, and possibly also their values, correspondingly. A more grounded theoretical foundation finally could help social banking to enter the academic field. This not only could help with the education of future social bankers, it could also help to develop new paradigms as an alternative to those old paradigms that have led us into the mess we are in.

Conclusion and outlook

To some, the above might sound obvious and/or over-simplified. Many practitioners also might find that the opportunities and threats and the strengths and weaknesses identified by us are not (or less) relevant in the context of their particular organization. Furthermore, we acknowledge, there is a considerable amount of vagueness in the approach sketched out above, not at least because of the broad categories in which we grouped the identified strengths and weaknesses. Thus, it is unlikely to be applicable by any social bank in the form presented here.

Still, we feel there is a value in the general concept and we would argue that social banks could benefit from this approach if they *consciously* and *systematically* identified their particular opportunities and threats and strengths and weaknesses, and then planned their strategy accordingly.

Referring back to the title of this chapter and to our conviction that more and bigger social banks are needed to support more and bigger projects fostering sustainable development, we feel indeed that 'social banking is at the crossroads': at least some of its organizations have the potential to grow into the league of conventional banks, to increase their outreach and impact. Others might – willingly or not – stay small and focus on serving a limited group of local clients.

Social banks today face unique opportunities to grow and increase both their indirect and direct impact. For this purpose, they can build upon a number of important strengths, of which we consider their strong value base and corresponding operating principles to be key. However, for their growth, social banks also face some noteworthy challenges, especially regarding their values, and they also have to work on a number of important weaknesses, including their limited size, visibility and their limited financial means. As such, there is no growth guarantee, neither for individual social banks nor for the overall social banking sector. This assertion is also reflected in a recent study by ZEW (2010) described further above.

Particularly noteworthy, both the ZEW survey and our own analysis find that the current weakness of conventional banks in terms of the trust they have lost during the financial crisis, currently manifests as a major strength of social banks. But the word to look out for in this context is 'current'. If the memory of the current financial crisis fades (and it will), conventional banks, which increasingly 'green(-wash)' their businesses, are likely to regain at least some of the trust they once enjoyed, and with it possibly also some of the customers that had changed sides (and, it is important to note, 'some' customers for conventional banks spells 'many' customers for social banks). Add to this the still unforeseeable changes in banking regulation in the aftermath of this crisis, which might or might not disproportionally affect smaller banks, including social banks, it is clear that the future of social banking is by no means certain, and to a good extent beyond their own control. Thus, if the social banks are too self-content, relying on their very own strengths and on the current weaknesses of conventional banks, and continue their business as usual, they might well survive, but in a niche not so much bigger than the one they used to live in before the crisis – and hope for the next financial crisis, which then is likely to come.

However, it seems plausible to argue that the better social banks perform, not only with respect to their financial profitability but also with respect to their social impact – and the better they measure and communicate this impact – the better are the chances that their voices will be heard – not only by (future) customers but also by the regulators. This could also translate into them growing out of their niche for good.

As mentioned at the outset of this chapter, we would like to see this happen in a more holistic system of an 'ecology of finance', comprising a variety of different organizations – some tiny, some large, some with a local and some with a global focus, some with a banking licence and some without, some dealing with money as we know it and some dealing with alternative currencies instead, some taking interest and some not, some specializing in gift money and some not – all competing and cooperating to find and realize the solutions to the pressing economic, social and ecological problems, which we all need to survive and develop as a community of human and other beings.

In such a system, we further envisage, banks would have much more to offer than just their core business of handling money. Specifically, to us, a key strength of banks that we failed to address explicitly in our analysis above lies in their role of intermediaries able to link and enable people – with or without money. Based on this, banks even might start to redefine and widen their business models to become 'bazaars', or 'ba*nk*zaars', for people to meet, discuss, and exchange and transform ideas rather than just money – to identify, develop and realize innovative solutions to the vital problems we face.

To many this vision might sound a bit too ambitious. However, as Wilhelm-Ernst Barkhoff (1916–94), co-founder of the GLS Bank once pointed out:

> We can only overcome the fear of a future we are scared of with images of a future we aspire to.
>
> [Die Angst vor einer Zukunft, die wir fürchten, können wir nur überwinden durch Bilder einer Zukunft, die wir wollen!]

References

Arup, K. (2010) 'Promoting transformation and sustainability: Merkur's aim', in: *Networking Social Finance*, Brussels: INAISE, 90–4.

Bateman, M. (2010) *Why Doesn't Microfinance Work? The Destructive Rise of Local Neoliberalism*, London: Zed Books.

Bendig, M., Habschick, M. and Evers, J. (2010) 'Der neue Kosmos – Social Banking', *Die Bank*, 8: 70–3

Bhole, B. and Ogden, S. (2009) 'Group lending and individual lending with strategic default', *Journal of Development Economics*, 91: 348–63.

Chapple, A., Walia, V. and Remer, S. (2007) *New Horizons: Creating Value, Enabling Livelihoods – Opportunities in Microfinance for the UK Financial Services Sector*, London: Forum for the Future.

Clark, A. (2009) 'Goldman Sachs breaks record with $16.7 billion bonus pot', *Guardian*, 15 October.

Counts, A. (2008) *Give us Credit*, Hoboken: John Wiley & Sons.

De Clerck, F. (2009) 'Ethical banking', in Zsolnai, L. (ed.) *Ethical Prospects – Economy, Society, and Environment*, Berlin, Heidelberg and New York: Springer, 209–27.

Descours, A., Donnedieu, R., Thiery, N. and Verjus, C. (2010) 'La Nef: a banking organization involved in ethical finance', in *Networking Social Finance*, Brussels: INAISE, 99–100.

Deutsche Bank (2009) *Gesellschaftliche Verantwortung – Bericht 2009*. Online, available at: www.db.com/csr/de/docs/CSR_GER_Gesamt_Doppelseiten.pdf (accessed 10 June 2010).

European Commission (2008) *Financial Services Provision and Prevention of Financial Exclusion*. Online, available at: ec.europa.eu/social/BlobServlet?docId=760&langId=en (accessed 15 June 2010).

GABV (2010) Global Alliance for Banking on Values. Online, available at: www.gabv.org (accessed 11 November 2010).

The Global Reporting Initiative (2008) *Sustainability Reporting Guidelines & Financial Services Sector Supplement*, Amsterdam: The Global Reporting Initiative.

Hawken, P. (2004) *Socially Responsible Investing – How the SRI Industry has Failed to Respond to People who want to Invest with Conscience and what can be done to change it*, Sausalito: Natural Capital Institute.

Kohn, S. (2008) 'Exploiting poverty caused the financial crisis', *Huffington Post*. Online, available at: www.huffingtonpost.com/sally-kohn/exploiting-poverty-caused_b_127401.html (accessed 20 May 2010).

Labatt, S. and White, R.R. (2007) *Carbon Finance*, Hoboken: Wiley.

Lochmaier, L. (2010) *Die Bank sind wir – Chancen und Perspektiven von Social Banking*, Telepolis/Heise Verlag.

Luo, X., Li, H., Zhang, J. and Shim, J.P. (2010) 'Examining multi-dimensional trust and multi-faceted risk in initial acceptance of emerging technologies: an empirical study of mobile banking services', *Decision Support Systems*, 49: 222–34.

Lüthi, K. (2010) 'Opinion leader in Swedish social banking', in *Networking Social Finance*, Brussels: INAISE, 124–8.

Lützel, Ch. (2010) 'Creating opportunities for money to "make sense"', in *Networking Social Finance*, Brussels: INAISE, 83–6.

N.N. (2005) *International Convergence of Capital Measurement and Capital Standards ('Basel II')*, Basel, Switzerland, Basel Committee on Banking Supervision.

nef (New Economics Foundation) (2009) *The Ecology of Finance – an Alternative White Paper on Banking and Financial Sector Reform*, London: New Economics Foundation.

Niven, J. (2010) 'Triodos Bank – the power of three', in *Networking Social Finance*, Brussels: INAISE, 99–100.

Østervold, J. (2010) 'Cultura Bank: a serious business without the goal of maximum profit', in *Networking Social Finance*, Brussels: INAISE, 129–33.

Pachauri, R.K. and Reisinger, A. (2009) *Climate Change 2007: Synthesis Report*, Geneva: IPCC.

Pehrson, L. (2010) 'From financial crisis to sustainability – is that possible?', in *Networking Social Finance*, Brussels: INAISE, 50–63.

Porter, M.E. (2004) *Competitive Strategy*, New York: Free Press.

Saunders, A. (2000) *Financial Institutions Management: a Modern Perspective*, Boston: McGraw-Hill.

Scheire, C. and de Maertelaere, S. (2009) 'Banking to make a difference', Preliminary Research Report, Artevelde, Artevelde University College.

Social Investment Forum (2009) *2007 Report on Socially Responsible Investing Trends in the United States*, Washington, DC: Social Investment Forum.

Solo, T. (2005) *The High Cost of being Unbanked*, Newsletters, Washington, DC: The World Bank Group.

Weber, O. (2005) 'Sustainability benchmarking of European banks and financial service organizations', *Corporate Social Responsibility and Environmental Management*, 12: 73–87.

Weber, O., Fenchel, M. and Scholz, R.W. (2008) 'Empirical analysis of the integration of environmental risks into the credit risk management process of European banks', *Business Strategy and the Environment*, 17: 149–59.

World Bank (2009) 'The global economic crisis: assessing vulnerability with a poverty lens', A Policy Note. Online, available at: siteresources.worldbank.org/NEWS/Resources/WBGVulnerableCountriesBrief.pdf (accessed 5 June 2010).

World Economic Forum (2009) *The Future of the Global Financial System – A Near-Term Outlook and Long-Term Scenarios*, Geneva: World Economic Forum.

zeb – rolfes.schiereneck.associates (2009) 'Konsequenz der Finanzkrise: Kreditinstitute sollten wachsende Nachfrage nach "Social Banking" ernst nehmen'. Online, available at: www.zeb.de/de/presse/pressemitteilungen/pressedetail.html?detailid=98 (accessed 1 December 2009).

ZEW – Zentrum für Europäische Wirtschaftsforschung (2010) 'Sonderfrage: Social Banking', *ZEW Finanzmarktreport*, 18, 3. Online, available at: ftp://ftp.zew.de/pub/zew-docs/frep/072010.pdf (accessed 30 July 2010).

8 The future of social banking

Olaf Weber

Introduction

> Ethical finance represents a concrete alternative for the more responsible customers and an example for the rest of the banking system. At the same time, and despite its spectacular growth, it is a tiny fraction of the finance sector. It would be naive to believe that just scaling up this experience could, with its own propulsive push and its strength, bring a change in the whole system.
>
> (Baranes 2009)

In this final chapter we want to summarize and discuss important aspects to look at for the future of social banking. The discussion will be based on the earlier chapters of this book and on interviews with representatives of four European social banks and one representative of a European socially oriented foundation. Specifically, the interviewees were Eric Nussbaumer (President of the Board of Directors of Alternative Bank Switzerland (ABS), Edy Walker (Executive Board of ABS), David Niven (Head of Communication, Triodos Bank), Lars Pehrson (CEO Merkur Bank), Lars Hektoen (CEO Cultura Bank) and Julian Kühn (Executive Board of GLS Treuhand, Bochum, Germany).

We will structure our discussion broadly along the chapters of this book to discuss the following themes:

- the size of social banks;
- future challenges for social banking products and services;
- future strategies for future clients;
- the measurement of the impact of social banking;
- lowering transaction costs;
- future human resources management;
- communicating the interaction between social support and financial returns;
- the growth of social banks – increasing the impact without diluting ethics.

The size of social banks

Based on the analyses of this book, it must be confessed that social banks can only have a significant impact if they grow. The bigger they are, the more clients they are able to attract and the more projects they are able to finance. Thus, social banks – individually and/or as a group – have to grow in size to provide more influence on the society and sustainable development. Banks the size of small regional banks will not have the power to create the social change that they are striving for. This does not mean that every social bank has to grow rapidly, but rather that they have to cooperate whilst giving individual social banks the freedom to grow at their own pace. In Germany, for instance, the German Savings Banks are organized in a strong association (see www.dsgv.de) with a common strategy, common IT and common products. But each savings bank within the association has a certain amount of independence. However, with a total balance sheet of more than €1,000 billion, the savings banks in the association have a significant impact on the economy and the society (see www.dsgv.de). It is needless to say that social banks are far away from such a size, and the possible impact that comes with it. But nevertheless the savings banks example shows how local savings banks are able to create a powerful institution in the financial market. There are already some social banking associations that might be used to achieve similar results, such as the International Association of Investors in the Social Economy (INAISE), the Global Alliance for Banking on Values (GABV) or the European Federation of Ethical and Alternative Banks (FEBEA). But whatever the ultimate organizational form, in order to gain more power and social impact social banks should cooperate even more in order to appear as a strong group with common goals.

Future social banking products and services

We could show that there are two major challenges of social banking products and services. The first challenge is to guarantee that capital invested by social banks flows into projects, enterprises or other initiatives that really provide a positive impact on society, the environment and sustainable development. The second challenge is to design the financial mechanisms of products and services in a way that they meet the goals of the social banks – i.e. to make them sufficiently profitable for the social banks to be able to sustain and increase their outreach and impact. Thus, what would be suitable future social banking products and services? We feel two areas are particularly worthwhile looking at in this context, microfinance and socially responsible investment (SRI).

Microfinance products and services

Microfinance products are examples of products with a social impact that are not like the typical loans of social banks in Europe and the United States. We saw earlier in the book that these products can be highly profitable as well. They are not relying on the classical mechanisms of lending, collateral and credit history, but on mutual guarantees and the willingness of borrowers to be able to provide for their own costs of living. As the first microfinance institutions from the South like BRAC started their business in the United States and other social banks like the German GLS developed microfinance products and services for clients in industrialized countries the concept seems to have moved away from its original, development oriented purpose. In the meantime many microfinance institutions offer products and service for small and medium sized enterprises, especially start-ups, as well. Thus the microfinance website www.themix.org shows that loans in Eastern Europe and Central Asia increased much more than loans to borrowers in African, South American or Asian countries (see Figure 8.1). And here now is a higher amount of microcredit outstanding in Europe than in the other continents.

Additionally Figure 8.2 shows the average loan per borrower in 2007. It is obvious that the average loan in Eastern Europe and Central Asia is much higher than in developing countries in Africa and in Asia and even higher than in Latin America and the Caribbean and Middle East and North Africa.

Thus the figures show two tendencies, higher loans per borrower and an increase of loans in Eastern Europe and Central Asia. Microfinance seems to have left its niche and is being used as a means to foster economic development in European countries as well. There is one example in Germany where a microcredit fund was initiated. The capital of €100 million for this fund came from the European Social Fund and from the German Federal Ministry of Labour and Social Affairs. Loans are provided to micro-, small- and medium-sized enterprises. Thus the successful microfinance model seems to have penetrated Europe as well. Box 8.1 shows the principles of microfinance in Europe as presented by GLS (see http://mikrokreditfonds.gls.de/startseite/haeufige-fragen/was-ist-anders.html).

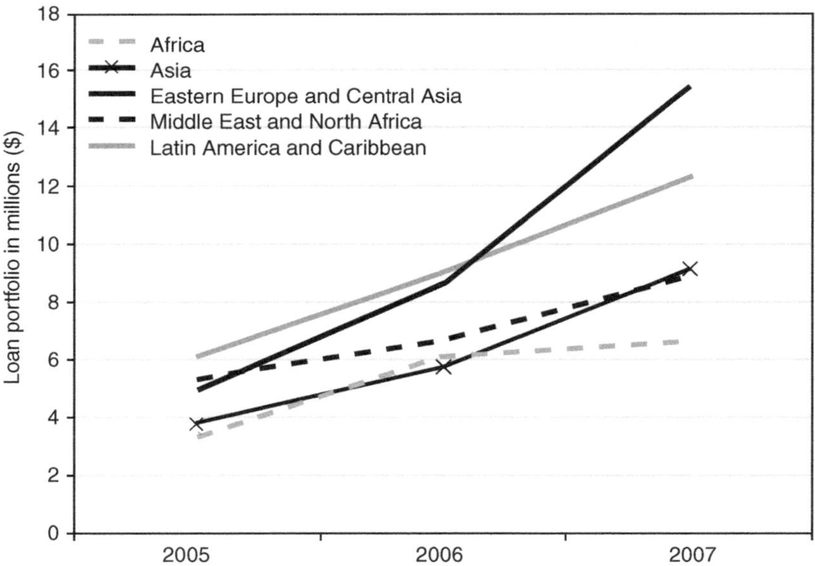

Figure 8.1 The increase of microfinance between 2005 and 2007 in different regions.

Box 8.1 Microcredit at the GLS Bank

What's the difference to standard bank loans?
(translated by the author)
The fascinating thing about successful microfinance institutes is:

- someone who has no access to banks gets a loan anyway;
- granting the loan is fast and easy;
- the default rates are small.

For more than 150 years cooperative credit associations developed these products. Furthermore they were developed by microfinance institutions in the 1980s for regions with lower economic development. They are broadly known to the public since Mohhammad Yunus was awarded with the Nobel Peace Prize.

Loans based on business plans are generally more complex and riskier than microcredit methods that are used by microfinance institutions in Germany:

- Stepwise loans: a small amount, i.e. €2,000, will definitely be repaid. This could be at very small rates. Thus, for a credit decision it is sufficient to rate the motivation to repay in a reliable way without the use of complex documents. If successful, a credit history could be developed up to €20,000.
- Monitoring: the borrowers of some microfinance institutes have to answer three questions per month about their current situation. The answers are analysed automatically. On this basis, before it comes to a default, the microfinance institute is able to intervene personally and in time.
- Social control: similar to a conventional bank in a village the microfinance institution is able to create a personal interaction with the borrowers and their environment. This could be provided by concentrating on a certain region, on a group of migrants or on members of an association.
- Savings: enterprises can become eligible for a loan by providing monthly savings. Loans could be granted that are three or even ten times higher than the amount of savings.

As the model is still in its infancy for the German market there is no data on the success rate yet. However, it seems to be the first time that financial methods used in developing countries have entered into the high-tech European financial market. Thus, in the future, microfinance, inside or outside of developed countries, will become a more important part of social banking going along with new principles of lending that are not based on collateral and credit history anymore.

Socially responsible investment

Socially responsible investment (SRI) presents another success story in the last decade. SRI related products and services like mutual funds are part of both conventional and social banking. Though they are still niche products, SRI

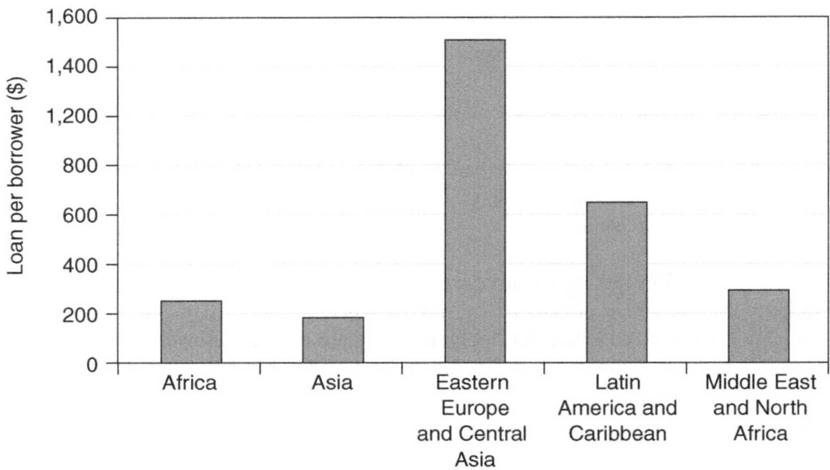

Figure 8.2 Microcredit loans sum per borrower in US$ in different regions.

products and services showed a tremendous growth in recent years. However, many of these products are based on a modified best-in-class concept (whereby shares of these companies are selected that are the leaders relative to their peers in the same sector) that sometimes is added by some exclusion criteria regarding certain products, organizations or sectors (for a more detailed description of SRI products, see Chapter 5 in this volume). Thus, Hawken found in an analysis of more than 600 SRI funds globally that over 90 per cent of the Fortune 500 companies are part of the portfolio of SRI funds. He found that '[t]he cumulative investment portfolio of the combined SRI mutual funds is virtually no different than the combined portfolio of conventional mutual funds' (2004: 16).

One issue is risk. As firms that have a positive impact on society or the environment are often smaller innovative firms or are not traded on conventional stock exchanges the financial risk connected to these companies is often higher than for equities of bigger companies. Furthermore, retail investment products are often only allowed to invest in equities that meet certain regulatory standards with respect to reporting financial issues. SMEs often do not meet these standards and thus cannot be integrated in retail mutual fund products. Thus offering investments in smaller companies with a social impact is related to higher financial risk to the investor. Therefore, in the future, social banks could develop SRI products that meet expectations with respect to social and environmental impact on the one side and financial risk and return on the other side. To reach this goal, further cooperation with regulatory bodies could prove useful as the successful example of Triodos implementing the fiscal green scheme in the Netherlands in 1995 shows (Jeucken 2001).

Future strategies targeting new clients

In this section we concentrate especially on products and services for clients who want to invest money with an impact. As Lars Hektoen, the CEO of the Norwegian Cultura Bank, states, his and many other social banks originated from different movements, like environmentalist, unionist or anthroposophist groups. But to widen the impact social banks are aiming for, the original customer basis has to be broadened (personal communication). Thus new groups of clients have to be addressed and consequently new types of products and services have to be developed as well. One example for a new product for a new group of especially younger clients is presented in Box 8.2.

> **Box 8.2 The ABS educational account**
>
> The Swiss Alternative Bank AG offers an account for students, apprentices or younger people in other kinds of educational training. In addition to the ethical values and operations of the bank these clients pay smaller fees for the services and get a higher interest for their account. The product was developed in cooperation with a student group. It intends to attract younger clients with whom a long-term relationship can be established.

Another group of potential clients of social banking are the so-called Lifestyles of Health and Sustainability (LOHAS). This group connects a sustainable lifestyle with consumerism (Cortese 2003) and accounts for a more than $300 million market. Without discussing the ethics of this group it becomes clear that it differs from the original type of clients of social banks that is based on environmentalism, the workers' movement or anthroposophy. Nevertheless LOHAS are clients that invest in socially responsible investment products and thus could be addressed by social banks as well. Products and services suitable for this group probably should connect wealth-management products and services with a social or environmental impact. This argument is also supported by Edy Walker, member of the executive board of the Alternative Bank Switzerland:

> Social banks should create products that give their clients the opportunity to have a real impact on the one side and make social banks less dependent on the credit business with interest rates that are highly dependent on the policy of the national banks and with strong competition from conventional competitors.
>
> (Edy Walker in a personal interview)

Thus, with the LOHAS, there is strong group of clients looking not for savings and depository accounts but for assets and investment products in securities with an impact. They want to directly support enterprises and projects with an impact on the environment, society or sustainable development. They are not looking for classical investments listed on the stock exchanges where the investment mainly goes to those that were the former owner of the securities. Thus what could social banks do to meet the needs of the clients that represent a new field of sustainable private equity? What could be a future strategy?

Let us begin by citing Eric Nussbaumer, the President of the Board of Directors of the Swiss Alternative Bank (personal interview):

> Social banks have to leave the path of being a cooperative savings and credit banking with certain ethical or moral principles. In the future this will not be enough to differentiate from other banks that offer sustainable or ethical products and services as well. Social banks have to define and measure their social impact. They have to think about their societal effect and the benefit that they offer for the society. One central task will be to define criteria and indicators to measure the impact of social banking. This task can be tackled if products and services are designed with respect to their social impact as well. The social impact is the main characteristic of a social banking product.
>
> (Eric Nussbaumer in a personal interview)

What does that mean for the future strategy of social banking? To start with, most of the social banks in Europe and the United States are essentially credit and savings banks with a certain ethical background that guides their savings and lending principles. Thus they follow the example of the credit unions and credit cooperatives presented in Chapter 2. A main part of the business is regional and is mainly based on using exclusion criteria. This means that a loan will be given if the borrower does not violate these exclusion criteria. Thus more or less conventional business is a part of social banks as well. However, at the current time of relatively low interest rates and conventional banks trying to attract typical clients of social banks the credit business becomes harder for social banks.

Furthermore, as stated above, there is more and more competition with respect to socially responsible investment (SRI). SRI products and services are successful on the market. But they are mainly developed and distributed by conventional banks and financial institutions. These institutions are able to develop and distribute mutual retail fund products – something often impossible for smaller social banks because of the expenses and the complexity involved in creating such products

Third, during the financial crisis many clients left the global conventional banks. But where did they go? Of course there was a rise in demand, especially for savings accounts and deposits, at social banks. However there was a comparable rise in clients at regional, but conventional, smaller banks as well. For instance, the amount of savings in the Swiss Raiffeisen Group increased by 10.6 per cent between 2007 and 2008 and by 6.4 per cent between 2008 and 2009 (see www.raiffeisen.ch). This means that many clients who were willing to change to banks that behave more ethically did not perceive the difference between conventional regional institutions and social banks, or the difference did not matter to them.

Thus what could be a strategy for social banks to differentiate their products and services from their conventional counterparts? As the above quote by Eric Nussbaumer suggests, social banks should identify, describe and differentiate themselves by their social impact. They should not be the banks that only avoid the ethical downside of the financial business but should reach a positive societal impact. Therefore they have to direct their strategy, their products and services and their communication to reach the highest societal impact possible. On this basis the business changes from responsible business to impact business, from mainly using exclusion criteria to positive criteria.

Examples of products and services of this nature are specialized impact funds that only invest in equities and other securities that have a societal or environmental impact. These products already exist in the case of microfinance. ResponsAbility (www.responsability.ch) or Sarona (www.saronafund.com) are already offering funds that invest in microfinance institutions or enterprises in developing countries (see Chapter 5 in this volume). These concepts could be used in regional investments in developed countries as well.

However, to be able to decide about products and services and the impact that can be made by these, there have to be indicators to measure the societal impact. Thus the following section concentrates on the measurement of the impact of social banking.

The measurement of the impact of social banking

What is the impact of social banking on society, the environment or sustainable development? As stakeholders start to put pressure on conventional banks to report and reduce their financed emissions (Barclay 2008), social banks should also report about their impact on society and the environment. They will have to demonstrate the societal and environmental impact connected with their business to be recognized as truly social banks in future as well. The measurement of the impacts should be transparent, valid, reliable and objective. The goal is to inform stakeholder like clients or investors about the impact of the products and services of a social bank on the society and the environment. The reported results should be comparable to other banks and financial institutions and comprise environmental and societal issues. They should inform the clients of a social bank about the blended return of their investment, the financial and the social impact.

In addition to measuring the impact of certain products or services the measurement of the relation between capital invested with a social or environmental impact compared to the total capital invested should be measured and be transparent. During the financial crisis the number of clients of social banks increased. However the growth mainly took place in the segment of these clients that want to place money with a bank in the form of savings accounts or deposits. During the same time the number of potential borrowers providing acceptable risks did not increase the same way as the savings and the deposits, the banks were not able to provide the loans in such a short time period or the banks could not provide that many loans because their own equity was too low. Thus a certain amount of capital of social banks is invested in government bonds and other low-risk assets. These assets often are not providing the kind of societal or environmental impact that clients of social banks imagine. Thus social banks should develop indicators to report about their impacts in a transparent way that provides the necessary information for their clients. An indicator could be 'loans outstanding for projects or enterprises selected by positive social or environmental impact criteria/balance sheet sum' or 'loans outstanding for projects or enterprises selected by positive social or environmental impact criteria/total loans'. These indicators could also be split into different impact fields like education, healthcare, CO_2 reduction, etc. One example for a transparent presentation of the impact of environmental banking is provided by the Alternative Bank Switzerland. They report about the impact of fixed deposits connected with loans to renewable energy projects and enterprises (see Box 8.3).

Box 8.3 CO_2 reduction caused by loans for renewable energy projects

In 2009, again, we calculated the environmental impact of our financing and development loans in the field of renewable energies. In 2008 we financed 73 (70) projects with an amount of 17.2 million Swiss francs. The result: clients that invested CHF 100,000 for one year in a development fixed deposit 'Alternative Energies' allow for the mitigation of nine tons of CO_2 emissions per year.

While the measurement of the impact of social banking with respect to the mitigation of CO_2 emissions is relatively easy and transparent, the measurement of social or societal impacts is more complex. The quantification of social impacts like educational or health impacts needs more elaborated methods. However, even the simple indicators 'school enrolment/loans outstanding for schools' or 'school enrolment finance/balance sum' provide some interesting information for clients that have their savings accounts or deposits with social banks. Thus the Global Impact Investing Network initiated a project to create a framework 'for defining, tracking and reporting the performance of impact capital' (www.iris-standards.org). Though the project concentrates more on charity money, it could be taken as a model for measuring the impact of social banking.

Lowering transaction costs

Often the transaction costs for social banks are higher than for conventional banks. In microfinance the administrative costs for microfinance are even about 30 per cent of the given loan (www.themix.org). There are other studies that also estimate the transaction costs of the social capital market as high as 22 to 43 per cent of the value of the capital raised (Meehan *et al.* 2004). Because social banks have to integrate social, environmental, ethical and other non-financial indicators and factors into their decision-making processes the amount of time and input per loan sum is often higher than at conventional banks. These costs cannot be compensated by lower default rates compared to other banks because comparable small or medium sized banks often rely on secured mortgages that have a very low default rate. In addition to that the loan costs between social banks and other comparable banks do not differ that much anymore.

Nevertheless the integration of environmental and social exclusion or positive criteria produces costs connected with additional efforts for analysing social, environmental and ethical issues. Thus a future challenge for social banks will be to guarantee the capital flow between those who want to support social or environmental projects and the projects that should be supported. The question is whether e-banking or e-trade services can be used in that field to lower transaction costs without giving up competency in social banking and being a reliable intermediary in this field. An example for the new concepts in lending is the so-called peer-to-peer lending. This kind of lending connects lender and borrowers directly and is named as one of the most promising future developments (Sviokla 2009). Thus also private persons can directly lend to other persons or projects without having a financial institution as intermediary. The peer-to-peer platform provides services like bundling smaller amounts to loans, the rating of the lender and some security services. They charge a fee for the services, but do not earn interests on the loans. Based on Internet technology this kind of banking is able to connect these who want to channel their capital into social projects and enterprises and those that have the project ideas but need the capital. However, social banks could take the role of an intermediary who guarantees the social impact of these projects that are available on the peer-to-peer platform. This is, at the present state of these platforms, not given yet.

Human resources management

In this section we will highlight two issues of likely importance for the future development in social banking: workplace democracy, and training and education for employees in social banks to be able to connect social and financial issues. These issues were presented earlier in Chapters 4 and 7.

As described in other chapters of this book social banks grew from very small institutions with flat and grassroots democracy oriented structures to medium sized banks underlying massive regulations and managing billions of capital during a relatively short time period of about 15 to 20 years. As Lars Hektoen, the CEO of Cultura Banks mentions: because of that '[T]the step from a tight family type business to a larger organization has to be mastered in a way that does not sacrifice the responsibility of each co-worker and the proximity to our clients and stakeholders' (personal communication). Thus general assemblies as a method of discussing businesses in these banks are no efficient measure anymore. On the other hand one major quality of social banks is to give all employees the opportunity for participating in the banks' decision-making processes and ethical discussions. Social banks are relying on the competence of their employees as other organizations do as well.

Thus, given that social banks do not have the opportunity to offer the best payment in the banking sector other incentives have to be offered to attract excellent employees. In order to rethink and to organize the organizational participation process in the bank in 2008 the Swiss Alternative Bank, for instance, started a project to develop a new charter to define the basics of participation on the workplace. The result is presented in Box 8.4.

Box 8.4 Participation at the Alternative Bank Switzerland

This is the way the institutionalized participation works.

By fixing the rights to participate we want to avoid the necessity to negotiate who has the right to participate or to decide for every topic. Comprehensive employee-participation rights are in place at the ABS. Furthermore an association of all employees of the ABS exists.

- Decision-making: a representative of the association of the employees is member of the board of directors and is the representative body of the employees of ABS.
- Participation in decision-making processes: the executive board and the association of the employees mutually create motions for the board of directors with respect to changes of the regulations for employees (consented decision-making).
- Co-determination: the association of the employees has the right of co-determination in the fields affecting the rights and responsibilities of the employees. The executive board and the association of employees commonly define those topics that are subject to co-determination. They regularly meet to discuss how co-determination comes into practice (i.e. participations in working groups, common hearings, forums).
- Information: all employees have the right of comprehensive, goal oriented, timely and transparent information about topics that affect their rights and responsibilities.
- Proposals: all employees are invited to express their proposals and opinions for the further development of ABS.

Thus the future challenge for social banks will be to offer attractive workplaces and to attract excellent employees given financial constraints compared to other players in the financial sector. Participation, an attractive work–life balance and the offer to create a social and environmental impact combined with state-of-the-art banking practice will be the main recruiting arguments for social banks.

But how to guarantee that social banks are able to recruit employees who share the ethics of social banks and provide the expertise that is needed to manage a bank in a highly regulated but risky environment? The positive attitudes of the employees to the missions and vision of social banks will not be sufficient to guarantee excellent performance in the workplace. Also Lars Pehrson, CEO of the Danish Merkurbank, named the need for qualified employees as one of the future challenges of social banks (personal communication). Nevertheless, to date mainly two types of employees have been recruited for social banks:

- Former employees from conventional banks supporting the idea of social banking and therefore often being prepared to accept lower income. These employees often are well grounded in banking knowledge.
- Employees that are connected with the social or environmental movement. These employees are often well grounded in social or environmental issues.

Christina von Passavant (Chapter 4) presented challenges connected with recruiting these different types of employees. However, it becomes clear that both groups are often missing some competencies that are needed for social banks, related to the banking or the social part of 'social banking'. A solution to this problem could be the implementation of a training and education programme for social banking. The Institute for Social Banking that was founded by a group of European social banks offers a solution for this present and future challenge to social banks. The institute is described in Box 8.5 (see also www.social-banking.org).

Box 8.5 The Institute for Social Banking

In late 2006, a dozen European socially oriented banks and foundations joined up to found the Institute for Social Banking (ISB), a charitable association to engage in training and research activities in the context of social banking and social finance. Amongst its current members are Triodos Bank from the Netherlands, GLS Bank from Germany, Banca Etica from Italy, and Alternative Bank from Switzerland.

The ISB members are united in their conviction that those working in socially oriented banking and finance need, besides the conventional banking and finance tools and techniques, additional competencies as compared to their peers in conventional banking and finance.

Thus the ISB is developing a platform for various courses and seminars tailored towards the needs of the employees of social banks on all different levels, be they senior functional managers, high potentials, or just newcomers.

But ISB members also strive to raise awareness for the topic of social banking and social finance both in the general public and to attract prospective future employees such as current students of business and finance courses.

Finally, the ISB members realize the importance of making social banking and social finance subject to rigorous research, both in-house and externally, so to systematically improve the foundations for current and future practice both in the individual organization and in the overall sector.

Together, the above motives led pioneering socially oriented banks to join their forces and to set up the ISB, some key characteristics of which shall be sketched out in the following points:

- a practice-oriented MA in Social Banking and Social Finance for professionals in the financial sector, to systematically research their own work practices;
- a summer school for banking and finance professionals as well as interested others;
- experts' seminars for senior functional managers from its member organizations;
- introduction seminars for junior employees of its members;
- interactive seminars and a public lecture series for students at various universities;
- a social banking module in a BA Business Administration at a German university;
- an ISB Paper series wherein innovative questions on alternative banking and finance are approached by ISB students and affiliates.

Communicating the interaction between social support and financial returns

What is the interaction between social support – one important goal of social banks – and financial returns? Is there a cause–effect relation between the social goals of social banks and a smaller financial return? On the one hand social banks are a kind of facilitator for social change and sustainable development and on the other hand they are banks based on the classic products and services of the banking sector. In 2008 the Return on Equities (RoE) of microfinance institutions was 8.9 per cent (Gonzales 2009) and the balance sheet growth of the three biggest European social banks between 2006 and 2008 was between 15 and 55 per cent.

Thus social banks and microfinance as a part of social banking seemed to be a successful business in recent years. Shareholders of the Alternative Bank Switzerland, for instance, earned a dividend of about 1.5 per cent over the last years, together with a constant increase of the value of the shares. However, social banks and microfinance institutions are criticized, on the one hand, for making profits with the poor or those who need societal support and, on the other hand, for not being in the business of increasing profits as famously postulated by Friedman (1970). To date, achieving societal support and making profits often is seen as a contradiction: charitable institutions are there for supporting societal needs and banks exist to make profits. But how can social banks communicate their concepts, visions and goals?

One means of communication is the foundation of an association or organization, such as the Global Alliance for Banking on Values (GABV) that represents social banks and communicates their common goals. According to its website:

> (t)he Global Alliance for Banking on Values (GABV) takes a leading role in the debate about how to build a sustainable financial future, and fosters joint projects between its members to help deliver it. It is a both a talking and, crucially, a doing organisation.
>
> (www.gabv.org)

The association was founded in 2009 and consists of 11 of the world's leading sustainable banks from Asia, Latin America, the United States and Europe. They share the common commitment to 'find global solutions to international problems – and to promote a positive, viable alternative to the current financial system' (www.gabv.org/Banks). Such an association could serve as an entity communicating the goals of social banks. Other organizations that are able to communicate the impact of social banks on society are the International Association of Social Finance Organisations (INAISE) and the Federation of European Ethical and Alternative Banks (FEBEA).

The growth of social banks: increasing the impact without diluting ethics

The growth of social banks, especially in recent years (see Chapter 1 of this book), showed the increasing interest in their products and services and provides a stronger impact of social banks. However, there are at least two challenges connected with this growth:

1 The balance sheet growth is mainly caused by additional savings and deposits while the growth in loans was smaller especially during the last financial crisis.
2 The growth has to be managed in a way that the social impact and the ethical background remain the main characteristics of social banks – i.e. in a way that does not dilute the core values of social banks.

The increase in savings and deposits in the last years was higher than that in loans and mortgages. The latest annual report of GLS for instance reports an increase of the balance sheet of 33.3 per cent, an increase of account deposits of 37.2 per cent and an increase in loans and mortgages of 16.9 per cent between 2008 and 2009. Other social banks show similar figures indicating a stronger increase in account deposits than in loans and mortgages. We showed the relations between the loans sum and the balance sheet in Chapter 1 as well. Furthermore, compared to bigger conventional banks, the business of social banks mainly relies more on loans and mortgages. Consequently, the returns of social banks decreased because they had to pay the interest for the deposit accounts and could not increase the income by loans at the same amount. At the same time the amount of liquidity rose and social banks were forced to invest a part of the capital in non-risky but also conventional investments. Thus it became harder to channel the capital to social and environmental projects (see above, pp. 9–10) and at the same time to make profits that are necessary to maintain the business. Consequently, social banks have to look intensively for projects that can be financed by loans. Additionally they have to look for other ways to channel the capital into projects with a social impact to reach a certain independency from returns caused by the credit business.

Referring to the second challenge, keeping the difference and the distance to conventional banks that offer more and more socially responsible investment products as a part of their product portfolio will be decisive for the further development of social banking. Social banks have always been the innovators in socially responsible finance and banking (Weber 2005) and should keep this role in the future as well. However, during the last financial crisis not only social banks were able to achieve an increase in account deposits, but conventional smaller cooperative banks and savings banks as well. Therefore, social banks have to differentiate themselves better from both conventional smaller and bigger banks. Conventional cooperative banks represent a kind of regional banking that is not especially based on ethical principles. Bigger conventional banks use social and sustainable finance products as value drivers in addition to their conventional products (Weber 2005). At present the unique selling position of social banks is a portfolio that only consists of products and services with a social and environmental impact. The future challenge will be to keep and communicate this unique market position. This will be reached by expanding first the range of products with a specific social impact based on positive criteria and second by expanding the products and services beyond the lending business.

Conclusion

What is the future of social banks? In this chapter we tried to present strategies for social banks to manage their future development in a sustainable way. These strategies should guarantee an increase of the social impact of the banks based on a solid business model that is necessary to be able to perform well in the banking business. Though these banks grew significantly with respect to their balance sheet and public awareness, their future development is still uncertain and further growth is not guaranteed. It will be decisive whether social banks will be able to develop innovative and successful products and services with a positive social and environmental impact that are attractive to many clients. In addition to that social banks will have to measure and to show the social impacts of their products and services in a clear and transparent way that is understandable also for those potential clients that are not well grounded in social banking. In order to reach these goals social banks have to further develop their human resources management to find and train these employees that are able to create these successful products and services.

From a more conceptual point of view the relation between the social and the financial return of social banking activities and products has to be analysed and communicated. More and more clients of social banks want to know more about the social and financial return of their investments or savings. In this field there is a lot of fascinating work to be done. However, if social banks manage these tasks successfully, then a further growth of social banks that increases their social impact without diluting their ethics should be possible.

References

Baranes, A. (2009) 'Towards sustainable and ethical finance', *Development*, 52: 416–20.

Barclay, B. (2008) *Financing Global Warming: Canadian Banks and Fossil Fuels*, San Francisco: Rainforest Action Network.

Cortese, A. (2003) 'Business; they care about the world (and they shop too)', *The New York Times*, 20 July.

Friedman, M. (1970) 'The social responsibility of business is to increase its profits', *The New York Times Magazine*, 33: 122–6.

Gonzales, A. (2009) *Microfinance at a Glance*, Washington, DC: Microfinance Information Exchange.

Hawken, P. (2004) *Socially Responsible Investing. How the SRI Industry has Failed to Respond to People who want to Invest with Conscience and what can be done to change it*, Sausalito: Natural Capital Institute.

Jeucken, M. (2001) *Sustainable Finance and Banking: the Financial Sector and the Future of the Planet*, London: Earthscan.

Meehan, W., Kilmer, D. and O'Flanagan, M. (2004) 'Investing in society', *Stanford Social Innovation Review*, spring: 34–43.

Sviokla, J. (2009) 'Forget Citibank – borrow from Bob', *Harvard Business Review*, February: 25.

Weber, O. (2005) 'Sustainability benchmarking of European banks and financial service organizations', *Corporate Social Responsibility and Environmental Management*, 12: 73–87.

Notes

2 Social banking: a brief history

1 Many thanks to David Suttie (translation), Bledi Balliu and Mauro Ferrari (technical support activity) for their important help.

2 This work will focus primarily on these issues, bearing in mind that there are numerous additional examples of social banking in other parts of the world (e.g. the United States, etc.), which would be interesting to study. Only some paradigmatic hints in the Canadian and Japanese experience are mentioned. It is hoped that future work will cover all these aspects.

3 It is recalled that at least six Councils have treated and have addressed the issue of usury and several encyclical letters were written for this practice. The last of those letters was the *Vix Pervenit* of Benedict XIV in 1745.

4 'Usury is taking longer than we have given'. Le Goff (1986: 20) (cited by Ieronimus, Breviarium in psalmos, LIV –PL 26, col. 1042–). Also, Gerolamo expresses the same idea (347–420; cited in Le Goff 1986), cf. Giacchero (1981: 319).

5 S. Thomas follows the Aristotelian economic optics of the idea that money is sterile, it cannot produce fruit. In fact, Aristotle distinguished between an economy, which he called *chrematistiké* (the creation of wealth generated by the accumulation of money for itself) and *oikonomiké* (functioning to satisfy family and community needs). It is clear that only the latter was for the community, while the former was individualistic. Interest, therefore, was not lawful because it was not beneficial for the community.

6 'Money … was first invented for trade; its first natural use was to enable trade. Therefore it is not right, in itself, to receive a price for the use of borrowed money, which is what usury consists of'. Also, St Bonaventure argued that money itself is unproductive: 'quia pecunia, quantum est de se, per se ipsam non fructificat, sed fructus venit aliunde' ('money, of itself, does not bear fruit; fruit is borne elsewhere'). Cf. for both citations Le Goff (1986: 23).

7 Passages in the Torah, which explicitly preach against the collection of financial interest, can be recalled from Exodus, Leviticus and Deuteronomy. Proclamations are based on the brotherhood of blood of the Jewish community: it ruled the solidarity of *mishpaha* (clan) and the exclusion of *nokri* (foreigners) from the privileges and obligations of the community; it also prohibited Jews from taking any *neshek* (interest) from their brothers, making it permissible, however, against the *nokri*. The prohibitions relating to the usury in the Old Testament are: first, in Exodus: 'If though lend money to any of my people, even to the poor with thee, thou shalt not be to him as a creditor; neither shall ye lay upon him interest' (Exodus 22: 24); second, in Leviticus: 'If one of your countrymen becomes poor and is unable to support himself among you, help him as you would an alien or a temporary resident, so he can continue to live among you' (Lev. 25: 35–7); third, in Deuteronomy:

> You may charge a foreigner interest, but not a brother Israelite, so that the LORD your God may bless you in everything you put your hand to in the land you are entering to possess. If you make a vow to the LORD your God, do not be slow to pay it, for the LORD your God will certainly demand it of you and you will be guilty of sin.
>
> (Deuteronomy 23: 20–1)

8 About this time, it was customary to say that the word poor started conflicting with the word rich, which previously had been represented by other words (such as powerful, soldier, etc.). Meanwhile, the opposite of poverty was held to be not arrogance, but greed.

9 St Anthony of Padua, during the Lent of 1231 a few months before his death, in what was his spiritual testament, wrote to the poor victims of usury (with particular reference to the family of the Scrovegni, known moneylenders in Padua):

> Accursed race! They grew strong and numerous on earth, and have lion's teeth. The moneylender respects neither Lordship nor men; his teeth always work, intent to rob, crush and swallow the assets of the poor, orphans and widows … And look at his hands, which dare to give alms, his hands dripping with blood the poor. There are moneylenders who exercise their profession in secret, others openly, but not in style, seem compassionate to others, finally, vicious, desperate, they are most openly and do their job in the sunshine.

The language of his preaching, which largely has been handed down, was simple and direct: 'The nature begets the poor, bare it comes to the world, naked you die. It was the evil that created the rich, and who desire to become rich stumbles into the trap of the devil.'

10 Soon, their demands became excessive and the interest asked seemed like punishment, so in 1291 King Philip IV expelled them from France; Edward III in 1240 drove them from England where they were able to return only in ten years under the auspices of the Pope, however they were expelled after a short time.

11 The reflections on the ethics of money of St Anthony, Dominican and Bishop of Florence, in his *Summa Teologica*, are interesting and still valid today.

12 In particular, for the previous Franciscans, those of *regula non bullata*, money was considered 'dust to walk on with feet'. God did not allow you to profit from individuals' needs.

13 Merchants and big businessmen recurred with clever artifices to disguise their interest.

14 The action of establishing the Banco di Ascoli contains a statement, which seems to be from A.K. Sen's pen or a UN document: the institution was established 'to support and nourish the poor of Ascoli and other places, especially the shameful ones and those who blush and experience discomfort in seeking alms from door to door'.

15 The Statute of Monte di Pietà of Perugia read: 'per subventione et aiutorio de le povere persone… nelle loro estreme necessità'.

16 Hence they did not finance all but only those who already had something and were able to develop an economic practice. For the excluded ones, a welfare practice was continued until their culture and availability allowed for an improvement in the quality of life. Today, in microcredit practice, not everybody receives financing, but only those who are available for a comprehensive training course.

17 Initially there were 500 Monti institutions in Belgium, France and then Spain. The Monti was still a primarily Italian phenomenon of the central North (because the countries of the Reformation, such as England, regarded Mons Pietatis as synonymous with Catholicism). Other than Monti, which was not derived from the principle of reciprocity, there were experiences of 'social economy' *ante litteram* as Fuggerai di Hausburg, a village built by the wealthy Fugger for poor families: this type of

experience was not born at random at the same time as the Protestant Reformation, and gave life to forms of 'philanthropic capitalism' of the Anglo-Saxon style. The Fuggerei was founded in 1521 by Jakob Fugger the Rich as a residential area for needy citizens of King August. It was the oldest public housing complex in the world. The annual rent (excluding expenditures) per apartment had nominal value of a Rhine guilder, at that time 88 cents, as well as three daily prayers for the founder and his family. In 140 apartments of 67 houses there were around 150 people. The most famous resident of Fuggerei was the foreman Franz Mozart, the composer's great-grandfather, W.A. Mozart. Actually Fuggerei is a 'city within a city' with a church, walls and three doors. The public house complex is still funded nearly exclusively through assets of the foundation (forestry and immobile economy). The area is administered by 'Fürstlich und Gräflich Fuggersche Stiftungs-Administration'.

18 In the same decades Martin Luther also takes aim at usury, attacking this practice with the same determination of the Church Fathers and Popes. Indeed, in his two sermons on usury in 1519 and 1520, Luther not only confirms that loans of money must be free, but also condemns the payment of foreseen and allowed compensation under canon law. Furthermore, the production of Shakespeare's *Merchant of Venice* achieved the effect of reviving further doctrinal disputes of usury in England: the ideals of the comedy included man's relationship with money. The criticism turned attention to usury topic, which presented itself as an important issue both economically and morally.

19 Even though the Franciscans worked very hard in the promotion of Monti di Pietà, they almost never had any part in the management themselves, it being entrusted to the local ruling classes.

20 This move was the contribution of Sir George Rose. During the session in the House of Commons on 15 November 1957, the financial secretary of the British treasury – J. Enoch Powell – talked about the Trustee Savings Banks' Bill (Vol. 577 cc1269–99):

> I beg to move, that the Bill be now read a Second time. This Bill relates to the fortunes of a very remarkable institution, an institution, which, I think, may be fairly described as characteristic of the British – characteristic of the British in its long continuity, in its power to combine sturdy independence with common sense, cooperation, and in the ability, which it has shown over a long period to adapt itself to changing circumstances. The origin of the trustee savings bank goes back to the very last years of the eighteenth century, to the middle of the first Industrial Revolution. It took its origin in circumstances, which socially, politically and economically are about as different from those of today as can well be imagined, yet over all that period it has survived and its usefulness has grown rather than diminished until today there are 84 of these trustee savings banks, with a total of £1,250 million invested in them. It is ironical to note that in these recent weeks, which have not been a very easy period for national savings, those forms of national savings, which have done best have been the very newest and the very oldest – the Premium Bonds and the savings banks. This is an institution, in which almost from the beginning hon. Members of this House have taken a special interest. Its earliest legislative basis was given to it by a Bill of 1817, which was moved by my predecessor the right hon. George Rose, friend and colleague of the younger Pitt.

21 The first saving bank in the United States – the Philadelphia Savings Fund Society – opened on 20 December 1816, and by 1830 was emulated by many other similar companies.

22 The Central Commission of Benefaction was an emanation of the Central Congregation, established by the Habsburg administration during the economic crisis of 1815–18, with the task of organizing and managing philanthropic activities to support the poor and promote the local economy. When in 1823 the Commission completed

its tasks, the problem of how to use available resources remained, thanks to shrewd investments over the previous years. The Habsburg administration proposed establishing the Cassa di Risparmio di Milano, based on the Vienna model. In subsequent years, the success of this initiative was evidenced by activity expansion through the Lombardo territory, and established from acquisition the names of Cassa di Risparmio delle Provincie Lombarde. Currently, the Central Commission of Charity is still the name used to identify the organ of Cariplo Foundation's address.

23 See Matteucci (1998: 23), which distinguishes between banks based on association, whose Board of Directors is appointed by the shareholders, and banks based on institutions, whose Board is appointed by the founder company.

24 In England, there were 122 in 1830.

25 For the historical record, there is an interesting anecdote: in Umbria the idea of adopting means and the Statute of Savings Banks was taken by mons. Gioacchino Pecci in 1843. (Later, Pecci was Apostolic Delegate in Perugia. Then he became the Bishop of the Diocese and subsequently Pope with the name of Leo XIII, in 1878.) In 1843 Don Vincenzo Tizzani was appointed bishop of Terni. He took inspiration from Pecci and wrote a letter on 30 January 1846 to Joseph Massarucci, to ask a united effort for the establishment of a popular bank or a savings bank, denouncing 'the failures, which continuously resulted through usuries exploitation of poor industrial classes'.

26 Italian banks were spread over the whole territory in different ways, especially between the north and south. The lack of space was a problem of real and economic significance.

27 Italy in 1876 saw the success of postal savings, which became state law the year before, on 27 May 1875. The number of postal books had risen in one year with to 57,000. But 20 years later, in 1912, the postal savers grew to six million. Postal savings were administered by the General Directorate of the Postal Service. By this measure, the legislature was regulating and enhancing the success of deposits and loans services, launched in 1861, when the regulation on the service of money deposits and payment of money orders came into effect. Fuelled by emigrants' remittances, the service had become a significant source of revenue for the postal administration, which after 1862 started supplying an international money service too. The activity of savings postal banks had a constant growth in the period from 1876, when there were about 300, up to the early twentieth century. Then, in the late nineteenth century, postal books were also introduced for Italians living abroad, the funds being collected in schools and savings banks on military ships. Funds were placed, even today, in public utilities' works and used for the extinction of local debts.

28 When Schulze-Delitzsch died in 1883, there were another 3,000 with 1.2 million members.

29 The great merit of Schulze-Delitzsch was his confidence in man, in his abilities and in the relationships between individuals. He favoured participatory and colloquial principles over fundamentalist and rigid ones, and did not exclude, a priori, from financial services those who didn't have the financial merits at the time in the cooperative context. The National Bank comes to light in a characteristic context from a pressing consideration of a 'social issue' that meant poverty, illiteracy and the absence of any prospect for urbanized masses whose relative number increased, coinciding with the industrial revolution, at an exponential rate. Combining technological progress and economic development of the lower classes was a challenge of the era to those who tried to respond with logic in a philanthropic way or, on the other hand, with the research of an extreme associationism like utopian socialists. The person as an individual was destined to disappear in a multitude of assisted people or in the anonymity of collectivism.

30 The basic idea was simply to teach poor people how to improve their own conditions. This meant replacing charity with self-help: bringing people together to help each other in a cooperative manner. A structure was necessary to carry out this idea. The

system of credit cooperatives was based on mutual togetherness between small farmers to meet their needs.

31 www.creditocooperativo.it. Social And Mission Report Cooperative Credit, 2008.

32 Surely we don't want to support an approach where the banks would be either completely good or completely bad: private banks and large institutions have played a big role in supporting major industry and infrastructure. But these merits and objectives are different from those social ones. With a pure commercial orientation, the presence in rural territories is given less attention, but it is possible in the cities. This has undoubtedly helped, but perhaps not in the right way, a wealth due to important industrialization and commercialization, but not redistributed equally among all workers.

33 Introduction to the Principles of Morals and Legislation, written in 1780 but not published until 1789.

34 A case from Italy is interesting in this regard: popular banks in the Veneto region initially provided social loans and were based on mutuality. But in the end this behaviour was not subsequently supported by facts. Indeed Don Manzini, a priest from Verona who founded many rural banks, stated:

> from one part, socialism, which cries out to impoverished people: lifting, it's time! And it is a crime. From the other part, the law says to hungry people: Be patient and pay! And people are dying of hunger. On one hand Popular Banks denied that they were reduced and corrupted in bourgeois banks, because poor farmer hardly finds a discount, on the other hand usury is more disgusting and fatal.
>
> (cited in Milano 2001: 57)

35 In the first half of nineteenth century, many rural banks failed, dragging thousands of people into despair.

36 From Greek '*anthropos*', man, and '*sophia*', wisdom: a true and proper science of humans.

37 The basic idea is that each person individually has the opportunity to evolve morally and cognitively. This individual evolution brings about experience, which exists in a hidden reality apart from current sensory perception. Therefore the world is knowable and the fact that our knowledge is limited today depends on our limited sensors. The limits of sensual perception may be gradually overcome by those who proceed in the evolutionary process and will develop perceptual and cognitive faculties that are impossible at present. This is reflected in the history of those who anticipated developments very early: the saints. This phenomenon makes people acknowledge the mystery of Golgotha and the resurrection of Jesus Christ as central points of the entire evolution of earth. This ability to anticipate developments arises from the evolution of cognitive abilities that are developed through scientific thinking and can lead to a feeling of self-awareness and to a desire to investigate the spiritual world. The definition of Spiritual Science or Anthroposophy originated from these activities.

38 The idea was from a group of parents in Bochum who had a dream: build a school for their children that applied Steiner's pedagogy. The state did not contribute and it needed lots of money, but banks were reluctant to grant funding. People in Bochum gathered together and decided to set up their own banking institution.

39 The new bank soon had to face dozens of requests from schools and kindergartens for a similar focus, but also from a biodynamic farm, host communities, eurythmics courses, projects for promotion of alternative medicine and other initiatives related to Steiner's movement.

40 This reminds us that all bank activities are based on three basic conditions: first, all human beings have the right to develop and to exercise freely their individual capacity; second, all humans have the right, if they wish and think that they have the ability, to participate in social life; third, to be sustainable, the economy can not be conceived and developed only through responsible projects, which take into account the importance of general interests, and of each person's needs and respect for the laws of nature.

41 It also shows that the underlying value of ethical banks is constructed by the transparency from the harvest moment to the use moment; processes assume the same importance for products, funds are evaluated not only from a financial economics point of view, but also from the social and ethical one; financial instruments are studied as the last element of the business planning process: the bank is a privileged interlocutor in the evaluation of business issues and in setting and covering financial needs; and the grassroots base of the bank's operation allow it to realize people's real needs and to examine new intervention hypotheses; democracy, participation and sobriety show core values of the bank, both in internal and external relationships.

42 Balances and various ratios are absolutely positive, so that for example its sufferings are much less than 0.5 per cent.

43 The Cooperative Bank is an interesting case. It is the only financial institution to correlate relief in the social economic sector in the United Kingdom and proposed a goal of 'making the banking system ethical'. Since 1992 it has shown a very strict ethics policy, defined in an elaborate charter on the basis of a survey taken with its customers who wished to combine ethics and finance. The main ethical criteria contained in the charter are the defence of human rights, fair trade and the fight against the arms industry. With over 2,300 branches scattered throughout the country, the Cooperative Bank has about a half a million customers, among them, as its name indicates, many cooperatives.

44 Considering the reputation of microfinance and microcredit, it is not necessary to explain in detail here what they are. For a catalogue and listing of these subjects' activities, please refer to many sites of different networks and NGOs. For products and services refer to Chapter 5 in this volume.

45 Regulation (CE) no. 1435/2003 of the Council of Europe on 22 July 2003 related to the statute of Società Cooperativa Europea (Sce).

46 See note 4.

47 Nevertheless, many of them – especially savings banks and rural banks – continued to operate with fairly good results (and in any case they were the only ones) in social and regional banking markets. But this (with all its ups and downs) is another story.

3 Why do we need social banking?

1 World Health Organisation, Fact sheet No. 266, August 2007, www.wpro.who.int/NR/rdonlyres/33FA546E-7813–4E51-BA89–48759FF45360/0/climate_factsheet.pdf (accessed 26 March 2010).

2 Evidence supporting the paradox is also reported by Blanchflower and Oswald (2004) for the UK, Frey and Stutzer (2002b) on a large sample of countries using data from the World Database of Happiness and the U.S. Bureau of Census and Veenhoven (1993) for Japan over the period 1958–87. In spite of it, the Easterlin paradox is not in itself a regularity that is always confirmed across countries and time. When Castriota (2006) repeated the Easterlin exercise on Eurobarometer data for some European countries in the last decade he found that the paradox applies to Germany but not to Italy where a quite strong positive relationship between the happiness and per capita income is found.

3 Corporate reductionism ignores that a large share of economic value is produced by non-profit-maximizing entities (cooperative firms, social enterprises, etc.) and that profit maximization is the ultimate cause of self-destruction of many banks in the global financial crisis under the explosive mix of asymmetric information among firm members (managers, traders and shareholders) and short-run performance incentives (stock options and traders' bonuses).

4 As it is well known one of the discoveries of the Greek philosopher and scientist Archimedes was the lifting power of levers. His most famous saying was 'give me a lever and I will lift the world'. In this sense, voting with the wallet is the lever needed to make the economic system more socially and environmentally responsible.

5 In essence, in the 'originate-to-hold' model, banks retain ownership of loans, bear the risk of non-repayment and therefore have incentives to monitor the borrower and to loan responsibly. In the 'originate-to-distribute' model, they sell the loan to an insurer and therefore lose the link with the borrower and the above-mentioned incentives.

6 These banks include Banche Cooperative and Banche Popolari in Italy, building societies and credit unions in the UK, mutual savings and loans and credit unions in the United States. These banks account for a 33.7 per cent market share in deposits and 29.5 per cent in loan volumes in the Italian banking industry and represent in terms of branches 60 per cent of the total in France, 50 per cent in Austria and about 40 per cent in Germany and the Netherlands (Bongini-Ferri 2007). In 2007, EU cooperative banks held an average market share of 25 per cent for loans to small and medium enterprises (SMEs), while an average of 29 per cent of their loans were SME loans (source: EACB). At world level financial cooperatives serve over 621 million people in the G20 nations alone, 'provide US$3.6 trillion in loans, hold US$4.4 trillion in savings and have US$7.6 trillion in total assets'. Among top 50 rankings by shareholder equity in 2008 the first coop bank is Crédit Agricole, ranked seventh, followed by a series of banks ranking from the twenties to the forties, such as Rabobank, Caisse d'Epargne, Banque Populaire, Crédit Mutuel. Beyond these figures, the interest of academicians, politicians and readers towards non-profit-maximizing banks is increasing after the global financial crisis, in which the specific characteristics of this kind of banks seem to have protected them better from the crisis.

> According to the *International Co-operative Alliance Statement* of co-operative identity, a co-operative is an autonomous association of persons united voluntarily to meet their common economic, social and cultural needs and aspirations through a jointly-owned and democratically-controlled enterprise. Co-operatives are based on the values of self-help, self-responsibility, democracy, equality, equity and solidarity. In the tradition of their founders, co-operative members believe in the ethical values of honesty, openness, social responsibility and caring for others.
>
> (from http://icba.free.fr/IMG/pdf/G_20_MARCH_09.pdf, accessed 30 April 2009)

7 The origin of modern microfinance traces back to the creation of Grameen Bank in 1983 after a pioneering activity of Muhammad Yunus who started in 1976 to experiment with the effects of lending small sums to poor borrowers without asking for collateral. The development of microfinance has been astounding. The Grameen Bank has now six million borrowers and the *Microcredit Summit Campaign* at the end of 2009 documents the existence of around 10,000 microfinance programmes around the world reaching approximately 155 million borrowers (2007 data) and, among them, 82 million in straight poverty conditions with a market potential of around 1.5 million clients. The most outstanding element of the performance of MFIs is their extremely low share of non-performing loans. According to the most systematic source of aggregate data on MFIs – the Micro Banking Bullettin (www.mixmbb.org/en), which created a panel of 200 MFIs from different continents – the average MFIs loan loss rate was 1 per cent in 2005. The literature provides various interpretations for this surprising performance. The most reputed among them are the role of group lending with joint liability (Ghatak 2000; Stiglitz 1990 and Armendariz de Aghion 1999), which is however neither adopted by all MFIs nor by the same Grameen after its 2000 reform, and the capacity of MFI loan officers of accumulating soft information in the Berger and Udell sense (2002), which is crucial to assess the creditworthiness of small businesses.

8 For liquidity services we mean that banks match liquid liabilities with illiquid assets. This is one of the main roles of credit intermediaries giving real investors the possibility of running their projects even when depositors draw their money back. As it is easy to understand liquidity services are also at the root of banks' fragility.

9 As Amartya Sen clearly explains in his 1977 paper *homines economici* are 'rational fools'. This is because the standard anthropological approach followed by economists assumes that individuals are motivated only by self-interest (which is obviously true for the most part) and not by sympathy (passion for others) and commitment (moral duty even when it is against self-interest).

10

> The rich can evade the consequences of non-payment; the poor cannot. They value access to credit so highly, and dislike the loan sharks so much, that they are only too grateful for a once-in-a-lifetime opportunity to improve themselves.
>
> (Muhammad Yunus, founder of Grameen Bank)

11 Among examples of the liaison between socially responsible consumers and microfinance are dedicated bond issues (see the case of Banca Popolare Etica) with yields, which are below the market rate and the decision of Etica sgr, the ethical investment company controlled by Banca Etica, to transform its entry fee into a guarantee fund for microfinance initiatives.

12 From this point of view, and with respect to fair trade, microfinance for pays the lack of certification and labelling criteria. In such a void the microfinance system risks leading many traditional intermediaries or even moneylenders to exploit the term. This is why one of the most discussed issues in the field is the creation of social rating schemes.

13 From this point of view it is acknowledged that the microfinance loan structure based on high frequency instalments may not help to finance long-term high-risk innovative projects.

14 The principle states that absolutely precise measurements are impossible, given the interference to the measured quantity inevitably introduced by the measuring instrument. An example typically used by physicists is the impossibility of observing a subatomic particle. Electron microscopes shower their subjects with electrons, and translate the electron 'echoes' into images. Electrons, however, are comparable in mass to their subjects and consequently knock them out of their natural states. A macroscopic example of this phenomenon is when the thermometer measures the temperature of a cup of tea. While measuring, the thermometer touches the tea and thereby lowers the temperature in the cup, however slightly.

15 We refer for example to the experimental results on ultimatum games (Camerer and Thaler 1995), dictator games (Andreoni and Miller 2002), gift exchange games (Fehr *et al.* 1993; Fehr *et al.* 1998), trust games (Berg *et al.* 1995) and public good games (Fischbacher *et al.* 2001; Fehr and Gächter 2000).

16 In February 2004, a survey by the market research company TNS Emnid in Germany on a representative sample of the population found that 2.9 per cent of the interviewees bought fair trade products regularly, 19 per cent rarely and 6 per cent almost never. Thirty-five per cent of respondents said that they supported the idea, but did not buy (www.fairtrade.net/sites/aboutflo/aboutflo). In a parallel UK survey, Bird and Hughes (1997) classified consumers as ethical (23 per cent), semi-ethical (56 per cent) and self-interested (17 per cent). Eighteen per cent of the consumers surveyed declared that they were willing to pay a premium for SR products.

17 According to recent literature (Ulhaner 1989; Gui 2000; Gui and Sugden 2005) relational goods are *a specific kind of local public goods, which are simultaneously consumed when produced.* Examples of relational goods are, on a small scale, love or family relationships and, on a large scale, many kinds of social events (club or association meetings, live sport events, etc.). Relational goods are *local public goods* since non-excludabilty and non-rivalry are limited to participants. They are simultaneously consumed and produced since participating in them is both an act of production (my presence contributes to the increase the value of the good) and consumption (I enjoy it while producing it).

They are a special kind of public good as well since they should be better defined as anti-rival than non-rival. This is because their very same nature is based on the interpersonal sharing of them. As a consequence, participation to their production and consumption actually creates a positive externality on partners and contributes to the quality of the public good itself. For the same reasons partners do not see non-rivalry and non-excludability as negative elements, which prevent them from exploiting all private benefits of the good, but as positive elements, which increase its value (my satisfaction is actually increased, or even crucially determined, by the fact that the other is also participating and taking pleasure).

18 Even though the literature on self-esteem is much less extensive, the debate between economists and psychologists on the causality nexus between self-esteem and life events has taken a very similar direction with respect to that of life satisfaction. According to Tafarodi and Swann (2001) self-esteem is 'the intrinsic perception of one's self in relation with other people' and is strictly related to self-confidence, representing the perceived ability of accomplishing one's own goals in life, since 'those who are liked enjoy a clear advantage in achieving their goals'.

19 Social capital generally identifies the degree of cohesion of a given community under several aspects. The most important of them are trust on institutions, interpersonal trust (under the form of trust and trustworthiness) and willingness to pay for public goods. For the role of social capital in economic systems see Putnam (1993), Zak and Knack (2001) and for its effects on economic growth see Knack and Keefer (1997).

20 t stands for the income tax rate.

4 Inside social banks

1 These criteria are similar to those proposed by the Ethos Foundation in the discussion around the compensation systems of businesses listed on the stock exchange.

6 Financing change through giving and donations: an integral part of social banking

1 There are some famous studies about giving by socioligists, anthroposophers, philosophers and theologians. The best known might be Marcel Maus' *The Gift*, first published in French in 1923/4 and translated into English in 1956. In this work on reciprocity and gifts, Mauss understands gift giving as a form of exchange that creates obligations for gift recipiants to pay back the giver. With this understanding, he stays within the logic of tradeoff. Other research, in theology and philosophy, for example, goes beyond this. French philosophers like Jacques Derrida (1992) talk about the possibility of gift giving without any expectations. Also, research on gift economies looks at a whole different paradigm, which leaves economics of scarcity behind. See my description of Bennholdt-Thomson's understanding of gift economy (pp. 125–126).

2 In the social sciences, gift economy has evolved as a term used to describe a society where goods and services are freely given without any explicit agreement for immediate or future rewards. Often this form of giving leads to a more just redestribution of wealth within a society (Wikipedia, online).

3 Men in this area typically work in farming or in the trades such as carpentry or plumbing.

4 This is a very interesting fact. The macro-economic data of Juchitán show that it is not as prosperous as other regions. And of course, these data show that other states, such as the United States, are much wealthier. But this wealth does not translate into better nutrition for children in the United States.

5 Anthroposophy is a spiritual philosophy, founded by Rudolf Steiner (1861–1925) at the end of the nineteenth and the beginning of the twentieth century. It is born out of a philosophy of freedom. It is a practice of spiritual research, developed on the basis of European idealistic philosophy. Anthroposophists are active in the fields of alternative medicine, biodynamic farming and Waldorf/Steiner education (Waldorf Answers 2010).

6 For example through tax deductions.
7 Gemeinnützige Treuhandstelle was later renamed GLS Treuhand.
8 In Germany there is a legal debate about whether or not it should be possible for independent, unaffiliated foundations to use up their base capital. Leading opinion tends towards maintaining the base capital.
9 GLS Treuhand also supports loans given by GLS Gemeinschaftsbank to charitable organizations. This is done, for example, through credit guarantees, hypothecation of assets, or loan capital.
10 All religions seem to have rules about giving. For examle, in the Judeo-Christian tradition, giving is a way of ensuring prayers of the benefactors for oneself. Here, giving isn't altruistic. Nevertheless, as Volz (2008: 185) points out, the flow of money and goods from the rich to the poor balances the distribution a little better. What motivates people to act in this way is the ethics of sister/brotherhood. It includes sharing, distributing and partaking in wealth.

7 Social banking at the crossroads

1 The author works at the Institute for Social Banking ('ISB'; www.social-banking.org). But this chapter represents his own views, not necessarily those of the ISB or its member organizations. The author owes deep gratitude to his wife, Laxmi. Without her continuous support this chapter would not have been possible. All mistakes are the author's responsibility. Constructive criticism and suggestions for improvement are explicitly welcome.
2 Here, it should be acknowledged that the socially and/or environmentally oriented activities of conventional banks (even if looking only at their CSR or sponsoring activities, not their normal business activities, e.g. in the area of green-/clean-tech, etc.), in absolute figures, certainly exceed the sum of all activities by social banks. For instance, Deutsche Bank, in its 2009 CSR Report, claims to manage around €3.1 billion in sustainable funds, to have arranged for microcredits worth €1.2 billion for 2.6 million people (since 1997), to have sponsored educational programmes for 275,000 people, and to have spent about €81 million on CSR activities (Deutsche Bank 2009: 113).
3 In essence, the economic, social and environmental issues are the commonly referred to 'three pillars of sustainability'. We therefore will subsequently also use the terms 'sustainability' or 'sustainable development' to capture all three aspects simultaneously.
4 It should be noted here that individual banks report their (net) profits differently. As such, Figure 7.2 does not serve to compare between different banks' profitability, it only serves to highlight the general trends in the profitability for each individual bank relative to the size of their respective balance sheet.
5 It should be noted here that because of regulations regarding equity and liquidity, no bank can have a 100 per cent conversion rate of loans to balance sheet. There are also differences between regulations in different countries. Broadly speaking, however, conversion rates around 75 to 80 per cent would be desirable – i.e. 10 to 15 per cent over what is to be found in the social banking sector today.
6 Instead of using the term 'threat', we are inclined to use the term 'challenge', which comes closer to what we actually mean. However, since the SWOT analysis is a well-established tool, we have decided not to rephrase it into SWOC analysis – to avoid unnecessary confusion.
7 We acknowledge that this differentiation between both opportunities and threats and between strengths and weaknesses might seem somehow vague and sometimes ambiguous. In each opportunity lies a threat and vice versa. The transitions between them are fluid. The same holds for strengths and weaknesses.

At the same time, we emphasize again that there is no *the* 'social bank', and any generalization about 'social banks' will always do injustice, at least to some of them.

So, our differentiation between social banks' opportunities and threats, and strengths and weaknesses is at best indicative. It should serve as a basis for discussion, and not present a universal verdict.

8 With respect to the 'conservative' attitude towards PR/marketing, as well as with respect to the limited funds in this context, one has to point out that the oldest and biggest social banks such as Triodos, GLS and ABS by now are spending substantial funds on (fairly) modern PR and marketing. Still, they seem a far cry from the activities of their conventional peers in this field.

9 The relatively low equity capital of most social banks is partly a consequence of their already discussed relatively low profitability, which does not allow for building up much equity on their own strengths, but partly also because of their ownership structure as cooperatives with many small members. The equity provided by these members is insufficient for many social banks that want/have to lend more of their excess funds. This means attracting more and/or bigger shareholders (e.g. pension funds, such as is the case with Triodos Bank). The latter has the advantage of being more efficient. But, overall, many social banks will find it difficult to attract new large members who are as willing to accept no or very low returns on their investments in the social banks, as were the banks' original members, or to generate sufficient profit to be able to pay at least average dividends to shareholders.

10 However, it is also fair to say that the majority of SRI products available today do not comply with the operating principles of most social banks. This is because many of the SRI products currently on the market are based on modified best-in-class concepts, sometimes added to by some exclusion criteria regarding certain products or sectors. As such, they often comprise – very conventional – firms like Microsoft, JPMorgan Chase or Exxon Mobil, and therefore would not really appeal to the majority of (established) clients of social banks (see Hawken 2004).

11 Herein 'social' does not refer to 'social' in terms of being concerned about the well-being of others but to the 'social' interaction facilitated by 'social' media software in combination with suitable hardware mobile-Internet devices such as laptops, smartphones and tablets etc.

12 Whilst not in our focus, it is worth mentioning that the new ICT technologies are also of increasing relevance for the financial sectors in the South, where poor infrastructure and difficulties to reach dispersed communities have been a major obstacle for establishing a fully functioning banking sector covering more than just a tiny fraction of the population. Here new companies, such as M-Pesa in Kenya, are being set up – often by mobile-phone companies – to provide mobile banking services to reach the rural population (cf. Chapple *et al.* 2007).

13 These discussions are arguably more pronounced in those social banks that were not just set up to address more specific – e.g. social or environmental – problems, but were based on a certain worldview such as anthroposophy. At least in some of these banks, some of the early employees feel that there was a lack of engagement with the initial ideas and ideals behind this worldview. Indeed, if one is to compare the development of some mission statements and other public documents of these banks, one would hardly find the word 'anthroposophy' in prominent places anymore.

14 Again, it should be noted here that there are considerable differences between individual social banks. The problem mainly exists for small cooperative banks, but not so much for the larger social banks. Triodos or Alternative Bank Switzerland, for instance, pay a dividend, but do not find it difficult to raise additional capital. GLS does not pay dividends on its cooperative shares but does so on its dormant equity.

15 To be independently audited, sustainability reports normally should comply with international standards such as ISO 14,000 or the GRI. However, these standards are pretty much 'one size fits all'. A similar case could be made with respect to the much

discussed 'labels' for 'ethical', 'green', or 'sustainable' banking products, as most of these labels, as of now, provide no information on the company behind the labelled products/services.

16 The Institute for Social Banking (ISB), which the author is working for, arguably is the only institution so far that aims to address this gap in the educational market explicitly with a focus on social bankers systematically and with an international orientation, for instance with a Masters in Social Banking and Social Finance, with a summer school on social banking and with various specialists seminars targeted at social bankers on different levels. Apart from the ISB, a small number of training institutions offer courses that could be also of relevance to social bankers but target a much wider audience. With a view to universities, to our best knowledge, there are no comprehensive and advanced courses on social banking available yet.

17 We opted to consider this as 'strengths' of social banks rather than an 'opportunity' for them because we felt it would be cynical to call the failure of the conventional banks that resulted in so much damage for many people an 'opportunity' for anyone.

Index

Page numbers in *italics* denote tables, those in **bold** denote figures.

Taylor & Francis

eBooks

FOR LIBRARIES

ORDER YOUR FREE 30 DAY INSTITUTIONAL TRIAL TODAY!

Over 22,000 eBook titles in the Humanities, Social Sciences, STM and Law from some of the world's leading imprints.

Choose from a range of subject packages or create your own!

- Free MARC records
- COUNTER-compliant usage statistics
- Flexible purchase and pricing options

Benefits for your user

- Off-site, anytime access via Athens or referring URL
- Print or copy pages or chapters
- Full content search
- Bookmark, highlight and annotate text
- Access to thousands of pages of quality research at the click of a button

For more information, pricing enquiries or to order a free trial, contact your local online sales team.

UK and Rest of World: **online.sales@tandf.co.uk**

US, Canada and Latin America:
e-reference@taylorandfrancis.com

www.ebooksubscriptions.com

A flexible and dynamic resource for teaching, learning and research.